celebrity family trees

celebrity family trees

THE WORLD'S MOST CELEBRATED AND SCANDALOUS DYNASTIES

ed wright

BARNES & NOBLE

NEW YORK

CONTENTS

INTRODUCTION

THERE IS NO DOUBT THAT IT IS AROUND THE FAMILY AND THE HOME THAT ALL THE GREATEST VIRTUES, THE MOST DOMINATING VIRTUES OF HUMAN SOCIETY, ARE CREATED, STRENGTHENED AND MAINTAINED.
WINSTON CHURCHILL

The great Russian novelist Leo Tolstoy, whose crazy family features in this book, began his masterpiece *Anna Karenina* with the observation that "Happy families are all alike; every unhappy family is unhappy in its own way." Celebrity families are rarely happy. For every celebrity success there are usually tragedies, black sheep, freaks and thwarted mediocrities traveling in the wake of the luminaries. For them, the accident of birth that many of us would consider fortunate, brings only pain, suffering and a sense of worthlessness.

Contained within these pages are families who have made their way to celebrity through political, business, showbusiness, intellectual or artistic achievement, or often a combination of the above. Most of them have been able to sustain their fame over several generations, some of them over centuries. You will see power, genius, eccentricity, charisma and sexiness in their many aspects. However, you will also see murderous rivalries, incest, serial philandering, insanity, narcissism and appalling parental neglect. You will be reminded, too, that the bonds of family, whether supportive or destructive, are almost impossible to escape.

Being in a celebrity family definitely has its advantages. For starters, various members get to live in mansions, own massive art collections and drive expensive cars. Even better, they often don't even have to work. And when they do, family connections are there to help them into a well-remunerated gig—when Napoleon Bonaparte became Emperor of France and conquered most of Europe, he granted his relatives monarchies and duchies all over Europe; some may question whether George W. Bush would have become US President of the United States if it weren't for his pop and grandfather.

This kind of thing goes on in Hollywood families, such as the Farrows, Fondas and Barrymores, too. It seems as if almost every member of these families has tried acting at some point. Not all of them have succeeded, of course. We know Bridget Fonda well, but not many have heard of her brother, Justin. We think of Mia Farrow but not of sister Stephanie. The fame of these siblings exists second-hand in their surnames.

The world becomes small in the echelons of the ultra-famous and it's interesting how incestuous the realm of celebrity families is. Members of them tend to hang out with, sleep with and get hitched to members of other celebrity families. Hotel barons Conrad and Nicky Hilton married Hollywood beauties Zsa Zsa Gabor and Elizabeth Taylor respectively; Elizabeth Taylor's son, Christopher Wilding, married Aileen Getty; Jane Fonda married Roger Vadim who was once married to Brigitte Bardot; while Ethel Barrymore turned Winston Churchill's marriage proposal down. The Darwins, Bonapartes and Du Ponts had a penchant for marrying their cousins, while George W. Bush's genealogy has links to sixteen former US Presidents as well as Princess Diana, Winston Churchill and the native American princesss Pocahontas.

Then there's the networking. Not content with belonging to one of Hollywood's first families, Drew Barrymore, for instance, had Steven Spielberg for a godfather to help smooth her path to fame. The networking champions in this book, however, are indisputably the eccentric and controversial British Mitford sisters who, collectively, were the only family in the world of their time who could say they were on close terms with the Kennedys, the Churchills *and* the Hitlers.

JACQUELINE BOUVIER WITH HER SHORTS-CLAD FIANCE, SENATOR JACK KENNEDY, AT THE KENNEDY FAMILY SUMMER HOUSE, 1953.

SIGMUND FREUD, AGED 16, WITH HIS MOTHER, AMALIE FREUD, C.1870. FREUD'S MOTHER WAS OVERLY DOTING TO HER FAVORITE SON, SIGMUND, AND HER SUPPORT AND LOVE WERE CRUCIAL TO HIS LATER SUCCESS.

Those who strive for fame are often misfits with gifts and serious will power. This striving is strongest in those who come from the outside to achieve political power. The Corsican outsider Napoleon Bonaparte struggled to make his family the most powerful in France, then Europe; while Austria's Adolf Hitler—bullied by his father, as well as being a failed artist—harnessed his diabolical will to command Germany. Other political dynasties have a longer relationship with privilege. The Nehru-Gandhi dynasty of India has provided three prime ministers in the short history of the world's largest democracy, with Sonia Gandhi having recently turned the job down. The dynasty's founder, Motilal Nehru, was of high caste, an Anglophile barrister and the richest man in his state. With the exception of Pandit Nehru, the Nehru-Gandhis' qualification for the PM's job has been their surname. Still, happiness has been scarce in their particular family story, with assassination and family schisms being prominent.

The Churchills are another unhappy, yet pedigreed, political dynasty. They first came to fame four centuries ago, and have occupied positions of authority in Britain ever since. Yet the family's bright stars are outnumbered by its libertines, tragedies and losers. The current heir to the family's Duke of Marlborough title is a drug addict. Winston Churchill himself fought depression throughout his life. Then what about the less talented members of the family who had to live up to him? One of his daughters committed suicide, while his son Randolph was a vile alcoholic and was once considered the rudest man in Britain.

Similar patterns can be found in the great American political families. Senator Prescott Bush initiated the family's political dynasty, but spent his free time hiding out at a country club drinking himself into oblivion. His son George Herbert went on to become president and his son George Walker also made it through a boozy youth to the top job, while his son Jeb is Governor of Florida and remains a possible presidential candidate. Jeb Bush's daughter, Noelle, who has been jailed for drug possession, is however, a classic case of a political dynasty's collateral damage. The sad story of JFK's sister Rose, with her botched unnecessary lobotomy and subsequent sequestration, is another.

Belonging to a celebrity family puts people under pressures that we regular citizens don't normally have to deal with. High achievers are usually extremely egocentric and they demand sacrifices of those around them in the pursuit of their goals. Even when their offspring achieve a modicum of success it can come at a cost. The Fonda children, Jane and Peter, are excellent examples of children who have followed in their father's footsteps, and have the emotional scars to prove it. In most families, individuals get to rise to the level of their natural ability. But many members of celebrity families are faced with steep descents to the natural level of theirs.

The souls of some celebrities are just plain ugly. Imagine if your grandfather was the richest man in the world and you were kidnapped because of it. Then imagine he was too mean to pay the ransom until your ear was cut off and mailed to your mother. That's what happened to Paul Getty III. When Patty Hearst was kidnapped she ended up joining the revolution of her captors, then served time for armed robbery—but at least the family money was used to try and rescue her.

Growing up famous and liberated from the expectation to earn your keep, magnifies the potential for perversity. Drug and alcohol addictions, suicide, sexual fetishism and madness abound in celebrity families. Sometimes engaging in the perverse can magnify your income, as Paris Hilton has shown by combining the family name with a porn video, to turn herself into a merchandizing empire that girls the world over are imitating. There's a marked trend today for girls in celebrity families to become models: Paris and Nicky, Amanda Hearst and her cousin Lydia Hearst Shaw, Lauren Bush, Stella Tennant, Sophie Dahl and Jasmine Guinness all belong to families in these pages. It's a far rarer occasion when a celebrity family member chooses to become an accountant.

Being smart, creative and famous is no guarantee of being able to keep yourself out of trouble. Take the Hemingway family, for example, with its unparalleled rate of suicide. Other literary families featured here include the wild Tolstoys of Russia, and the Dahls who have combined literature and Hollywood. One of the great theorists on the family, Sigmund Freud, also founded a dynasty whose descendants have survived transplantation from Vienna to Britain and the USA, where they've excelled in the media and the arts, producing novelists, painters, PR Svengalis, fashion designers and politicians.

One of the most brilliant families here, however, is the Darwin family. Their eminence began with the crippled pottery genius and inventor, Josiah Wedgwood, whose fortune subsequently helped the descendants of himself and his friend—renaissance man Erasmus Darwin (whose son married his brother's daughter)—make some of the greatest scientific discoveries of the 19th century, including the theory of evolution as we largely know it today.

A Darwinian question provoked by these celebrity family trees is whether it is nature or nurture that perpetuates the families' success? The logical answer is something of both. But when presented with the sheer evidence of tragedy, black sheep and misfits in these families, it's hard not to think that, if we are looking at evolution in progress, it's evolution that favors random selection. Contrasting the wide variety of genius on display is also ample proof to suggest that human nature has improved very little since all those millions of years ago when humans first descended from the trees.

PETER FONDA AND FAMILY PICTURED AT THEIR HOME IN LOS ANGELES, 1970. FRONT ROW FROM LEFT TO RIGHT: SON JUSTIN, DAUGHTER BRIDGET AND WIFE SUSAN.

HOW TO USE THIS BOOK

Every family has its saints, sinners, heroes and hopeless cases, but some families seem to have more than their fair share! *Celebrity Family Trees* takes a detailed look at twenty of the world's most notable families, providing insight into what makes the famous members of these families tick.

Rather than providing a chronological history from the dark ages of each family up until contemporary times, we highlight the most interesting people and stories in the family's history. Each family section includes a number of introductory pages, complete with photographs of key family members or family groups, witty pull-outs and features that sometimes take a bit of a swipe at our families—only if deserved, of course!

At the heart of the book, though, are the family tree spreads. These spreads show our famous families' trees in the traditional manner, laid out so you can see where all the family members fit into the big picture. Some of the larger family trees extend over more than two pages. We haven't always included every person in the family, but all the important marriage links and bloodlines are there, and the stars of each family are highlighted in gray boxes. In addition, our fun icons help you to pick out the family's drunks, devils and drug addicts at-a-glance!

CANDID PHOTOS ◄

Classic black and white and color photographs show our famous families at key moments in their history, relaxing at home with each other in casual mode, or in compromising situations.

PULL-OUTS ◄

Pull-out features provide witty insights into what our families get up to in their public and private lives. The "How They Rate" box, for instance, gives our families marks out of five for a variety of categories.

FAMILY HISTORY ◄

We provide a potted history of each family, focusing on the key moments in their history, sharing their highs and lows, and showing how they fitted into their contemporary world as well as how they burst from the bonds of being ordinary to achieve fame and fortune.

THE KENNEDYS

JOHN F. AND BOBBY AT A SENATE HEARING ON LABOR RACKETEERING, 1957.

WITHIN THE SPACE OF A CENTURY THE KENNEDY FAMILY GREW FROM POOR, BOG-IRISH IMMIGRANTS INTO AMERICA'S PRE-EMINENT POLITICAL FAMILY. ALTHOUGH THEY MAY HAVE BEEN OUTSTRIPPED BY THE BUSH DYNASTY IN TERMS OF HOLDING OFFICE, NO OTHER FAMILY HAS ENTERED THE POPULAR IMAGINATION TO THE EXTENT OF THE KENNEDYS WITH THEIR CHARM, AMBITION, TRAGEDY, IDEALISM, RUTHLESSNESS, SCANDAL AND GOOD WORKS.

In true Irish fashion, the family made its initial money selling booze, then made even more bootlegging it during Prohibition. In true American fashion, their wealth grew exponentially as a result of savvy speculation on the stock market. Yet, balancing this worldly performance was a powerful sense of spiritual purpose and the obligation to do good works. Few families have done as much for charity as the Kennedys. At a political level this created a Kennedy aura which combined ruthless pragmatism, a Macchiavellian sense of destiny with genuine idealism—a quality that has largely been lost in the 30-second-grab, spin-doctored politics of today. Of course this idealism lost its chance to be made a reality with the assassinations of JFK and Bobby, and the allure of the Kennedys is partly because they represent unfulfilled political potential. Yet, there is also a seamier, self-interested side to the Kennedys, prepared to sacrifice others (even their own) in the pursuit of the family's interest. The sad fate of Rosemary Kennedy is an example. Then again, few families have been as unlucky as the Kennedys, and the superstitious might think the Kennedy Curse is a consequence of hubris, of being stubborn enough to hold onto a dream.

HOW THEY RATE

WEALTH: ★ ★ ★ ★
Not short of a dollar but more interested in power, fame and public works than money.

HEALTH: ★ ★ ★
Their longevity is generally good, but they are extremely accident prone, while there is evidence of an addictive streak running through the family.

HAPPINESS: ★
Considering what has happened to them, it's hard to imagine them getting too much of a chance to be happy.

FAME: ★ ★ ★ ★
Huge at the time, though the pinnacle of Kennedy fame has probably passed.

SEXINESS: ★ ★ ★ ★ ★
Yes. JFK was a Presidential sex symbol and he cashed in on it, too. Male Kennedys are known for their womanizing. The good Catholics among them, both male and female, have shown their sexiness by the large size of their families.

BLACK SHEEP FACTOR: ★ ★ ★ ★
Heroin addiction, murder, serial adultery, election fraud. This is a family with a lot of Black Sheep moments.

ECCENTRICITY: ★
More of the all-American style charm.

INFLUENCE: ★ ★ ★ ★
On the surface their influence has been profound, though an argument might be made that the Kennedy myth exceeds the reality of their achievement. Still they are hardly lightweights on the world scene.

MONROE SINGS *HAPPY BIRTHDAY*, 1962.

JFK CHRONOLOGY	
1917	Born May 29.
1940	Harvard honors thesis on UK's Hitler A published as a book, *Why England Sl*
1941	Joins US navy.
1943	Earns medal for rescuing his crew whe by the Japanese during World War II.
1946	Elected to the US House of Represen
1952	Elected to US Senate as senator from
1953	Marries Jacqueline Bouvier.
1955	Almost dies during a back operation.
1956	Loses his bid for the Democratic nom Vice President.
1957	Daughter Caroline born. Wins Pulitze with *Profiles in Courage*, which chroni risked their careers for the sake of the
1960	Defeats Richard Nixon by a very slim the 35th President of the United State margin of 0.2 percent with 49.75 perc against Nixon's 49.55 percent.) Son John born.
1961	Becomes the second-youngest Ameri Bay of Pigs crisis after botched CIA-in
1962	Cuban Missile Crisis.
1963	Sends the Alabama National Guard to Alabama to protect two African–Ame won a court order against segregatior Son Patrick is born but dies after 2 da Signs the Nuclear Test Ban Treaty. Assassinated by Lee Harvey Oswald.

" And so, my fellow Americ
for you ... ask what you co
of the world ... ask not what
we can do
JOHN F. KENN

FAMILY TREE ICONS

Our slightly wicked icons appear on the family tree spreads. They occur next to a person's name only when they have been fully earned. They celebrate the geniuses and angels, and poke fun at the black sheep and casanovas. You'll find when you read the book that, oftentimes, families seem to specialize in one particular vice.

ALCOHOLIC   BLACK SHEEP   DEVIL   JETSETTER   MURDERED   SUICIDE   JAIL BIRD

ANGEL   CASANOVA   DRUG ADDICT   MILLIONAIRE   NOBLE   DRUGS & ALCOHOL   GENIUS

KEY TO LINES ◄

Different patterned lines denote different types of links. The line key clearly explains these.

PEOPLE BOXES ◄

Each family member has his or her own box. A solid line indicates a male and a dotted line indicates a female.

KEY PLAYERS ◄

The most important members of each family are highlighted in gray boxes. You might not have heard of a few of them, but you can be sure that they were instrumental in putting their family's name on the map.

KEY: CHILD ····► ADOPTED CHILD ·······► MARRIED ──── DIVORCED ─ ─ ─ ─ DE FACTO ········ SPLIT UP ──/──

{ kennedy family tree }

CELEBRITY FAMILY TREE / 146

PATRICK JOSEPH KENNEDY 1858–1929
The son of poor Irish Catholics who emigrated in a "coffin ship" to Boston, his father died in a cholera epidemic soon after his birth. He was the first Kennedy to get a formal education and won a scholarship to Boston College. He was a successful [...] Prohibition. The [...] cted to both [...] nate.

JOSEPH PATRICK KENNEDY 1888–1969
Joseph Patrick made his money during the stock market boom of the 1920s and pulled it out before the 1929 crash. He simultaneously operated as a Hollywood financier and had a stormy affair with the actress Gloria Swanson. As the son of a spirits importer, he made an illicit fortune supplying bootleg booze during the Prohibition era (1920–33). When Prohibition was repealed, he turned to politics. He was a backer of Franklin D. Roosevelt, who appointed him Ambassador to Great Britain from 1938 until 1940, but he lost favor for not supporting America entering the war.

ROSE ELIZABETH FITZGERALD 1890–1995
She married Joseph Kennedy in 1914 after a 7-year courtship. They had nine children of whom four would predecease her. Deeply religious, she shepherded her family through their many triumphs and tragedies until she died aged 104.

JOSEPH PATRICK KENNEDY JR 1915–44
His father had high hopes of a political career for his eldest son. He left Harvard Law School before his final year to become a US navy pilot. He earned his wings in 1942 and was sent to England where he flew missions as a bomber pilot. In July 1944, he heroically volunteered for a dangerous special mission designed to test a possible counter to Germany's V2 rockets. However, the plane he was flying laden with explosives blew up. Kennedy's body was never recovered.

ROSE MARIE "ROSEMARY" KENNEDY 1918–2005
Whether she was mentally handicapped or merely stigmatized as such for being slow in a family of powerful intellects, remains a moot point. However, she was competent enough to perform math and keep a diary. Yet adolescent mood swings and wild behavior made her a potential embarrassment to this image-conscious and ambitious family and her parents put her in for a lobotomy, which they had been told would cure her problems. Instead it reduced her to an incontinent, infantile state and she was packed off to a residential care unit in Wisconsin where she lived until her death 55 years later.

KATHLEEN AGNES "KICK" KENNEDY 1920–48
Known to her family as Kick, apparently because she was fun to be around, she worked for the British Red Cross during the war and married William Cavendish, heir to the Duke of Devonshire. Her mother, a staunch Catholic, was against the match on the grounds that he was a Protestant. Four months after their marriage, he was killed by a German sniper (his brother Andrew, who was married to Deborah Mitford, inherited the title). Kick then became the mistress of another English aristocrat, the married 8th Earl Fitzwilliam. Mrs Kennedy was even more appalled. As Kick and Fitzwilliam were flying to France to seek her father's blessing, their plane crashed into a mountain. Kick's mother and siblings did not attend her funeral.

EUNICE MARY KENNEDY 1921–
Perhaps out of sympathy or even guilt for the fate of Rosemary, Eunice Kennedy has spent most of her professional life helping the disabled, and especially the mentally retarded. In 1968, along with Anne McGlone Burke, she was one of the founders of the Special Olympics. She married Robert Sargent Shriver in 1953 and they had five kids.

JOHN FITZGERALD KENNEDY 1917–63
His early life showed both prodigious talent and tremendous reserve. Despite poor health from Addison's disease (a hormonal disorder) and osteoporosis, he joined the navy and became a hero when he rescued his crew when their boat was rammed by a Japanese destroyer. He entered the House of Representatives in 1946, moved to the Senate in 1952 and married Jackie in 1953. His 1956 nomination for the vice presidency failed, but he succeeded in becoming President against Richard Nixon in 1960. His presidency was dominated by international incidents such as the Bay of Pigs fiasco and the subsequent Cuban Missile Crisis. He was also instrumental in starting the Space Race, and sending the National Guard into the South to enforce Civil Rights. As a funky young couple, the Kennedys bridged politics and celebrity—something also noticeable in JFK's serial womanizing. However, the most resonant moment of his presidency was his assassination, while being driven through Dallas in a convertible, on November 22, 1963.

2 CHILDREN NEXT PAGE

JACQUELINE LEE BOUVIER 1929–94
Her high school yearbook quoted her ambition as "not to be a housewife." She became the White House wife instead. The daughter of a wealthy family, in 1947–48 she was named Debutante of the Year. After graduating from college, she worked as a photographer for the Washington Times-Herald, which was when she met the husband-to-be at a dinner party. As First Lady she modernized both the role and the White House. She displayed immense dignity when JFK was assassinated. In 1968, she married shipping magnate Aristotle Onassis. They remained married until his death in 1975, though the marriage had unofficially ended.

ROBERT SARGENT SHRIVER 1915–
After fighting in the US navy during World War II, he married Eunice Kennedy in 1953 and entered political life through working on his brother-in-law Jack's political campaigns. Like his wife, he was interested in philanthropic activity and was appointed the first director of the Peace Corps in 1961. He was selected by the Johnson administration to be the US Ambassador to France, a position which he held 1968–70. He also made unsuccessful runs for Vice President in 1972 and later President in 1976.

3 CHILDREN: MARIA, MARK & ANTHONY PAGE 149

4 MORE CHILDREN: ROBERT, PATRICIA, JEAN & EDWARD NEXT PAGE

COLLATERAL DAMAGE

AS THE THIRD SON OF ELEVEN CHILDREN, DAVID KENNEDY MIGHT HAVE FELT AGGRIEVED AT BEING LOST IN THE MIDDLE, BUT HIS FATHER, BOBBY, ALSO A THIRD SON, KNEW THIS AND PAID HIS DREAMY, INTROVERTED SON A BIT OF SPECIAL ATTENTION. WHEN HE BEGAN CAMPAIGNING FOR THE 1968 PRESIDENTIAL PRIMARIES, HE TOOK 13-YEAR-OLD DAVID WITH HIM. WHILE CALIFORNIANS WERE CASTING THEIR VOTES, DAVID AND BOBBY WENT FOR A SWIM AT MALIBU. DAVID GOT CAUGHT IN AN UNDERTOW AND BOBBY SWAM OUT AND RESCUED HIM. AS BOBBY KENNEDY WAS ANNOUNCING HIS VICTORY IN THE PRIMARY, DAVID WAS BACK IN THE HOTEL ROOM, ALONE, PROUDLY WATCHING HIS DAD ON TV THEN HIS DAD WAS SHOT IN FRONT OF HIS EYES. IN THE CONFUSION THAT FOLLOWED, DAVID WAS FORGOTTEN, AND IT WASN'T UNTIL SEVERAL HOURS LATER THAT HE WAS FOUND IN A STATE OF SHOCK, STILL STARING AT THE TV, BY THE ASTRONAUT JOHN GLENN AND AUTHOR THEODORE WHITE. DAVID WAS UNABLE TO SPEAK FOR DAYS AND THE EVENTUAL DECLINE OF THIS SENSITIVE BOY INTO A DRUG HAZE, WHICH ENDED WITH HIS OVERDOSE DEATH, HAD ITS ORIGINS IN THIS ONE APPALLING MOMENT.

what your country can do
country. My fellow citizens
do for you, but what together
om of man.
ATION SPEECH

► REVEALING QUOTES

We have selected some of the best quotations from our famous families. Sometimes the quotes reveal the personalities of an individual while, at other times, they give us an insight into what it's like to be part of a famous family.

FOLLOW THE LINKS ◄

For some of the larger families in this book, for example the Kennedys, we couldn't fit everybody on one page, so we have continued the family tree over to the next page. Just follow the signs to help you link up the first and second page of the family tree.

THE BARRYMORES

A BARRYMORE FAMILY REUNION AT JOHN BARRYMORE'S HOME. ETHEL IS SEATED IN THE CANE CHAIR WITH LIONEL ON THE LEFT, AND JOHN BARRYMORE HOLDS HIS BABY SON.

HOW THEY RATE

WEALTH ★ ★ ★
At times they have been rich and at others incredibly poor. Money does not seem to be the primary motivation of this family. The latest Barrymore star, Drew, has to be worth a lot of money, however, from the combination of her successful acting and producing career.

HEALTH ★ ★
Alcoholism is the big factor here, though both the mental and physical health are less robust than in many other famous families.

HAPPINESS ★ ★
Too much tragedy and indifference toward progeny is what prevents this family from a higher happiness rating—even if it is also full of good-time girls and boys.

FAME ★ ★ ★ ★ ★
Long-term Hollywood aristocracy.

SEXINESS ★ ★ ★ ★ ★
A stunning array of good lookers on both the male and female sides, with the odd character actor thrown in to stop them becoming formulaic in their beauty.

BLACK SHEEP FACTOR ★ ★ ★ ★ ★
There's a strong rebellious streak and a capacity for sex scandal and hell raising. A true black sheep in this family would be an accountant.

ECCENTRICITY ★ ★ ★
Drew Barrymore's father with his former reclusiveness takes the cake here. It's a fine line, but other Barrymores have tended to be idiosyncratic and charismatic rather than eccentric.

INFLUENCE ★ ★
In terms of Hollywood, enormous, but their clout and brilliance has pretty much stayed contained in the world of showbiz.

The Barrymores' acting pedigree predates Hollywood, since the dynasty's origins lie in the theaters of New York and Philadelphia in the middle of the 19th century. However, the first stars in this thespian family were actually Drews—a name of course that is acknowledged in the first name of the family's contemporary celebrity, Drew Barrymore.

Louisa Lane arrived in America in 1827 with her widowed mother. Both her parents had been entertainers, and Louisa soon made an impact on Broadway as a child star. She married comedian, Irish-born John Drew, in 1850 and together they managed the Arch Theater in Philadelphia. Louisa was the thinker and John the drinker—the genes for alcoholism have always been almost as strong as those for acting in this family. In 1861, Louisa took over the management of what was renamed Mrs John Drew's Arch Street Theater, a job she was to hold for 31 years.

The three children of the next generation were all actors too. Both John and Georgiana began their careers under the tutelage of their mother before joining the renowned troupe of the autocratic playwright and theater manager, Augustin Daly. It was here that Georgiana acted alongside and fell in love with an English actor called Maurice Barrymore. Meanwhile younger brother, Sidney, was making his mark as a comic actor, primarily as part of the husband and wife team, Mr and Mrs Sidney Drew. Sidney was also the first in the family to go into the movies.

THE BARRYMORES ARE SOMETIMES REFERRED TO AS "HOLLYWOOD'S FIRST FAMILY." NO OTHER FAMILY HAS SHOWN SUCH ACTING DEPTH, YET THEY ARE ALSO FAMOUS FOR THEIR ECCENTRICITIES, WILD BEHAVIOR AND ALCOHOL ABUSE.

DREW BARRYMORE IN 1986, AGED 10—ALREADY A CHAIN-SMOKING ALCOHOLIC.

The three children of Georgiana and Maurice—Lionel, Ethel and John—are perhaps the most talented and famous Barrymore generation. All three siblings were successful actors and Hollywood stars in their own right. Lionel and Ethel won Academy Awards, although, paradoxically, it was John (who didn't) who was rated both the best actor and biggest heart-throb of the three. His 1922 performance of *Hamlet* has often been considered the best of the 20th century. Despite his talent, John had an ambivalent attitude toward acting, and his troubled personal life—particularly the drinking—reduced him in later years to a parody of his former self, then finally killed him via cirrhosis of the liver.

THREE OF THE MOST FAMOUS MEMBERS OF THE BARRYMORE FAMILY PICTURED IN 1904. FROM LEFT TO RIGHT: JOHN, ETHEL AND LIONEL. IT WAS AROUND THIS TIME THAT THE THREE SIBLINGS MADE THEIR ACTING DEBUTS.

THE RANKINS

Although not a blood component of the Barrymore lineage, the Rankins—who married into the Drew family via Gladys Rankin (aka Mrs Sidney Drew)—are a Hollywood family in their own right. Gladys's sister, Phyllis, married the actor Harry Davenport (1866–1949) whose long career straddled stage, silent films and the talkies, including the role of Dr Mead in *Gone with the Wind*. He acted right up until his death. His final movie, the Frank Capra comedy *Riding High*, starring Bing Crosby, was released the year after Davenport's death. Harry was also one of the founders of Actors' Equity. First known as the White Rats, they closed down most of Broadway in a campaign for rights such as indoor plumbing in dressing rooms and a 6-day week. His first wife was Alice Davenport (née Shepard), a silent era comedy actress who appeared in some of Charlie Chaplin's films; while their daughter, Dorothy, was a Universal Studios star by the age of 17, who married Wallace Reid—an eventual Paramount matinee idol, who died from a morphine addiction in 1923. Their son, Wallace Reid Jr, did some acting in the 1940s and died in a plane crash off Santa Monica aged 73. Some of Harry's children by Phyllis also entered the movies game. Son, Arthur Rankin, acted in more than 140 films. His son, Arthur Rankin Jr, is a TV and film producer and director, whose credits include the 1966 version of *King Kong*, *The Wind in the Willows* and *The King and I*. Harry's daughter, Kate, was primarily a stage actress, while her son, Dirk Wayne Summers, appeared with his grandfather in *Gone with the Wind* before going on to write episodes of seminal TV series, such as *Kojak* and *Ironside*.

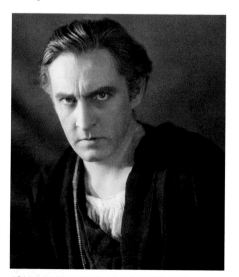

JOHN BARRYMORE AS HAMLET, 1925.

DIANA BARRYMORE, DAUGHTER OF JOHN BARRYMORE, RECUPERATING AT LENOX HILL HOSPITAL. DIANA WAS SUFFERING FROM BURNS TO HER RIGHT LEG, WHICH SHE RECEIVED FROM BOILING OIL IN A DOMESTIC COOKING ACCIDENT.

RASPUTIN AND THE EMPRESS (1932)

This is the only film all three famous Barrymore siblings appeared in together. Ethel played the Empress Alexandra; Lionel had the leading role playing the Mad Monk (Rasputin); and John played Prince Paul, his assassin. In real life, however, it was Prince Yusupov who assassinated Rasputin, but the story was changed because Yusupov was still alive. In fact his wife, Irina Romanov Yusupov, who was the model for the character Princess Natasha, sued the studio on the grounds the film implied she was a mistress of Gregory Rasputin. She was awarded over $100,000 in London and a reputed settlement of $250,000 in New York. Rasputin wasn't the only person assassinated in the film. The original direct, Charles Brabin, was taken off the film because he didn't get on with Ethel, who constantly disparaged him. He was replaced by Richard Boleslawski. Writer Charles MacArthur was nominated for an Academy Award for the film for best writing.

A TROUBLED GENERATION

The next generation of Barrymores were a troubled lot, with violence, drug abuse, suicide, under-achieving and weirdness all featuring. Although both of Ethel's sons to society stockbroker Russell Griswold Colt—descendant of the inventor of the Colt revolver—dabbled in acting, neither of them had success. Only her daughter, Ethel Barrymore Colt, made a name for herself, primarily as a Broadway musical specialist, before retiring into married life. Lionel's two children both died young. John's children—Diana (with his second wife, the poet and broadcaster Blance Oelrichs), and John Drew (with his third wife, actress Dolores Costello)—never managed a comfortable relationship with reality. The most talented of her generation, Diana Barrymore was once considered one of the "next big things" in Hollywood but she imploded. She considered herself a has-been by the age of 23 and spent the rest of her life fulfilling that prophecy, until she committed suicide aged 38.

John Drew also had a troubled upbringing. Sent to a military school he defied his mom's wishes and became an actor, leaping straight into movies without serving the more usual stage apprenticeship. His rebellious, violent nature and drinking made him difficult, but suited to roles in westerns. Toward the end of his life he became something of a derelict living in the wilderness.

Given her upbringing and the fact that she was an alcoholic and cocaine addict by the time most people are puffing on their first cigarette, it's amazing that Drew Barrymore has beaten the family addiction curse and emerged from a hellish adolescence to become one of the most engaging female stars in Hollywood, with lead roles in movies such as *Charlie's Angels*. She is also proving to be a savvy operator as a producer with her company Flower Films—evidenced by her involvement in movies such as *Donnie Darko*. Her love life, however, has proved somewhat less successful.

DANGEROUS LIVES

Nowadays, the biggest dangers that most Hollywood stars seem to face are from the pursuing paparazzi and their own addiction problems. But in the early years, acting was both a disreputable and risky profession.

★ **LOUISA LANE'S** mother married stage manager John Kinlock soon after her American debut. In 1830 they headed to Jamaica with Kinlock managing a company of actors. However, they were shipwrecked and marooned on a beach for 6 weeks until another ship could be found to rescue them. Eventually arriving in Kingston, Jamaica, the troupe was hit by yellow fever. Kinlock died, as did Louisa's half sister, and her mother nearly died.

★ **MAURICE BARRYMORE** was touring with a theater company in Marshall Texas when he went to a saloon with colleagues Ben Porter and Ellen Cummins. Jim Curry, a local drunk and thug, started calling Cummins a whore. Ben Porter, who had just proposed to her, objected, and Maurice Barrymore, who was managing as well as acting in the troupe, told Curry to leave them alone. Curry kept on with his abuse, so Barrymore—who had been British Middleweight Boxing champion—offered to take it up with Curry in a fight. After assuring them he was unarmed, Curry produced a gun and shot both Porter and Barrymore. Porter died, while Barrymore was seriously wounded and had to spend around 6 weeks in bed recuperating. Jim Curry's brother was the mayor of a nearby town and managed to buy the jury, who produced a "not guilty" verdict on the grounds of insanity.

★ **SCOTT RANKIN DREW** was the son of comedy actor Sidney Drew and cousin of Ethel, Lionel and John Barrymore. Not wanting him to go on the stage, his parents sent him to military school instead but, as with John Drew Barrymore, it wasn't enough to knock the thespian out of him. Although Scott Rankin Drew started out as an actor, it seemed his true talent was as a director. However, his parents' decision to send him to military school came back to bite them. In 1915, he joined the 180 American pilots who flew under the French flag as the Lafayette Flying Corp in World War I—America wasn't to enter the war until 1917. He survived until being shot down by the Germans just before the end of the war. His father was broken hearted and never recovered, dying a year later—proof that both love and war can be deadly.

JOHN DREW BARRYMORE (ABOVE) ONCE STARRED IN THE TELEVISION SERIES *KUNG FU*. IN HER 1991 AUTOBIOGRAPHY, *LITTLE GIRL LOST*, DREW BARRYMORE TOLD HOW HER FATHER WOULD PRACTICE HIS KUNG FU MOVES ON HER. ONCE WHEN SHE COMPLAINED ABOUT THE PAIN, HE GRABBED HER HAND AND STUCK IT INTO THE FLAME OF A CANDLE.

DREW BARRYMORE'S MOM, HUNGARIAN-BORN JAID, 1996. JAID POSED FOR THE SEPTEMBER 1995 ISSUE OF *PLAYBOY* MAGAZINE—JUST 8 MONTHS AFTER HER DAUGHTER DREW HAD POSED FOR THE JANUARY ISSUE.

> "I LEARNED EARLY ON THAT FAMILY, AS FAR AS MY MOTHER AND FATHER, WERE NOT AN OPTION."
> DREW BARRYMORE

DREW BARRYMORE WITH HER MOM, JAID, AND HALF BROTHER, JOHN BLYTH.

BLYTH AS A BARRYMORE

THE FIRST OF THE LONG LINE OF BARRYMORES, MAURICE WAS ORIGINALLY HERBERT BLYTH. HIS FATHER, JOHN BLYTH, WAS THE SON OF MINOR GENTRY. HE WAS BORN AT SNEATING HALL IN ESSEX, BUT LEFT AFTER HIS FATHER REFUSED TO LET HIM MARRY THE DAUGHTER OF ONE OF THEIR TENANT FARMERS WHO JOHN HAD GOTTEN PREGNANT. AFTER SHACKING UP WITH A WIDOW IN LONDON, HE LEFT FOR INDIA AND A FINAGLED HIS WAY INTO A JOB WITH THE EAST INDIA COMPANY IN CALCUTTA. HIS FIRST WIFE DIED FROM TYPHOID, AND HIS SECOND WAS THE HALF-CASTE DAUGHTER OF A BRITISH ARMY OFFICER AND AN INDIAN WOMAN—AND THEREFORE DEEMED UNFIT FOR POLITE, CULTURALLY CRINGING, CALCUTTA SOCIETY. THEY MOVED TO AGRA WHERE HERBERT WAS BORN. AT SOME POINT THE INDIAN BLYTHS WERE REUNITED WITH THEIR ENGLISH RELATIVES AND HERBERT SPENT TIME WITH THEM WHILE HE STUDIED AT HARROW SCHOOL IN ENGLAND, AND THEN OXFORD. HIS PARENTS WERE APPALLED WHEN HE DECIDED TO BECOME AN ACTOR SO HE CHANGED HIS NAME TO MITIGATE THEIR SHAME AT HIS CHOSEN VOCATION. (APPARENTLY, THE NEW NAME "MAURICE BARRYMORE" WAS TAKEN FROM A THEATER POSTER IN LONDON.) ALTHOUGH THE FOLLOWING TWO GENERATIONS OF BARRYMORES WERE CHRISTENED "BLYTH," IN A CLASSIC HOLLYWOOD SCENARIO, THE ILLUSION HAS PROVEN STRONGER THAN THE REALITY, AND DREW IS A BARRYMORE THROUGH AND THROUGH, WHILE HER HALF BROTHER, JOHN, HAS HUNG ONTO "BLYTH," BUT ONLY AS A MIDDLE NAME.

JOHN BARRYMORE, TOMB RAIDER

John Barrymore senior wanted to be cremated and to have his ashes laid to rest next to his father and mother in the family cemetery in Philadelphia. However, his brother, Lionel, and sister, Ethel, were Catholic and cremation was yet to be sanctioned by the Catholic Church. As a consequence, Barrymore's remains were entombed at Calvary Cemetery, Los Angeles, instead. In 1980, John Drew Barrymore decided in a boozy moment of filial piety, after hearing a rendition of *The Cremation of Sam McGee*, that his pop's last wishes should be respected. Enlisting the help of his son, he removed the "Good Night, Sweet Prince" marble monument at the front of the crypt and entered. The smell apparently was awful. Although Barrymore had been dead for 38 years, his body was still decomposing. Even worse, the casket liner had cracked and body fluids had formed a kind of glue between the casket and the floor of the crypt. They eventually got the casket into a van they had waiting outside and drove to the Odd Fellows Cemetery, which had the nearest crematorium, and handed the casket over for cremation. John Drew insisted on having a look inside the casket before they left. After viewing the body, he came out white as a sheet and crying. He got in the car and said to his son, "Thank God I'm drunk, I'll never remember it."

OH, I LOVE HUGGING. I WISH I WAS AN OCTOPUS SO I COULD HUG 10 PEOPLE AT A TIME!
DREW BARRYMORE

DREW BARRYMORE HIGHLIGHTS

1975 Born February 22.

1976 Makes her acting debut aged 11 months in a dog food commercial.

1980 Big screen debut aged 4 playing William Hurt's daughter Margaret Jessup in *Altered States*.

1982 Throws a chair at her father and doesn't see him again until 1989. While most kids of 7 were learning to read or clinging to their moms at the school bus stop, Drew was starring as Gertie in Spielberg's *E.T. The Extra-Terrestrial*. Even at this age, Drew already had an inkling that she might end up having to be her own driver.

1984 Has her first drink and takes up cigarettes. Nominated for a Golden Globe for her role in *Irreconcilable Differences*.

1985 Starts smoking marijuana.

1987 Gets into cocaine.

1988 Goes into rehab—twice.

1989 Comes out of rehab—ends formal education.

1991 Legally emancipates herself from her parents.

1994 Marries Jeremy Thomas for 6 weeks.

1995 Poses nude for *Playboy* and flashes her breasts on the David Letterman show as a present for the host's birthday. Her godfather, Steven Spielberg, gives her a quilt for her birthday with the offending issue of *Playboy* enclosed, together with a note saying "cover yourself up."
Sets up her production company Flower Films with business partner Nancy Juvonen.

1996 Plays Casey Becker in *Scream*.

1999 Produces and stars in *Never Been Kissed*.

2000 Produces and stars in *Charlie's Angels*. (Along with its 2003 sequel, it would gross over $500 million at the box office.)

2001 Marries comedian Tom Green.
Wins critical acclaim for her Flower Films movie *Donnie Darko*, on which she was executive producer.

2002 Divorces comedian Tom Green.
Starts dating Strokes drummer, Fabrizio Moretti.

2003 Produces and stars in *Charlie's Angels: Full Throttle*.

2004 Gets a star on the Hollywood Walk of Fame.

2005 Produces and stars in the baseball adaptation of the Nick Hornby novel *Fever Pitch* and becomes a Boston Red Sox fan in the process.

HOLLYWOOD WALK OF FAME

ALL TOGETHER, THIS EXTENDED FAMILY HAS ELEVEN STARS ON THE HOLLYWOOD WALK OF FAME. MOST OF THEM ARE IN THE MOVING PICTURE CATEGORY, WITH LIONEL BARRYMORE DOUBLING UP WITH ONE FOR RADIO, TOO. JOHN DREW BARRYMORE IS THE ODD MAN OUT. HIS STAR IS FOR HIS TELEVISION, RATHER THAN MOVIE, PERFORMANCES.

DREW BARRYMORE POSED NUDE FOR *PLAYBOY* IN 1995, THE SAME YEAR SHE FLASHED HER BREASTS TO TALK SHOW HOST DAVID LETTERMAN LIVE ON AIR.

{barrymore family tree}

THOMAS FREDERICK LANE 1796–1825

He was a provincial actor of considerable fame but died early, leaving his young family struggling to survive.

ELIZA TRENTER LANE 1796–1887

She was a professional ballad singer. When Louisa was born, England was mourning the death of King George III and the theaters were closed for a month. As such, Louisa was born into poverty. She decided to travel to America 2 years after her husband's death and found work at Philadelphia's Walnut Theater.

LOUISA LANE DREW 1820–97

Louisa was born in London, where she debuted on stage at the age of 1. She arrived in New York with her widowed mother in 1827 and began a stellar career as a child actress. As an adult, she worked for the Bowery Theater in New York before moving to Philadelphia with the Walnut Theater in 1838. Her marriage to John Drew in 1850 was her third. He took over the lease of Philadelphia's Arch Street Theater in 1853 but preferred touring with productions. In 1861 Louisa took over the management and it was renamed Mrs John Drew's Arch Street Theater. She ran it for 31 successful years, building it into one of the finest repertory theaters in America.

JOHN DREW 1827–62

Born in Dublin, he came to America and made his reputation as a comedian in the 1840s. His father was the treasurer of Niblo's Theater in New York. In 1853 he took on the lease of the Arch Street Theater, Philadelphia, which he ran as a stock company (repertory theater) with his wife as co-star and eventual manager. He died the year after his wife took over the Arch—he was the first of many in this illustrious family to fall victim to the demon drink.

JOHN DREW 1853–1927

The eldest son began his career under the tutelage of his mother at the Arch. In 1875 he joined the company of Augustin Daly in New York. His first success was while playing the character of Alexander Sprinkle in Daly's play, *Arabian Nights*, or *Haroun al Rashid*. He joined Charles Frohman's company in 1892, starring in modern comedies until Frohman was killed in the sinking of the *Lusitania* (which triggered America's entry into World War I) in 1915. From that point his career began to slide.

SIDNEY DREW 1864–1919

His mother claimed he was adopted, as her husband had been touring during the window of conception and was dead before Sidney was born. His first wife was Gladys Rankin, who also came from a famous acting clan. Billed as Mr and Mrs Sidney Drew, they toured America performing marital comedies. Later they went to Hollywood where he worked as an actor and director. After Gladys's death in 1914, he married a 24-year-old screenwriter and they went on to make the popular Mr and Mrs Sidney Drew series of films. When his son was killed in the war, Sidney had a nervous breakdown on stage in Detroit and died less than a year later from kidney failure.

1ST WIFE

GLADYS RANKIN 1874–1914

The daughter of producer McKee Rankin, Gladys wrote plays and stories under the masculine pseudonym George Cameron. Her marriage to Sidney Drew was also an artistic partnership. He directed and/or appeared in films based on her writing.

2ND WIFE

LUCILLE MCVEY 1890–1925

Lucille (aka Jane Morrow), daughter of a Missouri farmer, was an actress and writer when she met Sidney shortly after his wife's death. They married almost immediately, although he was more than twice her age. Together they created a series of domestic comedies. After his death she lost interest in films and died in 1925, at the age of 35, following a chronic illness.

In the early years of the Arch, Mrs Louisa Lane Drew often played 'breech roles,' such as Shakespeare's Romeo or Mark Antony. Her favorite role, however, was that of Mrs Malaprop, a character in "The Rivals" by 18th-century English playwright Richard Sheridan. After she'd retired from managing the Arch, it was said this grand dame of American theater would happily travel 1000 miles to play the role.

GEORGIANA DREW 1855–93

The woman who put the Drew into Barrymore. Like her brother John, she started her career under the direction of her mother at the Arch before moving on to Augustin Daly's troupe in New York. She performed alongside Maurice Barrymore in the Broadway play *Pique*, and married him the year after in 1876. Like her younger brother, Sidney, she was known for her comic roles, but it was her three children, Lionel, Ethel and John, who have sealed her place in American theatrical history.

MAURICE BARRYMORE 1847–1905

Born in India as Herbert Blyth, his father had belonged to the English gentry before getting an unmarried woman pregnant and running off to India with her. Herbert boarded at Harrow School in England, before studying law at Oxford University. In 1872 he was the amateur middleweight boxing champion of Britain. Having decided to abandon a career in law for the stage, he changed his name to Maurice Barrymore to deflect the shame of his family having a thespian in it. He acted in the English provincial theater, then went to the United States in 1875 and joined Augustin Daly's company, making his first appearance in Daly's melodrama, *Under the Gaslight*. A handsome actor, he was the leading man to many of the most famous actresses of the period. He met his future wife on stage and soon after, the Barrymore dynasty began.

MAURICE COSTELLO 1870–1950

The early days of film-making were nothing like the high-tech sets of today, peopled with tantrum-prone, overpaid stars. Everybody was expected to help in building the set. Costello was the first actor to refuse this duty. He claimed that he was hired as an actor and nothing else. As such, he often sat in a chair, reading a newspaper and drinking coffee, while the others worked. During the late 1910s and early 1920s he was one of the most successful and highest paid stars in Hollywood. Yet by the late 1930s his career had declined to the point where he was reduced to taking unbilled work as a background extra for a few dollars a day. In 1939 he was so broke that he sued his daughters for financial support.

MAE ALTSCHUK 1882–1929

She was a silent movie actress during the 1910s, where she was billed under the name Mrs Costello. She tried to prevent her beautiful and headstrong daughter from marrying John Barrymore, but failed—though her advice on his nature came true as he became completely dissipated due to drink.

LIONEL BARRYMORE 1878–1954

Perhaps the most multi-talented of the Barrymores he was an actor, painter, composer, novelist and, according to some sources, inventor of the boom microphone. He acted in over 200 films and won a Best Actor Oscar in the 1931 film *A Free Soul*. He is perhaps best remembered for his role as Mr Potter in the Frank Capra film *It's a Wonderful Life*. From 1938, arthritis forced him into a wheelchair yet, as a favorite of studio boss Louis B. Mayer, he was kept on the books and roles were adapted so he could play them from his wheelchair. He married twice and had two children, but neither survived infancy.

3RD CHILD JOHN BARRYMORE NEXT PAGE

ETHEL BARRYMORE 1879–1959

One of the three famous Barrymore siblings, Ethel was a well-known stage actress until she made her film debut in 1914. After turning down a marriage proposal from Winston Churchill, she married society stockbroker Russell Griswold Colt in 1909. She had one son to him that year, then a daughter and another son. They divorced in 1923. An avowed Catholic, Ethel never remarried, but continued with her acting. The highlight of her career came in 1945 when she won the Best Supporting Actress Oscar for her role in the film *None but the Lonely Heart*.

3 CHILDREN: SAMUEL COLT, ETHEL BARRYMORE COLT & JOHN DREW COLT NEXT PAGE

RUSSELL GRISWOLD COLT 1882–1959

2 CHILDREN: DOLORES & HELENE COSTELLO NEXT PAGE

S. RANKIN DREW 1892–1918

His famous parents sent him to military school, hoping he wouldn't become an actor. But the lure of the stage was too strong. At first he toured in plays with his parents and his cousin Lionel. A short significant career as a movie actor followed, before he became a promising film director. However, it was soldiery not acting that was to prove his undoing. In 1915, he volunteered for service with the Lafayette Escadrille Flying Corp and was shot down and killed by the Germans during the final months of World War I.

JOHN BARRYMORE
1882–1942

The most talented (and troubled) of his siblings, he was renowned as the best Shakespearean actor of his time. Initially he resisted the family business, working as a commercial artist and painter before turning to acting in order to support his nightclub lifestyle. He made his debut in 1903, though it was his 1922 *Hamlet* which wowed the world. He left Broadway for Hollywood superstardom in movies with the likes of Katherine Hepburn and Greta Garbo. With his dashing looks, "The Great Profile" was one of the most idolized actors of his day. But wild living, the maintenance of four wives and alcohol turned him into a shambolic mess.

> ' ONE OF MY CHIEF REGRETS DURING MY YEARS IN THE THEATER IS THAT I COULD NOT SIT IN THE AUDIENCE AND WATCH ME.   JOHN BARRYMORE '

1ST WIFE

KATHERINE CORRI HARRIS   1891–1927

2ND WIFE

BLANCHE OELRICHS   1890–1950

3RD WIFE

DOLORES COSTELLO   1905–79

She was once known as "The Goddess of the Silent Screen." Dolores appeared in numerous pictures throughout the 1910s and the early 1920s, mostly with her father and sister, Helene. Dolores met her future husband, John Barrymore, during the 1926 filming of *The Sea Beast*, a romanticized adaptation of *Moby Dick*. They married in 1928 and she took a career break to have two children with him. After her divorce from John in 1935, she returned to the screen, acting in films such as Orson Welles's *The Magnificent Ambersons* before retiring in 1943.

CHILDREN OF MAURICE & MAE COSTELLO

HELENE COSTELLO   1906–57

Sister of Dolores, her achievements included starring in *Lights of New York* (1928), the first full-length synchronous talking feature. She also worked as a reader for 20th Century Fox in the early 1940s. One of her four husbands was Lowell Sherman, an actor turned director, who directed Katherine Hepburn and Greta Garbo in early films. Helene and Lowell were responsible for convincing Dolores to divorce John on account of his drinking.

4TH WIFE

ELAINE JACOBS   1916–2003

3 CHILDREN OF ETHEL BARRYMORE & RUSSELL COLT

DIANA BARRYMORE   1921–60

One of the saddest tales of Barrymore dissipation, Drew Barrymore's half-aunt was the daughter of Blanche Oelrichs, the writer, suffragette, actress, broadcaster and second wife of John. Blanche also occasionally appeared and published under the pseudonym Michael Strange, and her most famous play, *Clair de Lune*, was made into a film in 1932. Although free-spirited, John and Blanche packed off the young Diana to a strict boarding school while they got on with their divorce, love lives and careers. Diana became a wild young thing and talented actress but problems with alcohol, bad luck and poor taste in men forced her to take desperate measures just to survive.

SAMUEL COLT   1909–86

Named after his grandfather who was a former Rhode Island Atttorney General and his great great uncle—who was the inventor of the Colt revolver—Samuel's career was less auspicious and peaked with a number of fairly minor roles in 1950s films, including *Johnny Trouble* (1957), in which his mother, Ethel, also appeared.

ETHEL BARRYMORE COLT   1912–77

She was a Broadway actress and singer during the 1930s before marrying a mining engineer. She made her Broadway debut at the Ethel Barrymore Theater—a theater named in honor of her mother who debuted as its star on its opening in 1928. In 1972 she returned to the stage in the Stephen Sondheim musical, *Follies*.

JOHN DREW COLT   1913–75

Like his brother's, John's career was also relatively lackluster, including a run of Broadway plays in the 1930s and an appearance as a stage manager in the 1947 film, *A Double Life*. Like his sister, he made his Broadway debut at the Ethel Barrymore Theater. Family inheritances may have dulled the thirst for work, but not that for alcohol, which, combined with cancer, was the cause of his demise.

JOHN DREW BARRYMORE JR 1932–2004

Another fairly tragic Barrymore who burned his talent with booze and drugs. His parents divorced in his infancy and he allegedly only saw his father once. His mother sent him to St. John's Military Academy, intending that he go on to college, not acting. But he rebelled and signed a movie contract at 17. He had a sporadic career including appearances in TV westerns such as *Rawhide* and *Gunsmoke*, but his violence and drug habits sabotaged his career. He was jailed numerous times for drunkenness and spousal abuse, then for drugs in the 1960s. He became more reclusive the older he got and ended up living like a hermit in the wilderness, though some say he simply became a derelict.

1ST WIFE

CARA WILLIAMS 1925–

John Drew Barrymore's first wife—he was her second husband. They were married 1952–59. Her previous husband was a jockey. Like her second husband, she was famous for her volatility. She was also a match for him in terms of talent. As an actress, she was nominated for an Oscar and Golden Globe for her role in *The Defiant Ones* (1958).

2ND WIFE

GABRIELLA PALAZZOLI 1937–

She was an Italian starlet who married John Drew Barrymore in a Roman church. They met during the 5 years he spent in Italy acting in B-grade films. They had a daughter, Blythe, who has stayed off her family's notoriety radar.

> When [Drew] came out of my womb, she had a publicist, a manager and an agent.
> ILDIKO JAID MAKO

3RD WIFE

ILDIKO JAID MAKO 1946–

The only child of her Hungarian parents, she was born in a camp for displaced persons outside Munich, Germany. A sixties wild child and actress, who worked under the name Jaid Barrymore, she was also a centerfold model on a number of occasions. At other times, she worked as a waitress to support herself and her daughter, Drew, and was instrumental in starting Drew's career in showbusiness, though it came at significant cost to their personal relationship. She dedicated her book, *Secrets of World Class Lovers*, to her daughter.

JOHN BLYTH BARRYMORE 1954–

He shares his father with Drew, and is the son of Cara Williams. He also became an actor but one of no special note. His father once made him help to disentomb his grandfather for the purposes of turning his burial into a cremation.

DREW BARRYMORE 1975–

Drew emerged from a seriously screwed-up childhood, which included becoming an alcoholic before she was 10, to become one of Hollywood's most bankable actresses. Her career lifted off at the age of 7 with the role of Gertie in *E.T.*, but then adolescence saw both drug and alcohol addiction. Having recovered, she has played leading roles in blockbusters such as *Charlie's Angels* and *The Wedding Singer*. She also has her own production company, Flower Films, which has raked in millions. Her love life has not been quite so successful. Both her marriages have lasted less than a year and she has also publicly claimed to be bisexual. However she's been going steady with Strokes drummer Fabrizio Moretti.

1ST HUSBAND

JEREMY THOMAS 1963–

2ND HUSBAND

TOM GREEN 1971–

DREW IS GODMOTHER TO FRANCIS BEAN, DAUGHER OF DREW'S BEST FRIEND, AND WILD GIRL, COURTNEY LOVE.

"I TRY TO MAKE MOVIES THAT I WOULD WANT TO GO SEE RATHER THAN ONES I WOULD JUST WANT TO DO AS AN ACTOR. I WANT PEOPLE TO HAVE MOVIES FULL OF ROMANCE AND HOPE AND EMPOWERMENT, SOMETHING THEY CAN ESCAPE INTO AND FEEL GOOD ABOUT. I LOVE HAPPY ENDINGS."
DREW BARRYMORE

THE BONAPARTES

NAPOLEON ON THE GREAT ST BERNARD PASS, JACQUES LOUIS DAVID, 1801. ALTHOUGH THIS PAINTING SHOWS NAPOLEON ON A HORSE, HE CROSSED THE PASS ON A MULE.

I n one generation the Bonapartes went from being minor nobility in Corsica, an insignificant outpost of the Genoese state, to the most important family in Europe with emperors, kings and queens spanning the whole continent. Most of this can be put down to one man, Napoleon I. His genius and ambition occurred at a lucky point in history where suddenly it was possible, thanks to the French Revolution, for the most talented person to rule a country. Of course, for Napoleon, one country wasn't enough. Having attained his position by merit, albeit with the backing of the army, he proceeded to do the opposite by installing his family as aristocratic rulers over the territories he conquered. Perhaps surprisingly, many of them proved popular and able rulers, sometimes to their brother's chagrin. There's much to prove the existence of leadership genes in the Bonaparte blood. Even the much-maligned reign of Napoleon III as Emperor of France has begun to look good with the benefit of hindsight, while another Bonaparte went on to become Attorney General of the United States and create the FBI. Other Bonapartes, such as the ornithologist Charles Lucien Bonaparte, became leaders in culture and science. But leadership genes or not, since the early 19th century, the Bonaparte influence and name has waned. Now, only one line of male descendants remains. When later generations look back at that time in history, the Bonapartes will perhaps appear like a century-long flash in the pan.

HOW THEY RATE

WEALTH ★★★★★
From a six-room house in Ajaccio, Corsica, the family ended up with two emperors, a few kings and duchies galore. Many members of the family married into the wealthiest families in Europe and even the US arm of the family married into money.

HEALTH ★★★
The health of this family is very uneven and their life expectancy not very high. From the look of the official portraits, male members of the Bonaparte family were prone to corpulence. Some of them also had problems in generating successors.

HAPPINESS ★★★★
Ambition often comes at the cost of happiness, yet there's something about this family which suggests they were not as screwed up as many others who climbed their way to the top.

FAME ★★★★★
Absolutely top class.

SEXINESS ★★
Most apparent in the female of the species.

BLACK SHEEP FACTOR ★★★
Pauline Bonaparte is one of history's great nymphomaniacs, while the family's penchant for revolutionary behavior scores points—as do the dissolute lives of a number of male Bonapartes, such as Lucien and Plon Plon.

ECCENTRICITY ★★★
Not especially, but the combination of Italian passion and French élan mixed with Corsican stubbornness makes for interesting characters.

INFLUENCE ★★★★★
They changed the course of history.

> The surest way to remain poor is to be honest.
> NAPOLEON I

NAPOLEON I'S FATHER, CARLO, C.1775.

BONAPARTE ORIGINS

THE BONAPARTE FAMILY IS A BRANCH OF THE CADOLINGI DI BORGONUOVO FAMILY, WHO WERE THE LORDS OF FUCECCHIO IN TUSCANY FROM THE 10TH CENTURY ONWARD. ONE OF THEIR DESCENDANTS, WHO HAD ACQUIRED THE NAME OF BUONAPARTE, SETTLED NEAR SARZANA, AN ITALIAN TOWN INLAND FROM THE COAST, BETWEEN GENOA AND FLORENCE IN THE MIDDLE OF THE 13TH CENTURY. THE FAMILY TRADITIONALLY WORKED AS NOTARIES—A KIND OF LEGAL OFFICER—AND OCCASIONALLY WORKED IN THE SERVICE OF MORE IMPORTANT NOBLES. GIOVANNI BONAPARTE, FOR EXAMPLE, CAME TO CORSICA AROUND THE TURN OF THE 16TH CENTURY AS A MANAGER FOR THE GENOESE GOVERNOR OF BASTIA, THEN THE CORSICAN CAPITAL. HIS SON FRANCESCO—A SOLDIER WHO SPECIALIZED IN USING A CROSSBOW ON HORSEBACK—SETTLED IN AJACCIO (NAMED AFTER THE GREEK HERO AJAX), THE TOWN WHERE NAPOLEON I WAS BORN 250 YEARS LATER, AND WHICH BECAME THE CORSICAN CAPITAL UNDER FRENCH RULE. THE MEMBERS OF THE BONAPARTE FAMILY, WHO WERE CONSISTENTLY *ANZIONE* (TOWN COUNCILORS) OF AJACCIO, OSCILLATED BETWEEN CIVIL SERVICE AND MILITARY SERVICE THEREAFTER.

NAPOLEONIC PARENTS

Carlo Bonaparte was tall for a Corsican and rather handsome. His wife, Letizia, was a local beauty whose dowry contained part of two vineyards, a public bread oven with an attached apartment and another apartment near the local abattoir. Letizia was extravagant in her penchant for buying clothes. On the face of it, they made a perfect couple: socially matched (both minor nobility), young, beautiful, smart and anxious to get ahead. Except for one thing: Carlo hadn't really wanted to marry her. Soon after the marriage was consummated, he abandoned her to pursue his legal studies in Rome. Meanwhile she gave birth to their first child who died in infancy. One wonders whether this neglect of her husband propelled her to over-invest in her children.

In Rome, Carlo led a profligate life and got himself into money trouble. He was something of a fop, promoting himself on his tenuous connections to the more prestigious Tuscan Bonapartes who, admittedly, had acknowledged the distant relationship. Eventually he left Rome in something of a hurry. One explanation is that he got a girl pregnant by promising to marry her if she slept with him. He also returned from Rome a fervent admirer of Corsican independence and its leader Pasquale Paoli. When Paoli set up his independent capital at Corte, Carlo enlisted at the new university which taught Enlightenment values such as liberty, equality and fraternity. He managed to ingratiate himself with Paoli and became his secretary in 1767. Paoli was also enamored of Letizia (all the clothes shopping had obviously paid off). In one incident she helped him charm the Bey of Tunisia when he came to Paoli's court bearing gifts, including a tiger.

In 1768, the Republic of Genoa offered Corsica to Louis XV of France as payment for a debt. Carlo made a passionate speech against the French "invasion" and was Paoli's guard during the battle that followed. Yet his nose for the main chance saw him alter his allegiances soon after the French conquest of the island. He was appointed assessor to the royal court for Ajaccio in 1769 and never doubted French authority thereafter. He was recognized as part of the French order of Corsican Nobility in 1771 and went on to become Corsica's representative to the court of Louis XVI of France at Versailles in 1778, a position he held for some years.

PSYCHOANALYST MARIE BONAPARTE, ARRIVING IN PARIS WITH FRIEND SIGMUND FREUD, 1938. MARIE FIRST WENT TO SEE FREUD ABOUT A CURE FOR HER FRIGIDITY.

NAPOLEON I

The greatest, and smallest, of the Napoleons was Napoleon I. He showed talent from an early age, was sent to France to complete his education at the age of 9 and won a scholarship to the top French military school, where he majored in artillery. At 16, he was commissioned a lieutenant in the French army, but spent much of his leave returning to Corsica to fight for the Independence movement, where he entered and lost his first battle. His artillery tactics helped achieve a French victory against the British at the Siege of Toulon in 1793 and he was promoted to Brigadier General. In 1795, his defence of the Revolutionary government against an armed protest of Royalist and counter-revolutionary forces earned him fame and the patronage of its leaders

After he married Joséphine in 1796, the former mistress of his new patron, Director Barras, he led the army of Italy on an invasion against the Papal States, earning himself "The Little Corporal" nickname for the easy camaraderie he enjoyed with his troops.

In 1798 he embarked on a campaign in Egypt that enjoyed victories but ultimately ran into problems. He returned in August 1799 with the French political climate unstable, largely due to the incompetence and corruption of the directors. He was approached by one of them, Sieyes, to lead a coup and on November 9, 1799 he seized power from the Directory and became one of four consuls, of which he was first and most powerful.

A YOUNG GENERAL BONAPARTE, 1796.

DETAIL OF JACQUES-LOUIS DAVID'S PAINTING *THE CORONATION OF NAPOLEON AND EMPRESS JOSEPHINE*, 1806–1807.

NAPOLEON I'S VICTORY SPEECH AT AUSTERLITZ

THE BATTLE OF AUSTERLITZ, 1805, WAS NAPOLEON I'S GREATEST VICTORY. ALTHOUGH OUTNUMBERED, HE DECEIVED THE RUSSIAN AND AUSTRIAN FORCE INTO BELIEVING HE WAS WEAKER THAN HE WAS, THEN ROUTED THEM WHEN THEY ATTACKED. THOUSANDS OF FLEEING ENEMIES DIED WHEN A FROZEN LAKE COLLAPSED UNDER THEIR WEIGHT. IN 1806, HE COMMISSIONED L'ARC DE TRIOMPHE TO BE BUILT IN PARIS TO COMMEMRORATE THE VICTORY. AFTER THE BATTLE HE GAVE HIS MEN THE FOLLOWING STIRRING SPEECH: "SOLDIERS! I AM PLEASED WITH YOU. ON THE DAY OF AUSTERLITZ, YOU LIVED UP TO ALL MY EXPECTATIONS OF YOUR BRAVERY AND BOLDNESS; YOU HAVE HONORED YOUR EAGLES WITH IMMORTAL GLORY. IN LESS THAN FOUR HOURS, AN ARMY OF ONE HUNDRED THOUSAND MEN, COMMANDED BY THE EMPERORS OF RUSSIA AND AUSTRIA, HAS EITHER BEEN CUT TO PIECES OR SCATTERED. THOSE WHO ESCAPED YOUR STEEL DROWNED IN THE LAKES. FORTY STANDARDS, THE STANDARDS OF THE RUSSIAN IMPERIAL GUARD, ONE HUNDRED AND TWENTY CANNON, TWENTY GENERALS, MORE THAN THIRTY-THOUSAND PRISONERS… THESE ARE THE RESULTS OF THIS DAY FOREVER RENOWNED. THAT SUCH VAUNTED INFANTRY, SO MUCH GREATER IN NUMBER, COULD NOT RESIST YOU MEANS FROM NOW ON YOU HAVE NO RIVALS, NO-ONE TO FEAR. IN TWO MONTHS, THIS THIRD COALITION HAS BEEN BEATEN AND UNSTRUNG. PEACE CANNOT BE FAR AWAY. BUT, AS I PROMISED TO MY PEOPLE BEFORE CROSSING THE RHINE, I SHALL NOT AGREE TO PEACE UNLESS IT PROVIDES US WITH GUARANTEES AND ENSURES THAT OUR ALLIES ARE REWARDED … SOLDIERS, WHEN EVERYTHING REQUIRED FOR THE HAPPINESS AND PROSPERITY OF OUR FATHERLAND HAS BEEN ACCOMPLISHED, I SHALL BRING YOU BACK TO FRANCE; THERE YOU WILL BE THE OBJECT OF MY MOST TENDER CARE. MY PEOPLE WILL GREET YOUR RETURN WITH DELIGHT, AND IT WILL BE ENOUGH FOR YOU TO SAY 'I WAS AT THE BATTLE OF AUSTERLITZ,' FOR THEM TO REPLY, 'THERE GOES A BRAVE MAN'."

FIRST CONSUL Napoleon I's administrative reforms in this role included the Napoleonic Code—the set of civil laws which replaced idiosyncratic feudal law and with the systematic regulation of matters such as property. It was complemented with Penal Code and Code of Criminal Instruction. These proved to be one of his most enduring legacies. With the exception of Scandinavia, Russia and Britain, every country in Europe utilized the Napoleonic Code in modernizing its civil law system, with many borrowing from the criminal codes, too. Perhaps the other most significant act of his time as consul was the Louisiana Purchase, where in recognition of the superiority of the British navy, he sold Louisiana (which at that time consisted of 22.3 percent of what is now the USA and stretched to the Canadian border) to the United States for less than three cents an acre.

EMPEROR NAPOLEON I

Following the quashing of an apparent Royalist plot to kill him, Napoleon crowned himself hereditary Emperor, reasoning it was necessary in order to wipe out the possibility of a Bourbon restoration. But it probably had as much to do with his inheritance of the social aspirations of his parents. One of his brothers, Lucien, strongly opposed this and went into voluntary exile as a result.

THE THIRD, FOURTH AND FIFTH COALITIONS

Having crowned himself King of Italy, too, Napoleon found himself at war again in 1805. He defeated the Austrians at Ulm, but lost as the British asserted their naval superiority at Trafalgar the very next day. Not long after, however, he achieved perhaps his greatest victory when he routed the Russians and Austrians at Austerlitz, forcing them to sue for peace. In 1806 he fought the Prussians and Russians, vanquishing Prussia before reaching an agreement with Tsar Alexander, which effectively divided Europe between them. When Portugal refused to comply with Napoleon's trade embargo against Britain, he sought Spanish support to invade. When they refused, he invaded Spain as well and made his brother Joseph king. In 1809 the Spanish revolted and the Austrians broke their peace. Napoleon fought a bloody draw against the Austrians in May before beating them in July. Having divorced Joséphine, he married Austrian Arch-Duchess Marie-Louise to secure the peace between the two empires.

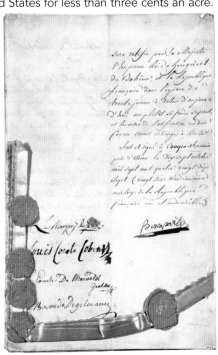

PEACE TREATY BETWEEN AUSTRIA AND FRANCE, 1797, WITH NAPOLEON BONAPARTE'S SEAL.

> "I closed the gulf of anarchy and brought order out of chaos. I rewarded merit regardless of birth or wealth, wherever I found it. I abolished feudalism and restored equality to all regardless of religion and before the law. I fought the decrepit monarchies of the Old Regime because the alternative was the destruction of all this. I purified the Revolution."
>
> NAPOLEON I

DEFEAT AND EXILE TO ELBA

Napoleon's defeat in Russia encouraged his enemies who formed the Fifth Coalition. After a number of victories, the French were pinned down by an army twice their size at the Battle of Nations in October 1913. Napoleon was left with an army of less than 100,000 men against the allies' 500,000 and retreated toward Paris. With the writing on the wall, Napoleon abdicated in favor of his son, but the allies refused to acknowledge this. When they occupied Paris, they demanded an unconditional surrender and abdication. Napoleon was exiled to Elba, an island off the coast of Italy, not far from Corsica.

THE RUSSIAN FOLLY

Although Tsar Alexander and Napoleon had a good personal relationship, by 1812 the Tsar's advisers were arguing for the reclamation of the part of Poland Napoleon had annexed. Three hundred thousand Russian troops, nearly three quarters of the entire army, were amassed at the Polish border. In response, Napoleon, who had introduced the modern ideal of universal conscription to Europe, put together a Grand Army of around 600,000 men. On June 23, 1812 he invaded Russia. The Russian forces avoided engaging the French army and adopted a scorched earth policy as they retreated, hoping to maroon the French without supplies for the harsh Russian winter. The two armies met at Borodino outside Moscow in September. One day's battle resulted in upward of 70,000 casualties and an inconclusive result. The French were able to take Moscow, but the Russians razed it to the ground, making it a pyrrhic victory. Napoleon began his retreat a month after. It was a disaster. Of the 650,000 men who went into Russia, only 40,000 returned.

THE VIEW FROM NAPOLEON I'S VILLA ON ELBA, WHERE HE WAS EXILED BETWEEN 1814 AND 1815.

100 LAST DAYS ON EUROPEAN SOIL

IN 1815, NAPOLEON ESCAPED FROM ELBA. HE ARRIVED IN PARIS ON MARCH 20 AND, RAISING A FORCE OF AROUND 340,000 MEN, HE GOVERNED FOR 100 DAYS BEFORE HE WAS ENGAGED AND DEFEATED BY THE ALLIES AT THE BATTLE OF WATERLOO. THIS TIME THEY EXILED HIM TO ST HELENA, AN ISLAND IN THE SOUTH ATLANTIC, WHERE HE DIED—OSTENSIBLY FROM STOMACH CANCER, THOUGH IT'S RUMORED THAT HE WAS POISONED WITH ARSENIC.

NAPOLEON II

Napoleon I dumped his beloved Joséphine so he could beget an heir. However, if there is a weakness in the Bonaparte family, it's their erratic patterns of reproduction—Napoleon I was one of thirteen, but five of them died. When matters of succession were at stake, children were particularly hard to come by. If power is an aphrodisiac, for the Bonapartes, the subsequent lovemaking was infertile. Napoleon I, for example, only managed one child who, with circumstance heavily stacked against him, nevertheless seemed a pale shadow of his father. He only became Napoleon II by virtue of the fact that when he was 3 years old his father abdicated in his favor. His technical reign only lasted a couple of weeks. Nicknamed "The Eaglet," for most of his short life, Napoleon II was a virtual prisoner of his mother's family, cosseted away in Habsburg Vienna, and received the consolation title Duke of Reichstadt in 1818. In 1832, he died of tuberculosis. In 1940, his remains were transferred, as a gift to France from Adolf Hitler, from Vienna to the dome of the Invalides in Paris, where he now rests beside his father.

NAPOLEON II, DUKE OF REICHSTADT, C.1831.

HOME IS WHERE THE HEART IS

ALTHOUGH NAPOLEON II'S BODY NOW RESTS BESIDE HIS FATHER'S IN PARIS, HIS HEART NEVER PHYSCIALLY LEFT VIENNA. IT CONTINUES TO LANGUISH IN THE HERZGRUFT ("HEART CELLAR"), A CHAMBER OFF A CHAPEL IN THE HOFBURG PALACE, WHERE FIFTY-FOUR URNS CONTAINING THE HEARTS OF DECEASED MEMBERS OF THE HABSBURG DYNASTY ARE PRESERVED.

NAPOLEON III

EMPEROR NAPOLEON III OF FRANCE AND HIS WIFE, THE EMPRESS EUGENIE, C.1870.

Louis Napoléon (Napoleon III) has long been presented as something of a bumbling oaf of an Emperor. Karl Marx, for instance, commented caustically in the opening to his book *The Eighteenth Brumaire of Louis Napoléon* that: "Hegel remarks somewhere that all great world-historic facts and personages appear, so to speak, twice. He forgot to add: the first time as tragedy, the second time as farce."

Louis Napoléon also incurred the wrath of Victor Hugo, France's greatest writer of the time. Yet despite his image, he managed to hang onto the job for longer than his more celebrated uncle, Napoleon I. However, although he lacked Napoleon's military brilliance and charisma, Louis's administrative actions, economic policy and civic improvements put France in a solid position toward the end of the 19th century.

Exiled from France, Louis Napoléon spent a peripatetic youth in Switzerland, Heidelberg and Italy, where he fought with his brother in the carabineri against the Austrians. When Napoleon II died, he became the Napoleonic heir of his generation and, encouraged by Bonapartists still in France, he made his first attempt to mount a coup in 1836, but failed. His second attempt to arrive at Boulogne by ship with an army resulted in his arrest and imprisonment for 6 years. Eventually, he resorted to democratic means. When the King was deposed in the revolution of 1848, Louis Napoléon returned to France and was elected president with more than 80 percent of the votes.

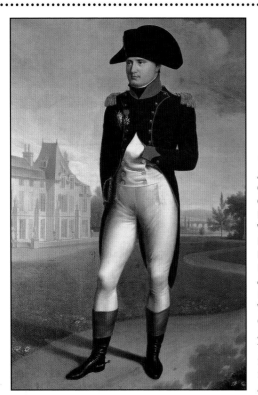

NAPOLEON COMPLEX

"NAPOLEON COMPLEX" IS A TERM DEVISED BY ALFRED ADLER TO DESCRIBE A TYPE OF INFERIORITY COMPLEX WHEREBY SHORT PEOPLE ATTEMPT TO OVER-ACHIEVE IN ORDER TO COMPENSATE FOR BEING VERTICALLY CHALLENGED. THOSE WITH NAPOLEON COMPLEXES ARE ALSO LIKELY TO BE OVERLY AGGRESSIVE AND ARGUMENTATIVE. INDEED THESE FIT WELL WITH NAPOLEON'S CHILDHOOD NICKNAME WHICH MEANT "THE RAMBUNCTIOUS ONE." YET NAPOLEON'S SHORTNESS IS ACTUALLY A MYTH. IN FRENCH PRE-METRIC MEASURE, HE WAS 5 FOOT 2 INCHES. HOWEVER, IN US MEASUREMENTS THIS TRANSLATES TO 5 FOOT 6 INCHES—THE CONFUSION ARISING FROM THE FACT THAT FRENCH INCHES WERE LONGER THAN ENGLISH ONES. FOR HIS TIME, NAPOLEON WAS AVERAGE HEIGHT. NAPOLEON'S AMBITION IS MORE LIKELY TO HAVE COME FROM THE PENCHANT OF HIS PARENTS FOR SOCIAL CLIMBING. IF WE ARE LOOKING FOR PHYSICAL REASONS TO OVER-ACHIEVE, IT'S POSSIBLE THERE WAS COMPENSATORY BEHAVIOR CAUSED BY NAPOLEON'S LACK OF SEXUAL POTENCY. HE ONLY FATHERED ONE SICKLY CHILD, AND A PIECE OF SKIN PURPORTING TO BE HIS PENIS—ALLEGEDLY DETACHED AT HIS AUTOPSY—WAS SAID TO BE "ONE INCH LONG AND RESEMBLING A GRAPE."

LOUIS THE EMPEROR When the Royalist-controlled National Assembly refused to change the constitution to allow him a second term as president, Louis Napoléon mounted a coup on December 2, 1851—the anniversary both of his uncle's coronation as Emperor and his victory at Austerlitz. The coup was sanctioned by the French people in a disputed referendum, but came at the cost of losing the support of Republicans such as Victor Hugo. An emperor at the age of 43, Louis Napoléon decided he needed an heir and therefore a wife. After being knocked back by a niece of British Queen Victoria, he married the beautiful Countess of Teba, Eugénie, in 1853. An 1855 asssassination attempt may have increased the urgency of his ardor and in 1856, Napoléon Eugène Louis was born.

Napoleon III's reign over France can be divided into two distinct periods: an authoritarian period followed by a liberal one. In the former, the press was heavily censored, political prisoners were shipped to harsh penal colonies such as Devil's Island, and Parliament was neutered with power tightly concentrated in the Imperial Executive. From around 1860, however, possibly due to the influence of his cousin Prince Napoleon, he made many concessions to the liberals, empowering Parliament and even making a leading liberal prime minister.

His foreign policy—until he was hoodwinked by Prussian Otto von Bismarck—for the most part consolidated French interests. He was successssful in the Crimean War, the second Opium War and Indo-China, although he dithered over backing the Confederate cause in the American Civil War, and his puppet emperor of Mexico, Maximillian, was defeated and executed.

Unlike his uncle, Louis Napoléon's greatest achievements were domestic. He changed the face of Paris by employing Baron Haussmann to flatten many of the narrow feudal remnants of Paris and build the wide boulevardes for which the city is now famous. Borrowing from his time in Britain, he introduced underground sewerage and a railroad network. He was also the first French leader to concentrate on managing the economy and to actively intervene in its laissez-faire operations in order to provide some kind of social support for the poor and disadvantaged.

None of this, however, saved him from the Realpolitik of Otto von Bismarck, Chancellor of Prussia. When Prussia went to war with Austria in 1866, Louis Napoléon was sentimentally unable to back the Austrians on account of his youthful fighting with Italian nationalists. The Austrians were thrashed and from then on Prussia and France competed for dominance in Europe. It was a battle Prussia won when Bismarck manipulated the French to fight, then routed them in the 1870 Franco-Prussian war. This was the end for Louis Napoléon. He was captured at the Battle of Sedan and deposed by the Third Republic. His remaining 3 years were lived in exile in England.

NAUGHTY PAULINE BONAPARTE

WHEN LOOKING AT THE HISTORY OF THE BONAPARTES, THERE SEEMS TO BE A LOT OF INFIDELITY AND, UNUSUALLY PERHAPS, THE WOMEN SEEMED TO BE GIVING AS MUCH AS THEY GOT. THERE WAS, FOR INSTANCE, SOME UNCERTAINTY CONCERNING THE PATERNITY OF NAPOLEON III. ACCORDING TO SOME SOURCES, IT WAS AN EXTRA-MARITAL AFFAIR THAT PARTLY PROVOKED NAPOLEON TO DIVORCE JOSEPHINE. HOWEVER THE PROMISCUITY AWARD GOES TO NAPOLEON'S FAVORITE SISTER, PAULINE, WHO CAME AND WAITED OUT HER BROTHER'S EXILE IN ELBA WITH HIM. BUT HER BROTHER WAS ABOUT THE ONLY MAN SHE REMAINED LOYAL TO. A RAVISHING BEAUTY BY THE AGE OF 16, SHE WAS CAUGHT IN AMORATA WITH A COLONEL LECLERC BY BROTHER NAPOLEON, WHO INSISTED THAT THEY TIE THE KNOT. HE THEN DISPATCHED THEM TO HAITI, PARTLY BECAUSE PAULINE SHOWED NO SIGNS OF ABANDONING HER FONDNESS FOR HAVING MORE THAN ONE LOVER. HOWEVER, LECLERC CAUGHT YELLOW FEVER IN HAITI AND DIED. PAULINE RETURNED TO EUROPE AND 8 MONTHS LATER MARRIED PRINCE CAMILLO BORGHESE, A MEMBER OF THE FAMOUS ITALIAN CLAN, AND THE RICHEST MAN IN ITALY. STILL, PAULINE'S EXTRA-CURRICULAR ACTIVITIES CONTINUED UNABATED AND, AT ONE POINT, HER HUSBAND WAS FORCED TO ARREST HER TO KEEP HER OUT OF OTHER MEN'S BEDS. NOT SURPRISINGLY, THE COUPLE BECAME ESTRANGED. NONETHELESS, PAULINE MANAGED TO CONTINUE HER HEDONISTIC LIFE. WHEN NAPOLEON GIFTED HER THE DUCHY OF GUANTALLA, SHE SOLD IT ON FOR 6 MILLION FRANCS. BUT SHE CASHED IN HER ASSETS AND CAME TO HIS AID IN ELBA, AND WOULD ALSO HAVE FOLLOWED HIM TO ST HELENA, HAD SHE NOT BEEN ILL. IT'S ALMOST AS IF THEY WERE TWO SIBLINGS WHO LIKED EACH OTHER SO MUCH BECAUSE THEY WERE OPPOSITES—THE UNTRAMMELED HEDONIST AND THE DISCIPLINED, AMBITIOUS LEADER. AFTER HER BROTHER'S DEATH, PAULINE CONTINUED HER PROMISCUOUS LIFE UNTIL SHE DIED FROM CANCER, AGED 44.

NAPOLEON IV

Once again the son of a Napoleonic emperor inherited unfortunate circumstances. After Napoleon III died, the Empress Eugénie bought a house in Hampshire, England, where she lived for the rest of her life. Her son, Eugène, dreamed of returning to France as Napoleon IV, and attended military college in England. He tried to join the British army but as a foreign national he was not allowed. Through his mother's influence with Queen Victoria he was allowed to go to South Africa as an observer, at the time of the Anglo-Zulu War of 1879. Soon after arriving, he went out on horseback on a mapping expedition, in an area thought to be cleared of Zulus. Approaching a small village, his party was ambushed by about forty Zulus. His colleagues leapt onto their horses and fled. However, something snapped in Prince Louis's saddle and he was unable to escape. He turned to fight and was killed. While Bonaparte pretenders remained, none have succeeded in having themselves acknowledged as Napoleon V.

IMPERIAL PRINCE EUGENE LOUIS NAPOLEON BONAPARTE, C.1871.

NAPOLEON I WAS PERCEIVED AS SOMETHING OF A BOGEYMAN IN BRITAIN. PARENTS WOULD WARN THEIR CHILDREN THAT IF THEY DIDN'T BEHAVE "OLD BONEY WOULD COME AND GET THEM." THEIR EXPRESSION OF DELIGHT (SHORT-LIVED) WHEN NAPOLEON WAS FIRST IMPRISONED AT ELBA INCLUDED ONE OF THE LONGEST PALINDROMES IN THE ENGLISH LANGUAGE, "ABLE WAS I ERE I SAW ELBA."

KEY: CHILD ••••••▶ ADOPTED CHILD •••••▶ MARRIED ━━━━ DIVORCED ━ ━ ━ ━ DE FACTO ━•━•━ SPLIT UP ─ ─ ─ ─

{ bonaparte family tree }

CARLO MARIA BONAPARTE
1746–85

He was a lawyer from minor Corsican nobility who served at the French Court, once the Genoese had gifted Corsica as a debt repayment. Before then, Carlo had been in the Corsican independence movement, and was made a lieutenant of the leader, Pasquale Paoli.

MARIE-LAETITIA RAMOLINO
1750–1836

Her family were minor nobility in the Republic of Genoa which controlled Corsica at the time. She married Carlo aged 14 and had thirteen children to him, of which eight survived. She was remembered as a no-nonsense mother.

JOSEPH BONAPARTE 1768–1844
The elder brother of French Emperor Napoleon I. In his own career he was a lawyer, politician and diplomat, but he prospered under the reign of his brother, who made him King of Naples (1806–1808) and King of Spain (1808–13).

JULIE CLARY (MARIE) 1771–1845
The daughter of a wealthy Marseille silk merchant and Joseph's second wife. Her sister, Desirée, became Queen of Sweden when her husband, Marshal Bernadotte, became King. In 1794, Julie married Joseph and they had three daughters.

ELISA BONAPARTE 1777–1820
Her sharp tongue and wit caused ructions between her and elder brother Napoleon, but he still made her Grand Duchess of Tuscany, where she ruled with considerable aplomb.

PAULINE BONAPARTE
1780–1825

Beautiful and promiscuous, her life was scandalous and her marriages were no impediment to her lust. However, when Napoleon was exiled she proved her loyalty by encouraging him to make his return for the 100 days that preceded his defeat at Waterloo.

CAROLINE BONAPARTE
1782–1839

She married one of Napoleon's closest lieutenants, Joachim Murat, in 1800 and her brother gave them the Duchy of Berg in 1806 and in 1808 the Kingdom of Naples. She ruled Naples while her husband was at war. In 1815 her husband was executed and she moved to Austria before returning to Italy.

NAPOLEON I OF FRANCE
1769–1821

The efforts of this man took his family from relative Corsican obscurity and made it the most powerful in Europe. Yet, there is no doubt he was a tyrant. While he put his siblings in positions of power, their sinecures were soon retracted after any signs of independent behavior. In some senses he was the military arm of the French Enlightenment, exporting many of the ideas of the French Revolution into feudal Europe as he conquered it—even though his empire was tightly run, using secret police, informants and ruling with an iron fist. The spread of his Napoleonic Code introduced the idea of systematic, rather than capricious, justice into European society. In military terms, he is considered one of the greatest generals of all time.

LUCIEN BONAPARTE
1775–1840

A firebrand French revolutionary, for much of his life he often fought with his brother. He was an ally of Robespierre during the Reign of Terror and Minister of the Interior when his brother was First Consul. But he fell out with his brother over his growing imperialism and went into self-exile in Rome. Sailing to the United States in 1809, he was captured by the British. He spent 4 years in Britain writing a long poem on Charlemagne. A cultured man, he was instrumental in re-establishing the Academie Française.

LOUIS BONAPARTE 1779–1844
His brother Napoleon appointed him King of Holland in 1810, where he earned the monicker "Louis the Good." Too good perhaps, since his brother forced him to abdicate for putting his Dutch subjects' interests ahead of the French. He married Joséphine's daughter Hortense.

JEROME BONAPARTE 1784–1860
The wild boy of the Bonaparte clan, he fought in his brother's Russian campaign, then at Waterloo. However, he was better known for extravagance than leadership and was almost permanently insolvent. Nonetheless, he became a Prince of France and President of the Senate.

> *Power is my mistress. I have worked too hard at her conquest to allow anyone to take her away from me.*
> **NAPOLEON I**

1ST WIFE

JOSEPHINE DE BEAUHARNAIS 1763–1814

She was born on a slave plantation owned by her father in Martinique. In 1779 she married Alexandre, Vicomte de Beauharnais. He was originally going to marry her sister, but she died, so Joséphine married him instead. She was arrested during the French Revolution and jailed while her aristocrat husband was guillotined. She married Napoleon on March 9, 1796. He crowned her Empress of France in Notre-Dame Cathedral in 1804, to his mother's displeasure. Unable to give him children, she agreed to a divorce so he could remarry in the hopes of having an heir. It was the first divorce under the Napoleonic Code.

JULIE JOSEPHINE BONAPARTE 1796–96

DAUGHTER ZENAIDE LAETITIA JULIE NEXT PAGE

CHARLOTTE NAPOLEONE BONAPARTE 1802–39

Charlotte married her first cousin Napoléon Louis, the second son of Louis Bonaparte and Hortense de Beauharnais, the daughter of Napoleon's first wife.

EUGENE DE BEAUHARNAIS 1781–1824

He accompanied his step-father in the 1799 Egyptian campaign and was wounded. Napoleon titled him Prince of France and Viceroy of Italy, before adopting him in 1806. He married the daughter of the King of Bavaria who made him Duke of Leuchtenberg that year He fought in the French army until Napoleon's abdication in 1814, then retired to Munich on his father-in-law's advice.

6 CHILDREN OF AUGUSTA & EUGENE PAGE 33

PRINCESS AUGUSTA AMALIA LUDOVIKA GEORGIA OF BAVARIA 1788–1851

2ND WIFE

MARIE-LOUISE 1791–1847

The daughter of the Habsburg (Austro–Hungarian) Emperor, she was married to Napoleon in 1810 to help (ultimately unsuccessfully) secure peace between the two empires. After Napoleon's fall she went to Vienna until her family gave her duchies in Italy. In 1821, soon after her husband's death she married her lover, Count Adam-Adalbert von Neipperg, with whom she already had children. After his death she married her Grand Chamberlain.

HORTENSE DE BEAUHARNAIS 1783–1837

After Napoleon adopted her in 1806, she married his brother, Louis, and became Queen of the Netherlands with Louis's accession to the throne. When he abdicated in 1810 in favor of their son Napoléon Louis, she became Regent. When Napoleon surrendered her title she was quickly demoted from Queen to Duchess. Her third son, Louis Napoléon, became President, then Emperor of France.

3 CHILDREN OF HORTENSE & LOUIS PAGE 33

1ST WIFE

ELIZABETH PATTERSON 1785–1879

This daughter of a wealthy Maryland merchant married Jérôme but his brother Napoleon opposed the marriage. When they tried to go to France to persuade him otherwise, she was refused permission to land in continental Europe. She went to England where she gave Jérôme a son. As a sweetener to the divorce she received a large pension and became a European society lady before retiring to the USA.

NAPOLEON II, NAPOLEON FRANCOIS JOSEPH CHARLES BONAPARTE 1811–32

Soon after his birth, Napoleon's only child became King of Rome. When Napoleon abdicated in 1814, he abdicated in favor of his son. However, most of Europe didn't recognize the title. Although Napoleon once claimed he'd rather see his son strangled than brought up as an Austrian Prince, he lived most of his life in quasi-captivity, as the relatively lowly Duke of Reichstadt, in Vienna, before dying from tuberculosis.

SON JEROME NAPOLEON NEXT PAGE

2ND WIFE

CATHERINE OF WURTTEMBERG 1783–1835

This daughter of King Frederich I of Württemberg was Jérôme's approved-of second wife. Of her father, who was rather obese, Napoleon once quipped that God had created him to discover how far skin could be stretched.

2 CHILDREN: MATHILDE & NAPOLEON JOSEPH CHARLES PAUL NEXT PAGE

3 CHILDREN: CHARLES LUCIEN JULES LAURENT, LOUIS LUCIEN & PIERRE NAPOLEON NEXT PAGE

DAUGHTER OF JOSEPH & JULIE

ZENAIDE LAETITIA JULIE BONAPARTE 1801–54

She joined her father when he was exiled to New Jersey for a few years. Her husband was her first cousin, ornithologist Charles Lucien Bonaparte. They had twelve children together.

CHARLES-LUCIEN JULES LAURENT BONAPARTE 1803–57

A famous ornithologist, he discovered the moustached warbler and a new kind of storm petrel. He married his cousin Zénaïde and lived in the US, then Italy, from where he was exiled for nationalist activity. He died in France.

LOUIS LUCIEN BONAPARTE 1813–91

Born in England, Louis lived in Italy and didn't visit France until after the Revolution of 1848, where he became a member of the French parliament, representing Corsica. He was also a linguist known for his pioneering work on the language of the Basques.

3 CHILDREN OF LUCIEN

SON OF JEROME & ELIZABETH

JEROME NAPOLEON BONAPARTE 1805–70

For many years the meat in the sandwich during his mother's argument with the Bonapartes, he was eventually allowed to use the name by his cousin, Napoleon III (against the wishes of his father), but without being admitted into the imperial family. His mother tried to circumvent this by persuading him to marry one of Joseph Bonaparte's daughters but he preferred an American heiress instead.

MATHILDE BONAPARTE 1820–1904

Her father married her off to the arts patron and fantastically wealthy Russian, Anatole Demidoff, in order for his debts to be paid, but the initial love match turned into a high-society public brawl involving infidelity, face slapping and the effective theft of Russian diamonds—which Mathilde wisely used to bankroll the presidential campaign of her cousin Louis Napoléon. He rewarded her by making her the second-highest ranked woman in France. Her salon was frequented by many of the greatest artists and thinkers of her time.

2 CHILDREN OF JEROME & CATHERINE

PRINCE NAPOLEON JOSEPH CHARLES PAUL 1822–91

Like his father, "Plon Plon" was known for his playboy lifestyle. He was also a key advisor to his cousin Napoleon III and represented liberal interests in opposition to the Empress Eugénie, such as the cause of Italian Unification under Count Cavour. His descendants, who maintain pretension to the Imperial title, are the last remaining males in the Bonaparte line.

PIERRE NAPOLEON BONAPARTE 1815–81

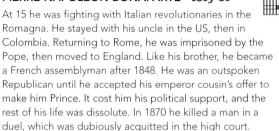

At 15 he was fighting with Italian revolutionaries in the Romagna. He stayed with his uncle in the US, then in Colombia. Returning to Rome, he was imprisoned by the Pope, then moved to England. Like his brother, he became a French assemblyman after 1848. He was an outspoken Republican until he accepted his emperor cousin's offer to make him Prince. It cost him his political support, and the rest of his life was dissolute. In 1870 he killed a man in a duel, which was dubiously acquitted in the high court.

ROLAND BONAPARTE 1858–1924

Forbidden by law from following a military career, he turned to geography and anthropology, traveling on scientific expeditions and amassing an enormous collection of specimens. He married Marie Blanc, daughter of Francois Blanc, Monte Carlo's chief property developer.

MARIE BONAPARTE 1882–1962

She became a psychoanalyst after she went to Sigmund Freud seeking a cure for her frigidity. It worked and she ended up having affairs with one of his disciples, and later the Prime Minister of France. Her husband was Prince George of Greece with whom she had two children. Perhaps her greatest influence on history was that she paid the Nazis a ransom which allowed Sigmund and most of his family to escape to England before the Holocaust began.

SUSAN MAY WILLIAMS 1812–81

The daughter of Benjamin Williams, co-founder of the Baltimore and Ohio Railroad—America's first—she married Jérôme Napoleon Bonaparte, who preferred her $200,000 dowry to the promise of a European princess.

JEROME NAPOLEON BONAPARTE II 1830–93

He studied at West Point and served in Texas with the Mounted Rifles before resigning from the US army to serve in the army of his cousin, Napoleon III of France.

CHARLES JOSEPH BONAPARTE 1851–1921

He graduated in law from Harvard and married the daughter of an attorney. The marriage was childless. In 1905 Theodore Roosevelt appointed him secretary of the US navy and in 1906 he became US Attorney General. In this position he was responsible for the creation of the FBI in 1908.

6 CHILDREN OF AUGUSTA & EUGENE

PRINCESS JOSEPHINE OF LEUCHTENBERG
1807–76

She became the Queen Consort to Oscar I of Sweden, the son of Marshal Bernadotte and Joseph Bonaparte's sister-in-law, Desirée Clary.

PRINCESS EUGENIE HORTENSE AUGUSTE DE BEAUHARNAIS   **1808–47**

Seems to have been a rather insignificant princess.

CHARLES AUGUSTE EUGENE NAPOLEON DE BEAUHARNAIS   **1810–35**

Married Queen Mary II "The Educator" of Portugal in 1835 and died 2 months afterward. A popular monarch, she went on to rule with her second husband until her death.

LUCIEN LOUIS JOSEPH NAPOLEON CARDINAL BONAPARTE   **1828–95**

Ordained to the priesthood on December 13, 1856 by Pope Pius IX, he was elected a Cardinal in 1868 and participated in the First Vatican Council.

AMELIE AUGUSTE EUGENIE NAPOLEONE DE BEAUHARNAIS   **1812–73**

Married Pedro I of Brazil, the father of her brother's wife, Queen Mary II of Portugal, and became Empress of Brazil.

THEODELINDE LOUISE EUGENIE AUGUSTE NAPOLEONE DE BEAUHARNAIS   **1814–57**

Married the Duke of Urach.

MAXIMILIAN JOSEPHE EUGENE AUGUSTE NAPOLEON DE BEAUHARNAIS   **1817–52**

Married Maria Nikolaievna Grand Duchess of Russia, daughter of Tsar Nicholas I of Russia, thus linking the Romanovs to the Bonapartes.

> The army is the true nobility of our country.
> NAPOLEON III

3 CHILDREN OF HORTENSE & LOUIS

NAPOLEON CHARLES BONAPARTE   **1802–1807**

Prince Royal of Holland and for a short time heir to his uncle Napoleon. When he died his body lay in state at Notre Dame Cathedral in Paris. He is buried at Saint-Leu-La-Foret, Ile-de-France.

SON OF ZENAIDE & CHARLES LUCIEN JULES LAURENT

NAPOLEON III, CHARLES LOUIS NAPOLEON BONAPARTE
1808–73

Third son lucky, he became President of the French Republic in 1849, then Emperor Napoleon III of France (1852–70). Often derided in history, the reign of Napoleon III was mostly a prosperous one where the Emperor introduced many of the amenities of the Industrial Revolution, as he had seen in Britain (underground sewerage and railroads, for example). He lost his seat because of the Franco–Prussian War (1870–71) after he was outwitted by Bismarck.

NAPOLEON LOUIS BONAPARTE   **1804–31**

He became Prince Royal of Holland on his brother's death and heir to Napoleon until the birth of Napoleon's son in 1811. His father abdicated the Dutch throne in his favor and he was King Lodewijk II for the week before his uncle's army invaded. After Waterloo he went into exile and married his first cousin, Charlotte, daughter of his uncle Joseph.

EUGENIE DE MONTIJO
1826–1920

She was Empress of France and daughter of a Spanish nobleman and his half-Spanish, half-Scottish wife. Louis Napoléon proposed to her after being rebuffed by the niece of Queen Victoria. She was smart and conservative and a considerable influence on her husband's reign as well as an adventurous trendsetter in fashion.

NAPOLEON EUGENE LOUIS JOHN JOSEPH
1856–79

Sometimes known as Napoleon IV, although he never reigned, his predecessor Napoleon I may well have turned over in his grave if he knew the way that this descendant died—speared by Zulus while fighting for the British Army. Still, according to all accounts, he died bravely against overwhelming odds following a deadly ambush. For their part, the Zulus later said that if they'd known who he was they wouldn't have killed him.

THE BUSHES

GEORGE H. W. BUSH PICTURED AT YALE UNIVERSITY, C.1947, CARRYING HIS BABY SON GEORGE W. BUSH ON HIS SHOULDERS. GEORGE BUSH SENIOR WOULD BECOME PRESIDENT OF THE UNITED STATES IN 1989, AND SON GEORGE W. WOULD FOLLOW IN POP'S FOOTSTEPS IN 2001.

HOW THEY RATE

WEALTH ★ ★ ★ ★ ★
The Bushes are representatives of America's plutocracy.

HEALTH ★ ★ ★ ★
For the most part, except for the seam of alcoholism in the family, the Bushes are robust, sporty characters with a good life expectancy.

HAPPINESS ★
Fathers who were brought up and perpetuated the school of tough love, ambitious matriarchs whose love is highly conditional and the sense of having to maintain a family momentum that has perhaps reached its pinnacle, are psychological factors that might help wealth and success, but are not the best recipe for happiness.

FAME ★ ★ ★ ★ ★
Doesn't get much better.

SEXINESS ★ ★
A subjective category, admittedly, but the Bushes are not known to inspire the idea of sex (with the exception of Neil's daughter Lauren). However, power is an acknowledged aphrodisiac.

BLACK SHEEP FACTOR ★ ★
Corporate corruption, drugs, sex and alcohol. However, Bush life narratives tend more toward either concealment or redemption rather than flagrant adoption of the "black sheep" mantle—although George W.'s brother Neil has come close.

ECCENTRICITY ★ ★
Not especially. There is evidence of a certain Protestant craziness, perhaps, and a fondness for practical jokes, but too much ambition and not enough brilliance for genuine eccentricity.

INFLUENCE ★ ★ ★ ★ ★
Major league—possibly more important in terms of US and world politics than the much vaunted Kennedys.

George H. W. Bush was a one-term President and two-time Vice President to Ronald Reagan. His son George W. is a two-term President and former two-term Governor of Texas, while brother Jeb is a two-term Governor of Florida, one of the nation's most populous states. Their grandfather, Prescott Bush, was the first to hold elected office—he was in the US senate for 11 years. Prescott's father, Samuel Bush, although not holding elected office, worked for the government during World War II and was an adviser to President Herbert Hoover.

The cosy relationship between the Bush family and business isn't suprising either, since they were a professional dynasty well before they were a political dynasty. While the Bush family is currently centered in the southern states of the US, such as Texas and Florida, its rise to eminence began in the 19th century in mid-west states such as Kansas, Missouri and via D. D. Walker's drygoods business and Samuel Bush's steel castings company. The family then entered the plutocratic stratosphere via Manhattan investment banking at the turn of the 20th century through George Walker, then Prescott Bush. The money they made here helped bankroll George H. W. Bush into the oil industry. Since then, the Bushes have continued their close relationship with the energy industry while they've branched into other businesses such as modeling, security, educational curricula and property development.

The Bushes are a family with a strong sense of identity and destiny. Much of this has been carried by a series of feisty women such as Dorothy (wife of Prescott) and Barbara (wife of George H. W.). The strength of the female line and the clannish awareness of the Bushes is shown by the maintenance of female surnames as middle names. Nonetheless, the family has its weaknesses, too, mainly through their fondness for hard liquor. Still, love them or hate them, it's hard to argue with the fact that, at this given point in history, the Bushes are probably the most important family in the world.

WHEN MOST PEOPLE THINK OF AMERICAN POLITICAL FAMILIES THEY THINK OF THE KENNEDYS, BUT THE BUSH FAMILY IS RAPIDLY BECOMING THE PRE-EMINENT POLITICAL FAMILY IN MODERN AMERICAN HISTORY.

BUSH ROOTS

While the tree in this book deals with George W. Bush's direct ancestors, in his 1995 book, *Ancestors of American Presidents*, New England genealogist Gary Boyd Roberts showed that Bush was distantly related to almost half the population of America. Six degrees of separation or what? Taking this into account, it's perhaps not surprising that he's related to fifteeen US Presidents (in addition to his pop), British monarchs, Winston Churchill and Pocahontas. With this kind of lineage it's hard not to think that George W. literally was born to rule.

According to Roberts the list of related presidents consists of George Washington, Millard Fillmore, Franklin Pierce, Abraham Lincoln, Ulysses S. Grant, Rutherford B. Hayes, James Garfield, Grover Cleveland, Theodore Roosevelt, William Howard Taft, Calvin Coolidge, Herbert Hoover, Franklin D. Roosevelt, Richard Nixon, Gerald Ford and George H. W. Bush. The socially-connected boy with an Ivy League education is about as far from the "log cabin" myth as it gets. The connection with Britain's Winston Churchill and Lady Diana Spencer (who share the same ancestors) is through the 15th-century Northamptonshire squire Henry Spencer, whose granddaughter Anne Marbury moved to Massachusetts during the 1600s. Anne was killed by native Americans but her direct descendant, Harriet Fay, married James Bush—the great great grandfather of George W. Bush.

Even more impressive, albeit buried much further back in history, are the ancestral links to monarchs Henry I, Henry II, Robert II of Scotland, William I of Scotland and Edward I of England. There's a link, too, to Pocahontas, the native American princess. She married tobacoo pioneer John Rolfe and a Bush ancestor married their only American great grandchild.

PRESCOTT SHELDON BUSH DOZES IN A CHAIR ON THE EVE OF HIS DEFEAT AS REPUBLICAN CANDIDATE FOR THE SENATE, NOVEMBER 1950.

' LET THE OTHERS HAVE
THE CHARISMA.
I'VE GOT THE CLASS.
GEORGE H. W. BUSH '

A FAMILY GATHERING AT GEORGE BUSH SENIOR'S SUMMER HOME AT KENNEBUNKPORT IN YORK COUNTY, MAINE, USA.

GEORGE W. BUSH DURING HIS UNIVERSITY YEARS AT YALE, WHERE HE GRADUATED WITH A BACHELOR OF ARTS DEGREE IN 1968, MAJORING IN HISTORY. BY HIS OWN ADMISSION, THE FUTURE PRESIDENT WAS AN "AVERAGE" STUDENT.

SMOKING BUSH

Bill Clinton very unconvincingly told the American public that he toked on a joint at Oxford but didn't inhale. George W. Bush, admirably, has refused to confirm or deny whether he smoked dope or snorted cocaine prior to 1974. His brother Marvin was busted for doing drugs at Andover, the exclusive New England prep school Bush boys are traditionally sent to. However, unlike his drug buddies, he was not expelled—daddy, George H. W., just happened to be on the Board of Trustees at the time. Less lucky was Jeb Bush's daughter, Noelle. Initially, she was busted for prescription fraud and sent to a drug treatment center. She was sentenced to 10 days in jail. However, she breached her court-ordered treatment plan by being caught in possession of sedatives. Then she went to jail for a further 10 days, but police raided her drug treatment center and found her in possession of cocaine. Oddly enough, simultaneously, her father was publicly arguing a "three-strikes" style of get tough on crime campaign.

NAZI BUSH

George H. W.'s grandfather Bert was an old-school robber baron. Both he and son-in-law Prescott were involved in business dealings through which they profited from Nazism. They were shareholders of a company that helped bankroll Hitler's rise to power. Interestingly, another prominent American lawyer who was fond of doing business with the Nazis was John Foster Dulles, Secretary of State under Eisenhower, whose brother was Allen Foster Dulles, who was head of the CIA—a position George H. W. Bush also came to occupy.

THIRSTY BUSH

WHEN LOOKING AT A BOOK FULL OF FAMOUS, MAINLY CAUCASIAN, FAMILIES, IT'S INTERESTING TO NOTE HOW OFTEN DYNASTIC ALCOHOLISM COINCIDES WITH DYNASTIC SUCCESS. THE HIGH-POWERED ARE OFTEN BIG BOOZERS. THE BUSHES ARE A CASE IN POINT. THE FOUNDER OF THE POLITICAL BUSH DYNASTY, PRESCOTT BUSH, USED TO TAKE HIMSELF AWAY FOR BENDERS AT EXCLUSIVE COUNTRY CLUBS, BUT STILL MANAGED TO CLIMB HIS WAY TO THE US SENATE. HOWEVER. HIS BROTHER, JAMES, TURNED HIS LIFE INTO A SHAMBLES WITH BOOZE. PRESCOTT'S GRANDSON GEORGE W. WAS A HARD-DRINKING PARTY BOY UNTIL HE WOKE UP DISSATISFIED WITH A HANGOVER AFTER HIS 40TH BIRTHDAY PARTY. SOME EXPERTS HAVE ASSOCIATED GEORGE W.'S IRRITABILITY AND INFLEXIBILITY WITH HAVING BOOZED AND GIVEN IT UP. THE CONDITION HAS THE CLINICAL NAME "DRY DRUNK SYNDROME." MEANWHILE, GEORGE W.'S TWIN DAUGHTERS JENNA AND BARBARA BECAME FAMOUS FOR THEIR DRUNKEN SHENANIGANS AT COLLEGE—A PHOTO OF A LEGLESS JENNA EVEN MADE THE TABLOIDS. MIND YOU, NEITHER OF THEM SEEMS TO HAVE COME TO ANY HARM AS A CONSEQUENCE. IN 2005, JEB'S SON, JOHN ELLIS JR, WAS ARRESTED FOR PUBLIC DRUNKENNESS AND RESISTING ARREST. OTHER RELATIVES, SUCH AS COMMENTATOR, COLUMNIST AND GEORGE W.'S COUSIN, JOHN ELLIS, ARE ALSO RECOVERING ALCOHOLICS.

A SCHOOL YEARBOOK PHOTO OF GEORGE W. BUSH (LOWER RIGHT, UPSIDE DOWN) WITH HIS BUDDIES AT PHILLIPS ACADEMY PREP SCHOOL IN ANDOVER, MASSACHUSETTS, USA.

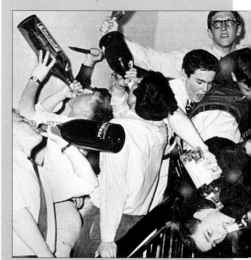

FASHION MODEL LAUREN BUSH, DAUGHTER OF GEORGE W.'S BROTHER, NEIL BUSH.

> I JUST WANT YOU TO KNOW THAT, WHEN WE TALK ABOUT WAR, WE'RE REALLY TALKING ABOUT PEACE.   GEORGE W. BUSH

DEADLY BUSH

ON NOVEMBER 6, 1963, 2 DAYS AFTER SHE TURNED 17, LAURA WELCH, NOW BUSH, WAS DRIVING HER CHEVROLET SEDAN WITH HER CLASSMATE JUDY DYKE SHORTLY AFTER 8 PM. AS SHE ENTERED THE INTERSECTION OF US HIGHWAY 349 AND TEXAS FARM ROAD 868, SHE DROVE THROUGH THE INTERSECTION'S STOP SIGN AND COLLIDED WITH A CHEVROLET CORVAIR SEDAN. WELCH AND DYKE SUSTAINED MINOR INJURIES, BUT THE DRIVER OF THE CHEVROLET, HER CLASSMATE AND CLOSE FRIEND MICHAEL DUTTON DOUGLAS, ALSO 17, WAS PRONOUNCED DEAD ON ARRIVAL AT MIDLAND MEMORIAL HOSPITAL. LAURA WELCH WAS NOT CHARGED OVER THE CRASH, BUT ONE WONDERS IF THIS INCIDENT MIGHT HAVE HAD AN IMPACT ON HER CHRISTIANITY AND DESIRE TO DO GOOD IN THE WORLD, QUALITIES THAT APPEAR TO HAVE BEEN PASSED ON TO HER CHILDREN.

SKULL AND BONES SOCIETY

If there is a Bush institution, it has to be Yale, one of America's top Ivy League Universities. More than thirty-five members of the Bush clan have been educated there. The first was George W.'s great great grandfather, the Reverend James Smith Bush, who graduated in 1844, while the most recent is George W.'s daughter Barbara, who graduated in 2004. Prescott Bush, George H. W., and George W. all went to college there, in all three cases as "legacy" students—let in because of relatives who were old boys. Only George W. didn't really enjoy the experience, perhaps because he arrived as a conservative Texan into a tumult of east coast liberal hippiedom and anti-war activity which culminated in 1968— the year he graduated.

Perhaps even more influential to the Bush clan is the Yale secret society, Skull and Bones. It was founded by an elitist student William Russell in 1832 with the idea of establishing a new world

SKULL AND BONES SOCIETY BUILDING.

order based on secret power networks. Each year fifteen students are selected to join and become known thereafter to their brethren as "knights." Prescott Bush was asked to join, and fellow Bonesmen who took an oath to help each other through life, such as the Harrimans, were instrumental in helping his career. Members pay a tithe to the Skull and Bones society throughout their working life and, according to one account, the "Russell Trust Association" is the wealthiest company registered in Connecticut.

Prescott was also the initiator of a controversial prank where he claimed to have kidnapped the skull of the native

American chief Geronimo—who had died in 1909—and put it in the "tomb" which formed the meeting house for the club. George H. W. was also tapped to become a member, as was his son George W. (Coincidentally, Bush's rival in the 2004 presidential election, John Kerry, was also a former member. If he had won the election, three of the USA's last four presidents would have been members.) For some reason, George W.'s daughter Barbara has not become a member of the Skull and Bones.

GEORGE H. W BUSH AND BABE RUTH, C.1946.

{ bush family tree }

SAMUEL PRESCOTT BUSH   1863–1948

The son of a reverend, he became an important industrialist and adviser to President Hoover. Between 1906 and 1927 he was the president of Buckeye steel castings who supplied, among other things, railroad equipment to the Harrimans, whose investment bank his son Prescott would later join. During World War I he was chief of the Ordnance, Small Arms and Ammunition section of the War Industries Board run by Bernard Baruch.

FLORA SHELDON   1872–1920

The daughter of Robert Emmett Sheldon, she was a housewife. Flora was killed by a car in Rhode Island, shortly before her son Prescott's wedding.

PRESCOTT SHELDON BUSH   1895–1972

US senator for Connecticut between 1952 and 1963 and, as such, the founder of the Bush political dynasty. After graduating from Yale (another family first) he served as an artillery captain in World War I. After a varied career as a salesman, in 1926 Prescott joined his father in law and his Skulls and Bones buddy, Roland Harriman, at Wall Street firm W. A. Harriman. In 1930 Harriman merged with banking firm Brown Brothers to form a private investment bank for the super rich. Prescott was made a partner. They had problems with Germany, first with the collapse of its economy and secondly through collusion with businesses close to the Nazis. By all accounts Prescott, like his father-in-law, was a fascist of a father and fond of applying the razor strap to his children's backsides. His temperament wasn't helped by his being an alcoholic.

GEORGE HERBERT "BERT" WALKER   1875–1953

By all accounts Bert Walker was a frightening man—a Missouri amateur heavyweight boxing champion with a foul temper, whose business practices, by today's standards, would have landed him in jail. Much of his angry passion came from his relationship with his own fiery father. When Bert married Presbyterian Loulie Wear, Bert's father, D. D. Walker, who was a fire and brimstone Catholic, refused to attend. While D. D. was a staunch southern Democrat, Bert became the family's first strident Republican. When self-made D. D., co-founder of Ely, Walker and Co.—the biggest drygoods supplier west of the Mississippi—started giving his fortune away, his sons tried to get him ruled insane. Bert went into business with E. H. Harriman, owner of the Union Railroad, whom his father had boycotted on account of his robber baron tactics. Bert then proceeded to make millions on Wall Street with his company G. H. Walker, much of it through insider trading. He sold short before the 1929 crash, thus ensuring the family's fortune, but earned the ire of Harry Truman for his corrupt and self-enriching involvement in the collapse of the Missouri Pacific railroad. He was also perfectly happy to do business with the Nazis.

JAMES BUSH   1901–78

James followed a similar path to his brother, Prescott—Yale, Skull and Bones, banking and alcoholism. Only the ending wasn't so happy. He was married four times, divorced three times and forced to resign as Vice President of a St Louis bank because of his drinking.

DOROTHY WALKER   1901–92

Born in Greenwich, Connecticut, Dorothy was the daughter of Bert Walker and Loulie Wear. She was a keen sportswoman, becoming runner-up in the first American girls tennis championship in 1918, and was a strong, devoted Presbyterian. She encouraged the spirit of competition in her children. Strong-willed, she forced her left-handed son and future President of the United States to play tennis and golf right handed.

{ "But let me tell you, this gender thing is history. You're looking at a guy who sat down with Margaret Thatcher across the table and talked about serious issues."
GEORGE H. W. BUSH }

PRESCOTT BUSH, JR 1922–

As his brother's political star rose, Prescott's wheeler-dealer instincts began to trade off the back of it, notably as an intermediary between Asian and American capital. At one stage he was sued by the Yakuza, the Japanese equivalent of the Mafia. His brother found him an embarrassment, but was unable to control his activities.

GEORGE HERBERT WALKER BUSH 1924–

He had a classic plutocratic East Coast upbringing and was a decorated World War II navy pilot whose plane got hit twice. Following Yale, where he captained the baseball team, Bush went into the oil game, securing employment with Dresser Industries (later part of Halliburton). His two unsuccessful pitches at the US Senate (1964, 1970) were punctuated by successful runs for the House of Representatives (1966, 1968). After Bush's 1970 loss, Nixon appointed him Ambassador of the United Nations then, after a spell in China, Gerald Ford appointed him Director of the CIA. When the Democrats got in, Bush went into investment banking. In 1980 he challenged Reagan for the Republican nomination for the Presidency and lost, but Reagan appointed him running mate and Bush became Vice President. They teamed up again successfully in the 1984 race. In 1988 he won the Presidency against Michael Dukakis, and presided over the fall of communism and the First Gulf War before losing in 1992, largely due to a lingering domestic recession. There has been controversy concerning Bush letting Saddam Hussein off the hook, possibly because of the prior CIA support for him. It is tempting to wonder whether the desire of Bush II to outdo his dad is part of the reason for his, at times, illogical bellicosity over Iraq.

BARBARA PIERCE 1925–

Very much the matriarch of the family and from a good East Coast family, whose most famous clan member was her distant cousin, US President Franklin Pierce. Her father was the President of McCall Corporation, a publisher of women's magazines, while her mother was a society lady who was killed in a car crash while her father was driving. Sister Martha was a *Vogue* covergirl, but Barbara was a sports-loving tomboy with an ugly duckling complex. She met George when they were 16 on a Christmas vacation. She married him while he was still fighting as a navy pilot in 1945.

6 CHILDREN: GEORGE, PAULINE, JEB, NEIL, MARVIN & DOROTHY NEXT PAGE

JOHN PRESCOTT ELLIS 1953–

A newspaper columnist, recovering alcholic and pundit, this cousin and childhood buddy of George W. and Jeb got into hot water when it was revealed that, while he was working as a consultant to Fox during the 2000 election, he leaked material from exit polls to his cousin's camp.

BILLY BUSH 1971–

A television personality and celebrity interviewer known for his light-hearted humor and irreverent attitude toward his subjects, he is the co-anchor of *Access Hollywood* and also the host presenter for the Miss Universe pageant.

NANCY BUSH 1926–

She married Boston insurance executive and Yale graduate Alexander Ellis.

JONATHAN BUSH 1931–

He's a Wall Street investor who's been fined in both Connecticut and Massachusetts for violating state company law

WILLIAM "BUCKY" BUSH 1938–

He became a banker in St Louis and has been accused of profiting handsomely out of the Iraq War.

GEORGE WALKER BUSH 1946–

Only the second son of a US President (41st) to become a US President (43rd). Like his father he went to Andover then Yale, where his conservative instincts were antagonized by the prevailing liberalism. After his college graduation he joined the Texas National Guard where, like his father in World War II, he was a pilot. During Vietnam, however, Bush, who stayed in the guard until 1974, never saw active service. Following his 6 years' service, he went to Harvard and is the first US President to hold an MBA. Like his father, he deployed his knowledge in the oil industry where he made the first of his millions. Something of a party boy businessman, he combined running oil companies with a fondness for boozing, then bought into the Texas Rangers baseball team, which he managed then sold, making a profit of $15 million. In 1978, he ran for the US Representatives but failed. In 1985 he gave up the grog and turned to God. He then helped his father's successful 1988 Presidential campaign. His own office-holding career began in 1994 when he was elected Texas Governor. In 1998 he won again in a landslide. He controversially won the 2000 election on a slogan of "compassionate conservatism" even though he failed to get a numerical majority of votes. His first term was marked by dwindling popularity until it was transformed by the September 11 attacks, when Bush appeared like a true leader and was an inspiration to his nation in a time of crisis. However, the Iraq War, which has defined much of his second term, has been less successful in terms of public opinion.

LAURA LANE WELCH 1946–

Although she went to the same junior high as her hubby, it wasn't until 1977 at a backyard BBQ that they met. Three months later they were married. She is an elementary school teacher and librarian. As First Lady she has promoted causes such as literacy and has added a humanitarian aspect to the Presidency.

> To those of you who received honors, awards and distinctions, I say well done. And to the C students, I say you, too, can be president of the United States.
> GEORGE W. BUSH

NEIL BUSH 1955–

As a child, Neil was such a goody two shoes that his siblings dubbed him "Mr Perfect." In his adult life, however, he failed to live up to the nickname. He was director of Colorado-based Silverado Savings & Loan, which collapsed, costing the taxpayer $1.3 billion. His divorce from Sharon, his wife of 23 years, was messy and included lurid tales of sex romps in Asia.

PAULINE ROBINSON BUSH 1949–53

George H. W. Bush's second child and first daughter died of leukemia. This apparently had quite an effect on young George.

MARVIN BUSH 1956–

After taking drugs in his youth, Marvin worked for a number of corporations, including the company in charge of security for the World Trade Center and United Airlines during September 2001. He's done campaign and fundraising work for the Republicans. The disease colitis led to an operation in the 1980s that has left him permanently having to wear a colostomy bag. His wife, Margaret, had ovarian cancer as a child and their two children are adopted.

JEB BUSH 1953–

Jeb is the two-term 43rd Governor of Florida. His school education followed the same path as his brother until he went on a high school exchange and taught English in Mexico. While there, he met his wife, Columba, the only woman he has ever seriously dated—though there are rumors of extra-marital activities. He graduated in Latin American Studies from the University of Texas and worked for a Texan bank in Venezuela before settling in Miami. He became a real estate salesman, then property developer, while at the same time he honed his political skills. He lost the gubernatorial election in 1994 but came back in 1998 and increased his majority in 2002.

DOROTHY "DORO" BUSH 1959–

The baby and only surviving daughter of the family, she's been married twice, trading up on Maine builder William LeBlond for Bobby Koch, former administrative assistant to powerful Washington democrat Dick Gephardt. Koch now is a lobbyist for the Californian wine industry while Doro is a fundraiser for her relatives' campaigns, as well as charitable causes.

GEORGE P. BUSH   1976–

George P. is a telegenic Texan attorney, whose half-American, half-Hispanic heritage, not to mention his family connections, puts him in an ideal position to pursue a political career.

BARBARA AND JENNA BUSH   1981–

After coming to notoriety for under-age drinking and college partying, George W. Bush's twin daughters are showing signs of developing social consciences, with Barbara volunteering in a South African hospital and Jenna school teaching in Washington DC.

NOELLE BUSH   1977–

Noelle is best known for her drug problems. A 2002 arrest for prescription fraud was followed by a court-ordered visit to a drug treatment center. She was jailed in July that year for being in possession of prescription pills—a violation of her court-ordered treatment plan. In September she was jailed for 10 days when police visited the drug treatment center and found her in possession of cocaine. During this crisis her father basically disowned her.

LAUREN BUSH   1984–

Lauren is most well-known as the model for the Tommy Hilfiger fashion label. She has also appeared as the covergirl for the famous Pirelli calendar.

JOHN ELLIS BUSH JR   1983–

Jeb Jr, or Jebby, is most famous for being charged with public drunkenness and resisting arrest in 2005.

PIERCE BUSH   1986–

Having overcome a high school diagnosis of ADD, Pierce is an earnest college kid with a keen interest in politics and a burgeoning public profile.

MARSHALL BUSH   1986–

She worked for her uncle's re-election as President in 2004 before going to college.

ASHLEY BUSH   1989–

Following in her big sister's footsteps, in 2005, Ashley, who much prefers theater to politics, made a splash on the high-society international debutante circuit, and looks set at least for a career in modeling.

CHARLES W. BUSH   1989–

No reports as yet of adolescent delinquency.

SAMUEL LEBLOND   1984–

ELLIE LEBLOND   1986–

ROBERT KOCH   1993–

GEORGIA KOCH   1996–

THE CHURCHILLS

> WE ARE ALL WORMS, BUT I DO BELIEVE
> THAT I AM A GLOW WORM.
> WINSTON CHURCHILL

With the 1st Duke of Marlborough, who some regard as the greatest ever military leader of Britain, and Winston Churchill, its best-known war-time prime minister, the Churchills are one of Britain's most formidable families. Around these indubitably great men are a range of strong-minded women, able statesmen, decadent aristocrats and, perhaps predominantly, men of more modest talents, whose family connections have facilitated political and military careers. There's also a strain of genuine blackguard too. One Churchill has even been regarded the most disreputable person to ever hold the title of English duke, while the current Marquess of Blandford may well challenge him to the title—that is, if he manages to outlive his father.

Generally the Churchills are a recalcitrant bunch, prone to melancholy, excessive expenditure and fits of rage. By all accounts, they're difficult to live with—this family was getting divorced well before it was considered acceptable, and often more than once. Both of the great Churchills are atypical in this respect, since they remained married and seemingly faithful to one woman throughout their adult lives. Other Churchills have approached their marriages with the pragmatic morality often practiced by the European aristocracy and compensated for the sensible dynastics with affairs.

Over the centuries Churchills have mixed it with kings, heiresses, arms dealers—even a professional juggler named after a sheep's stomach stuffed with variety meats and oats. But it's the tradition of callousness to the welfare of their offspring which is perhaps most off-putting to the modern eye. A stiff-upper-lip case of what doesn't kill you makes you stronger, but with genes of madness and genius thrown into the mix. Mind you, the current generation seems to be reasonably tame, though it's arguable that in these days of spin and shiftiness, Winston wouldn't have stood a chance.

BRITISH WORLD WAR II POSTER, C.1942.

HOW THEY RATE

WEALTH ★ ★ ★ ★
The Churchills always seemed to be better at spending money than earning it. Still, with Blenheim Palace in the family, things aren't that bad.

HEALTH ★ ★
Quite a few early deaths, the prevalence of depression, as well issues with alcohol, drugs and syphilis, means the health of this family is not great.

HAPPINESS ★
Lots of divorces, affairs and health problems make this, on average, one of the less happy families to grace the pages of this book.

FAME ★ ★ ★ ★
Winston was recently voted the greatest ever Briton. However, this is a family with long runs of dullness between its stellar moments.

SEXINESS ★ ★ ★
There's nothing like the promise of a title to get some women to drop their knickers—and from the look of the Churchill history, once they've started, they usually find it hard to stop.

BLACK SHEEP FACTOR ★ ★ ★ ★ ★
Or should it be the "Black Dog Factor," named for Winston's term for his bouts of black depression? With one Churchill described as the most disreputable man ever to be a duke of the realm, another the rudest man in Europe, and the current heir to the Duke of Marlborough a junkie, this family has produced enough black sheep to populate a large estate in Oxfordshire.

ECCENTRICITY ★ ★ ★ ★ ★
Whether they are brilliantly or boorishly eccentric, the Churchills are certainly up there with the best.

INFLUENCE ★ ★ ★ ★
Two great British leaders in the 1st Duke of Marlborough and Winston. Despite a constant string of politicians, the family hasn't done much since.

BLENHEIM PALACE, BUILT IN 1705, HOME OF THE DUKE OF MARLBOROUGH, AND BIRTHPLACE OF WINSTON CHURCHILL.

THE FIRST FAMOUS CHURCHILL

John Churchill, 1st Duke of Marlborough (1650–1722)

His family had lost most of their property supporting the Royals in the English Civil War, but the return of the crown saw this Churchill prosper. Rated as one of the great military tacticians in European history, as leader of the English army against the French during the War of the Spanish Succession, he was the first person to defeat the army of Louis XV and was made Duke of Marlborough out of royal gratitude for his series of crushing victories. His victory at the Battle of Blenheim in Bavaria in 1704 changed the power balance of Europe, putting a halt to France's expansionist inclinations for a century. For this he was rewarded by Queen Anne with the land and money to build Blenheim Palace, which remains the family seat today and was the birthplace of Winston Churchill. The influence of John Churchill over Winston was large considering he was the subject of the latter's six-volume history, *Marlborough: His Life and Times*. John Churchill was a man who stuck to his ideas rather than political loyalties, and this integrity as well as his ruthless ambition earned him enemies, and his periods of celebrated success were balanced by periods spent in the dog house, often on trumped-up charges and accusations. Perhaps this contributed to the clear-thinking irascibility which has continued to be a family trait. Noted for his ability to surprise an enemy on the battlefield, he showed unconventionality in other aspects of his life as well. Since he had no son, he managed to get a special act of parliament passed which enabled his daughter Henrietta to inherit his title and Marlborough remains the only English dukedom a female can inherit to this day—though it is unlikely, given the number of males in line, to ever happen again.

KNELLER'S PORTRAIT OF JOHN CHURCHILL.

RANDOLPH CHURCHILL'S AILMENT

WINSTON'S POP, RANDOLPH, WAS A MAN OF SOME ABILITY WHOSE CAREER AND LIFE WERE CUT SHORT BY A TERRIBLE DISEASE, WHICH BASICALLY SAW HIS BRAIN TURN TO MUSH. VARIOUS THEORIES HAVE BEEN POSITED AS TO WHAT THIS DISEASE WAS, BUT THE MOST COMMON IS THAT IT WAS SYPHILIS. SYPHILIS WAS THE AIDS OF ITS DAY, AN INCURABLE, SEXUALLY TRANSMITTED DISEASE THAT COULD TAKE DECADES TO KILL ITS VICTIM. A STORY OFTEN REPEATED IS THAT RANDOLPH CHURCHILL CONTRACTED SYPHILIS AS THE RESULT OF A UNIVERSITY PRANK, WHERE HIS FRIENDS GOT HIM DRUNK AND SENT HIM TO BED WITH A GRAY-HAIRED, ONE-TOOTHED WHORE. RANDOLPH APPARENTLY WOKE UP THE NEXT MORNING AND WENT STRAIGHT TO THE DOCTOR, WHO DOUSED HIS GENITALS WITH DISINFECTANT, BUT SADLY TO NO AVAIL—ALTHOUGH IT WOULD BE MORE THAN 20 YEARS BEFORE THE DISEASE WOULD TAKE HIS LIFE.

> *You seem to have no real purpose in life and won't realize at the age of twenty-two that for a man life means work, and hard work if you mean to succeed.*
> JENNIE JEROME CHURCHILL
> TO HER SON WINSTON

WINSTON CHURCHILL WITH GRANDSON NICHOLAS SOAMES.

" . . . ONE DAY I GOT INTO HIS BEDROOM PAST THE VALET WHO GUARDED HIS DOOR. HE LOOKED UP FROM HIS PAPER AND SAID, 'WHAT DO YOU WANT?' I ASKED HIM IF IT WAS TRUE THAT HE WAS THE GREATEST MAN IN THE WORLD. HE REPLIED, 'YES, IT IS TRUE. NOW BUGGER OFF'."

NICHOLAS SOAMES ON WINSTON CHURCHILL

JENNIE JEROME CHURCHILL

Once described as having the demeanor more of a panther than a woman—perhaps a consequence of her rumored Iroquois blood—Jennie was one of three daughters of Leonard Jerome, a financier and speculator who once owned the *New York Times*. Leonard was known for his lavish lifestyle which, at its pinnacle, included a mansion in South Manhattan with its own 600-seat theater. Jennie was a party girl and one legend credits her with invention of the Manhattan cocktail to celebrate the election of Samuel Tilden in 1874.

The Jerome sisters were pioneers in the trade between American heiresses and English aristocrats, for which there was a vogue in the late 19th century. The marriage of the 9th Duke of Marlborough to Consuela Vanderbilt in 1895 was another, more lucrative instance. Jennie married Randolph Churchill in 1874, against the wishes of both sets of parents—hers because they thought a second son was beneath her, and his because they thought all Americans were vulgar. Unfortunately for Jennie's husband, by the time she was married, her father had lost most of his fortune.

Their son Winston was born 7½ months after the wedding, and it has been suggested he was the reason they did marry. However, if it began as a union of passionate ardor, this wasn't to last. Her husband Randolph reportedly had the disease syphilis, and Jennie was not shy of seeking accommodation with other men. Her lovers included Edward VII and a king of Serbia, while her second son, Jack, was the consequence of another affair. After the death of husband Randolph in 1895, she married twice more: first to George Cornwallis West who was just 16 days older than her son Winston (who later threw her over for the famous stage actress Mrs Patrick Campbell), and then to Montague Phippen Porch, a British Civil Servant based in Nigeria.

In her later life Jennie also wrote a number of plays. She also helped her son publish his first books and they grew closer, partly from this talent they shared, but also as a result of Winston's rising political star. It was at a party his mother held for him that Winston first laid eyes on Clementine, his future wife. Jennie died in 1921, aged 67, from complications arising from surgery to remove a gangrenous leg.

JENNIE WITH SONS JACK (LEFT) AND WINSTON (RIGHT), 1885.

PRIME MINISTER WINSTON CHURCHILL, 1943, MAKING HIS FAMOUS "V FOR VICTORY" SIGN.

> IT HAS BEEN SAID THAT DEMOCRACY IS THE WORST FORM OF GOVERNMENT EXCEPT ALL THE OTHERS THAT HAVE BEEN TRIED.
> WINSTON CHURCHILL

WINSTON AND FIANCEE, CLEMENTINE, 1908.

WINSTON CHURCHILL

It was a career that spanned the last British cavalry charge and ended with the atomic bomb. However, if it wasn't for World War II, Winston Churchill's life would have probably remained a minor footnote in modern history. But his ability to lead his nation through some of its darkest hours and on to victory saw him recently voted the greatest ever Briton. Churchill's daily habits, however—which included drinking Scotch and sleeping during the day—were more those of a bohemian artist than a statesman. Indeed, one of his hobbies was painting, and he was eventually awarded the Nobel Prize in Literature for his multi-volumed histories—even though he would have preferred the Prize in Peace.

It was this facility with language which enabled Winston to succeed the way he did. His stirring speeches helped hold the nation of Britain together during World War II, and he coined post-war terms such as "the iron curtain," which defined the Cold War geo-political situation. His powers of language also gifted him the sense of humor and self-deprecation that, along with his mistakes, humanized his gargantuan genius ego, and enabled this impractical aristocrat to be popular with the British commoners.

His childhood was lonely and possibly the source of the depression that dogged him through his later days. His parents tended to the common upper-class opinion that children are best unseen and not heard. He was a poor student at school and, instead of going to university, Winston joined the army. He was initially stationed in a polo-playing regiment in India, but eventually saw the action he was restless for in India and Sudan. During the Boer War, he escaped from a prisoner-of-war camp and made his way back from behind enemy lines, then gained a commission in the South African Lighthorse and fought at Spion Kop before marching on Pretoria, where he and his cousin, the Duke of Marlborough, managed to get a Boer prison camp to surrender.

A SWIFT KICK

Come hither, all ye empty things,
Ye bubbles rais'd by breath of kings;
Who float upon the tide of state,
Come hither and behold your fate.
Let pride be taught by this rebuke,
How very mean a thing's a duke;
From all his ill-got honors flung,
Turn'd to that dirt from whence he sprung.

A poem by Jonathon Swift, author of *Gulliver's Travels*, inspired by the death of his political enemy, the 1st Duke of Marlborough.

POLITICS IN 1900 Winston was elected the Conservative Member for Oldham, England, in 1900. He deserted the Tories (Conservatives) for the Liberals in 1904 and joined the Cabinet when Asquith became Prime Minister, as President of the Board of Trade. In 1910 he was promoted to Home Secretary and he became First Lord of the Admiralty in 1911—a position he held through to World War I, where he was responsible for the modernization of the navy and for funding the development of the battle tank.

> "THERE IS NOTHING MORE EXHILARATING THAN TO BE SHOT AT WITHOUT RESULT."
> WINSTON CHURCHILL

WORLD WAR II Churchill's ill-conceived campaign in the Dardanelles earned him the epithet "Butcher of Gallipoli." He was demoted for this, and rejoined the army to command a battalion on the Western Front, but was back in the Cabinet as Minister for Munitions for the final year of World War I. After the war he caused controversy, but anticipated the direction of contemporary warfare by arguing for the use of chemical weapons dropped from planes on revolting Iraqi tribesmen. In 1924, Churchill rejoined the Conservative Party and he was a controversial Chancellor of the Exchequer in 1925, since his return of Britain to the Gold Standard almost caused a recession. While he was out of government during the 1930s he wrote much of his *History of the English Speaking Peoples*. An early advocate of re-armanent against Chamberlain's appeasement of Hitler, when World War II broke out, Churchill regained his old job as First Lord of the Admiralty. When Chamberlain resigned, George VI appointed Churchill Prime Minister. Churchill was as adept at keeping the Allies together as he was at inspiring the British people to grin and bear it under immense adversity—though he caused his generals palpitations with his often erratic attempts to meddle in military affairs. His post-war political career was marred by a series of strokes which affected his memory and powers of speech, and he was forced to retire from politics in 1955.

CHURCHILL CASHING IN

THERE WAS A NATIONAL OUTCRY IN BRITAIN IN 1998 WHEN IT WAS REVEALED THAT THE CHURCHILL FAMILY, LED BY GRANDSON, WINSTON CHURCHILL—WHO HAD INHERITED THE HUGE SUM OF $10 MILLION FROM HIS MOTHER'S WILL ONLY THE YEAR BEFORE—HAD BEEN PAID $22 MILLION FROM THE NATIONAL LOTTERY BY THE GOVERNMENT FOR PAPERS OF WINSTON CHURCHILL. THE FAMILY HAD THREATENED TO SELL THEM OFF AT AUCTION TO THE HIGHEST BIDDER—DESPITE THE FACT THAT THEY HAD ALREADY MADE $11 MILLION FROM THE COPYRIGHTS HELD BY THE ESTATE.

"THE BIG THREE," 1943—FROM LEFT TO RIGHT, JOSEPH STALIN, FRANKLIN D. ROOSEVELT AND WINSTON CHURCHILL.

> THE OLDER ONES WERE BROUGHT UP IN A DIFFICULT TIME OF MY GRANDFATHER'S LIFE, AND VERY MUCH IN THE VICTORIAN WAY. THEY HAD RATHER UNSATISFACTORY NANNIES, INCLUDING ONE WHO FILLED ALL THE NURSERY CHOCOLATES WITH MUSTARD BECAUSE SHE SUSPECTED THAT ONE OF THE CHILDREN HAD TAKEN ONE WITHOUT ASKING.

CELIA SANDYS, GRANDDAUGHTER OF WINSTON

churchill family tree

ARABELLA CHURCHILL
1648–1730

The elder sister of John Churchill, she was the mistress of King James II, and bore him four children. The relationship survived the death of his first wife, Anne, and subsequent marriage to Mary of Modena in 1673. Her two sons were made dukes and, following their father's deposing, one died in action while commander of the French Army of the Rhine.

JOHN CHURCHILL, 1ST DUKE OF MARLBOROUGH
1650–1722

SARAH CHURCHILL
1660–1744

As Lady of the Bedchamber to Queen Anne, her personal ascendancy over the monarch was a vital reason for her husband's military successes, as she fueled the martial flames in the Queen's heart. When she was replaced as the Queen's favorite by Abigail Masham, her husband's star began to wane and she became a fiery shrew.

HENRIETTA CHURCHILL
1681–1733

She was the second Duchess of Marlborough and Countess of Godolphin. A special act of parliament was enacted for the title to be passed to John's daughter, Henrietta, in the absence of a male heir. Henrietta, however, also failed to produce a male heir and when she died the title went Charles, the son of her younger sister, Anne.

ANNE CHURCHILL   1684–1716

The second and allegedly favorite daughter of the first Duke of Marlborough, she was a strong character and has been credited with converting her mother, a staunch Tory, to her father's pragmatic Whiggism (what might today be called Liberal).

CHARLES SPENCER, 3RD EARL OF SUNDERLAND   1674–1722

Winston was not the first member in his family to be Prime Minister. Charles was a talented politician and statesman who rose to become Prime Minister in 1718 before his career was ruined by his association with the South Sea Bubble fiasco. His marriage to Anne Churchill is why Winston Churchill is a relative of Princess Diana.

CHARLES SPENCER, 3RD DUKE OF MARLBOROUGH   1706–58

A career soldier, he was a Brigadier General and Commander in Chief of the British expeditionary force in the early part of the Seven Years War when he caught fever and died in Munster, Germany.

JOHN SPENCER   1708–46

The younger brother of the 3rd Duke of Malborough,

DIANA SPENCER   1735–1808

This unconventional eldest daughter of the 3rd Duke of Marlborough escaped an unhappy marriage to Viscount Bolingbroke to maintain a secret relationship with her lover, Topham Beauclerk. She concealed the birth of their illegitimate child and gained an expensive divorce—only the fifth-ever granted to an English noble family. To support herself, she painted portraits, illustrated books and provided designs for Wedgwood pottery, becoming a renowned artist at a time when upper-class women didn't have careers.

GEORGE SPENCER, 4TH DUKE OF MARLBOROUGH
1739–1817

He was a soldier until he inherited the dukedom, then he moved into the House of Lords. He was the first Earl Spencer and it is this lineage that leads to Princess Diana.

GEORGE SPENCER-CHURCHILL, 5TH DUKE OF MARLBOROUGH   1766–1840

The pinnacle of his political career came when he was Lord of the Treasury between 1804 and 1806. Although he was born and baptized with the name of George Spencer he had it legally changed to George Spencer-Churchill.

"Treat your friends as you do your best pictures, and place them in their best light."
JENNIE JEROME CHURCHILL

GEORGE SPENCER-CHURCHILL, 6TH DUKE OF MARLBOROUGH 1793–1857

He was the Conservative Member of Parliament for Chippenham from 1818–20, and Conservative MP for Woodstock from 1826–35, and 1838–40.

JOHN WINSTON SPENCER-CHURCHILL, 7TH DUKE OF MARLBOROUGH 1822–83

A statesman, he served as Lord President of the Council in Lord Derby's and Benjamin Disraeli's governments and was later Lord Lieutenant of Ireland from 1876–80.

GEORGE CHARLES SPENCER-CHURCHILL, 8TH DUKE OF MARLBOROUGH 1844–92

Once described as "one of the most disreputable men ever to have debased the highest rank in the British peerage." He was expelled from Eton and one of his sexual scandals ended up in a violent quarrel with the Prince of Wales—because they had both slept with the same man's wife.

> My most brilliant achievement was my ability to be able to persuade my wife to marry me.
> WINSTON CHURCHILL

RANDOLPH CHURCHILL 1849–95

His political career, which included being Chancellor of the Exchequer and Leader of the House of Commons, was cut short by an illness (commonly thought to be syphilis) which affected his temper and ability to think.

JENNIE JEROME 1854–1921

An appalling mother, experienced lover and generally fascinating woman, she was an American heiress whose dowry vanished, a collector of royal lovers and the mother of one of Britain's most famous figures who recovered from her indifference to win a world war.

CHARLES RICHARD JOHN SPENCER-CHURCHILL 9TH DUKE OF MARLBOROUGH 1871–1934

He became the 9th Duke upon the death of his father in 1892. He was often known as "Sunny" Marlborough, after his courtesy title of the Earl of Sunderland, but his disposition was the opposite. He married the American railroad heiress Consuelo Vanderbilt in New York in 1895, the celebrity wedding of that year. They were divorced in 1921, by which time the Vanderbilt dowry had been used to restore Blenheim Palace. His second marriage, also to an American, Gladys Deacon, was unhappy too. She dined with her husband with a revolver by the side of her plate. They eventually separated.

1 CHILD NEXT PAGE

JACK CHURCHILL 1880–1947

As children, he and Winston were close. One of the many Churchills to enjoy a career in the army, he rose to Major and was rewarded for his distinguished service in World War I.

3 CHILDREN NEXT PAGE

LADY GWENDOLINE THERESA MARY BERTIE 1885–1941

WINSTON CHURCHILL 1874–1965

The quintessential British bulldog, he was stubborn, cantankerous, often depressed and fond of booze and cigars. Yet he was also a talented painter, Nobel laureate for literature (though he had his eyes on the Peace Prize), "Butcher of Gallipoli," orchestrator of the Cold War and one of the greatest war-time leaders Britain has ever had.

5 CHILDREN NEXT PAGE

CLEMENTINE HOZIER 1885–1977

While the personal lives of many Churchills are marked by affairs and divorces, the marriage of Clementine and Winston was a success, lasting from 1908 until Winston's death. Curiously both came from unstable backgrounds. It's been alleged Clementine's father, Henry Hozier, was sterile and that she and her siblings were the biological children of her mother's affair with her sister's husband, Algernon Freeman-Mitford, grandfather of the famous Mitford sisters.

CHILD OF CHARLES RICHARD JOHN SPENCER-CHURCHILL

3 CHILDREN OF JACK & GWENDOLINE

JOHN GEORGE SPENCER-CHURCHILL   1909–92

The son of Jack Churchill, and nephew of Sir Winston Churchill, made his living by being an artist.

HENRY WINSTON PEREGRINE SPENCER-CHURCHILL   1913–2002

ANNE CLARISSA SPENCER-CHURCHILL   1920–

She later became the second wife of British Prime Minister Sir Anthony Eden, whose disastrous efforts in the Suez crisis occurred against her uncle's advice.

JOHN ALBERT WILLIAM SPENCER-CHURCHILL, 10TH DUKE OF MARLBOROUGH   1897–1972

Before inheriting the dukedom in 1934 he was a Lieutenant Colonel in the Life Guards.

DIANA CHURCHILL   1909–63

She married twice, and twice divorced. Her second marriage was to Conservative politician Duncan Sandys. She suffered a number of nervous breakdowns and eventually committed suicide.

5 CHILDREN OF WINSTON & CLEMENTINE

SARAH MILLICENT HERMIONE CHURCHILL 1914–82

A British actress, her most famous role was in the film *Royal Wedding* (1951) as Anne Ashmond, opposite Fred Astaire. She was also known for her problems with alcohol and was married three times, including to popular radio comedian Vic Oliver.

MARIGOLD CHURCHILL   1918–21

She died from septicemia while on a seaside holiday with the family's governess.

DUNCAN SANDYS   1908–87

The Secretary of State for Commonwealth Relations and for Colonies,1960–1964, he negotiated Britain's withdrawal from many of its outposts of Empire, and caused controversy by supporting Rhodesia's white-supremacist prime minister, Ian Smith.

RANDOLPH CHURCHILL   1911–68

Between 1940–45, he was a member of parliament, but after the war he tried many times to be elected without success. He was an irascible adult who drank himself to death and competed with friend Evelyn Waugh for the reputation as the rudest man in England. His daughter, Arabella, is from his second marriage to June Osborne.

> CRITICISM MAY NOT BE AGREEABLE, BUT IT IS NECESSARY. IT FULFILS THE SAME FUNCTION AS PAIN IN THE HUMAN BODY. IT CALLS ATTENTION TO AN UNHEALTHY STATE OF THINGS.
> WINSTON CHURCHILL

MARY CHURCHILL   1922–

The most sane of the Churchill children, she accompanied her father to the famous Potsdam conference after World War II. In 1947, she married politician Christopher Soames, who was Ambassador to Paris and the last British Governor of Zimbabwe. She has also written about her parents.

PAMELA HARRIMAN   1920–97

The notches on her bedpost are impeccable. Her husbands were Randolph, producer Leland Hayward, and wealthy Democrat politician Averell Harriman (whose firm gave a living to Prescott Bush), while her lovers included Gianni Agnelli (Fiat), Baron Elie de Rothschild and the McCarthy-era broadcaster Edward R. Murrow. After she helped bankroll Bill Clinton's presidential campaign, he named her the first woman US Ambassador to France in 1993.

JOHN GEORGE VANDERBILT SPENCER-CHURCHILL, 11TH DUKE OF MARLBOROUGH 1926–

He has been married unsuccessfully three times. His second marriage was to Athina Onassis, former wife of Winston's friend Aristotle. He is worth just under $375 million.

JULIAN SANDYS 1936–97

A barrister, his wife Elisabeth Sandys (née Martin) is the aunt of Chris Martin, lead singer of the band Coldplay and partner of actress Gwyneth Paltrow.

EDWINA SANDYS 1938–

She is an internationally renowned sculptor married to an American architect who has created works for UN buildings in New York, Vienna and Geneva.

CELIA SANDYS 1943–

As a teenager she hung out with Winston and Maria Callas on Aristotle Onassis's yacht. She has published books on the Churchills, including *Chasing Churchill* about her grandfather.

ARABELLA CHURCHILL 1949–

She is one of the organizers of Britain's famous Glastonbury Festival. She has two children, Jake (1973–) by first husband Jim Barton, and Jessica by second husband, juggler Haggis McLeod. She caused headlines in 1999 by promising to undergo a live facelift on the internet but eventually pulled out.

WINSTON CHURCHILL 1940–

He was Member of Parliament for Manchester Davyhulme 1970–97, when the seat was abolished, but did not achieve high office. His first marriage to Mary "Minnie" Caroline d'Erlanger ended in acrimonious divorce due to his extra-marital relationship with Soraya Khashoggi, former wife of the arms-dealer Adnan Khashoggi.

NICHOLAS SOAMES 1948–

Known for being a heavyweight in the physical rather than political sense, this British Conservative politician is a close friend of Prince Charles and holds reactionary Conservative views.

JAMIE BLANDFORD 1964–

Marquess of Blandford and heir to the dukedom, this eldest son is most famous for his addictions to cocaine and heroin. He has been arrested several times and spent a couple of short stints in jail. Although he will still inherit the title, his father has changed the inheritance so he will be unable to sell off the family estate if he lives that long.

RANDOLPH SPENCER CHURCHILL 1965–

JENNIE SPENCER CHURCHILL 1966–

MARINA SPENCER CHURCHILL 1967–

JACK SPENCER CHURCHILL 1975–

DIANA CHURCHILL

DIANA, THE ELDEST DAUGHTER OF SIR WINSTON CHURCHILL AND CLEMENTINE HOZIER, WAS A NAUGHTY CHILD AND GREW UP TO BE A TROUBLED ADULT. IN 1932 SHE MARRIED SIR JOHN MILNER BAILEY BUT DIVORCED IN 1935. IN THAT SAME YEAR HER FATHER ESCORTED HER TO HER SECOND WEDDING (PICTURED ABOVE) TO POLITICIAN DUNCAN SANDYS, WITH WHOM SHE WOULD HAVE THREE CHILDREN. THEY DIVORCED IN 1962. ALTHOUGH DIANA HAD HAD A CAREER IN THE WOMEN'S ROYAL NAVAL SERVICE, AND ALSO AS A SAMARITAN COUNSELING WOULD-BE SUICIDES, IRONICALLY SHE HERSELF EVENTUALLY COMMITTED SUICIDE IN 1964 BY SWALLOWING AT LEAST SEVENTEEN SLEEPING PILLS.

THE DAHLS

> FAIRY TALES HAVE ALWAYS GOT TO HAVE SOMETHING A BIT SCARY FOR CHILDREN—AS LONG AS YOU MAKE THEM LAUGH AS WELL. ROALD DAHL

MODEL SOPHIE DAHL SHOWING OFF HER WORLD-FAMOUS 38DD SIZE CLEAVAGE.

The Dahls are a prominent artistic family. Without doubt their most renowned member is Roald Dahl, one of the more unusual literary figures of the 20th century. Dahl's children's books are the work of a brilliant and subversive imagination and have captivated millions of children, while his macabre short stories have lodged in the mind of many an adult reader, and have also inspired a television series.

The darkness in Roald's work was mirrored by a life which was no stranger to tragedy. His father and one of his sisters died early, as did his daughter, while his son suffered brain damage in an accident, and yet another daughter had massive drug addiction problems that culminated in a suicide attempt. Roald's wife Patricia Neal was a top Hollywood actress until she was afflicted with a series of strokes at 39. Unfortunately, her career never quite regained the same heights.

While some of Roald and Patricia's children have tried to emulate the careers of their parents, the only unqualified success has been their daughter Ophelia who became an aid worker. However, the next generation of Dahls—whose current star is model Sophie Dahl—shows signs of being able to successfully combine the grandparental gifts.

FROM CHILDREN'S BOOK WRITERS, HOLLYWOOD ACTRESSES, PLUS-SIZED SUPERMODELS AND HUMANITARIAN AID WORKERS, THE DAHL FAMILY HAS MADE ITS MARK IN A VARIETY OF IMPORTANT FIELDS.

HOW THEY RATE

WEALTH ★★
Not enormous, but the royalties from Roald's books must still be worth a bit each year, and Sophie earns up to $5 million a year as a model.

HEALTH ★★
A lot of early deaths, from disease as well as chronic conditions, suggest that the Dahls are not particularly hardy stock.

HAPPINESS ★★
To some extent this seems like a family of difficult characters, some of them more troubled than others. There have also been too many tragedies for them to rate too highly on the happiness stakes.

FAME ★★★
A leading Hollywood actress, an incredibly popular author with a taste for attention, as well as one of the world's leading models, suggest the Dahls have covered some of the main fame bases pretty well.

SEXINESS ★★★★
Roald traded on his tall and handsome looks while Patricia had a homely but sexy screen presence. Sophie has been described as a "blow up doll with brains." Combined with the beautiful lesbian aid worker, Ophelia, the Dahls offer something for almost everyone to lust after.

BLACK SHEEP FACTOR ★
Roald was a rebel to begin with but at the same time the apple of his mother's eye. And, aside from the odd boarding school expulsion, there don't seem to be any genuine rebels in the family, only the sad case of Tessa and her drug addiction.

ECCENTRICITY ★★
Quirky and difficult but this doesn't quite mean that they're actually that eccentric.

INFLUENCE ★★★
Roald Dahl lives on in the minds of millions of children and one of his books received a major Hollywood film treatment as recently as 2005. Patricia, Sophie and Ophelia have all proven to be talented women who have been world leaders in their chosen fields.

ROALD DAHL AT THE MOVIES

While Roald Dahl is deservedly most famous for his books, he has also had an interesting Hollywood career. The best known screenplays he has written—some not based on his own novels and stories—were:

★ *You Only Live Twice* (1967): Dahl wrote the screenplay for the sixth James Bond movie starring Sean Connery, which was largely set in Japan. Dahl had hero-worshipped the Bond creator, Ian Fleming, when he was alive.

★ *Chitty Chitty Bang Bang* (1968): This classic children's story was also written by Ian Fleming. Dahl was commissioned to write the script but had a falling out with the director and didn't finish it. The subsequent movie was panned by the critics, though Dahl still made a lot of money from his percentage of the profits when it became a commercial hit.

★ *The Night Digger* (1971): This was a psychological thriller which was based on a Joy Cowley novel, which starred his wife Patricia Neal. Dahl wrote Patricia's stroke into the plot of the movie.

★ *Charlie and the Chocolate Factory*: While many of Dahl's novels and short stories have been made into movies, only *Charlie and the Chocolate Factory* has been turned into a movie twice. In the first one titled *Willy Wonka and the Chocolate Factory* (1971), Gene Wilder plays the eccentric and reclusive chocolate factory owner who invites five children into his magical world. Dahl himself wrote the screenplay for this version. A second version by director Tim Burton appeared in 2005, where Willy Wonka was played by Johnny Depp. Some people have claimed that the Depp portrayal of Wonka was like a cross between the original Willy Wonka and Michael Jackson.

ROALD DAHL WITH HIS SON, THEO, 1965.

ROALD DAHL TOP FIVE BOOKS

1. *Charlie and the Chocolate Factory*
2. *BFG* or *The Big Friendly Giant*
3. *James and the Giant Peach*
4. *Kiss Kiss*
5. *The Witches*

JOHNNY DEPP (CENTER) AND THE CAST OF THE 2005 MOVIE VERSION OF ROALD DAHL'S *CHARLIE AND THE CHOCOLATE FACTORY*.

> I DO NOT LIKE FILM DIRECTORS VERY MUCH. THEY LACK HUMILITY AND THEY ARE TOO DAMN SURE THAT EVERYTHING THEY DO IS RIGHT. THE TROUBLE IS THAT IT'S MOSTLY WRONG. OH, WHAT A MESS MEL STEWART MADE OF CHARLIE.
> ROALD DAHL

PATRICIA NEAL WITH GARY COOPER IN A SCENE FROM *THE FOUNTAINHEAD* (1949).

THE GARY COOPER AFFAIR

ACTRESS PATRICIA NEAL ALMOST SCORED HERSELF A "HIT" FROM GARY COOPER'S WIFE, WHO SENT HER THE FOLLOWING TELEGRAM AFTER SHE FOUND OUT ABOUT NEAL'S AFFAIR WITH HER HUSBAND—"I HAVE HAD JUST ABOUT ENOUGH OF YOU. YOU HAD BETTER STOP NOW OR YOU WILL BE SORRY." GARY COOPER WAS A KNOWN PANTSMAN WHOSE AFFAIRS ALSO INCLUDED THE ACTRESSES CLARA BOW AND GRACE KELLY. HE WAS 25 YEARS NEAL'S SENIOR. HOWEVER, AFTER HIS WIFE'S LETTER, THE AFFAIR DIDN'T STOP, AND NEAL FELL PREGNANT. COOPER PERSUADED HER TO HAVE AN ABORTION AND THE AFFAIR DIDN'T SURVIVE FOR MUCH LONGER. AFTER THEY BROKE UP, NEAL HAD A NERVOUS BREAKDOWN WHICH PUT HER ACTING CAREER ON HOLD FOR OVER A YEAR. THERE WAS ALSO A FAMOUS INCIDENT WHERE COOPER'S YOUNG DAUGHTER MARIA SPAT AT NEAL. HOWEVER, IN LATER YEARS NEAL AND MARIA BECAME GOOD FRIENDS.

DAHLOGRAPHIES

PATRICIA NEAL TOP FIVE FILMS

1. *Hud* (1963) Neal won a Best Actress Oscar for her role as Alma the housekeeper in this anti-hero cowboy movie starring Paul Newman.
2. *A Face in the Crowd* (1957) In this movie, directed by Elia Kazan, Neal plays a journalist who interviews a prisoner, hears he can sing and watches while he becomes a star.
3. *In Harm's Way* (1965) Directed by Otto Preminger, Neal plays the love interest opposite the navy admiral in search of redemption played by John Wayne.
4. *The Fountainhead* (1949) Neal co-starred with Garry Cooper who also became her lover in real life.
5. *Breakfast at Tiffany's* (1961) Neal played Mrs Failenson who "keeps" Paul, the failed writer and Holly Golightly's eventual lover.

Like many famous families, and particularly those with an artistic bent, the Dahl family have proven fairly prolific at putting their side of the story on record. Roald's two volumes of memoirs: *Boy*, which dealt with his childhoood, and *Flying Solo*, which chronicled his time in Africa and as a pilot in World War II, were bestsellers—even if their veracity is at times under question since Dahl was a renowned boaster. Not to be outdone, Dahl's former wife Patricia Neal published her memoir *As I Am* in 1988. In this she recounts her husband's bullying her back to health as well as his long-standing treachery which led to her divorce. Their daughter Tessa, whose life as a party animal cost her dearly, also produced a semi-autobiographical novel in 1988 called *Working for Love*, which received a lukewarm critical reception.

PARTNERS IN HEALTH

While the artistic achievements of Roald and Patricia's children might be described as moderate at best, there's no doubting the humanitarian work of their daughter Ophelia, who is a founding trustee and current director of the organization Partners in Health. At only 18 years of age, Ophelia went to Haiti as a volunteer aid worker. She worked on providing community-based medical treatment programs and in 1987 Partners in Health was founded to continue this. The organization deals particularly with HIV and tuberculosis, and its work has spread from Haiti to a number of other countries, including Guatemala, Peru, Rwanda, Siberia and even the ghettos of Boston, USA. It has won prestigious awards such as the Conrad N. Hilton Humanitarian Prize, while the Bill and Melinda Gates Foundation has granted it millions of dollars to continue its programs.

THE SPY WHO SHAGGED CLARE BOOTHE LUCE

After Roald Dahl was invalided out of active duty, as a consequence of injuries he suffered when his plane crashed in the Libyan desert during the war, he was sent to Washington as part of British Intelligence. His brief was to inveigle his way into society and keep an ear out for what the Americans were doing. As such, he became friends with Ernest Hemingway's wife Martha Gellhorn, and played poker with future president Harry S. Truman. At 6½ feet tall, Dahl was very appealing to women. One woman who became attracted to him was Clare Boothe Luce, a writer, politician and diplomat, who also happened to be married to Henry Luce, the influential publisher of *Time* and *Life* magazines. Having met Roald—who was 13 years younger than her—at a dinner party, Clare seduced him. Apparently when Dahl complained to his superiors that Clare had worn him out in bed, they told him to get back in there and mine the pillow talk "for the sake of Mother England."

ROALD DAHL'S DAUGHTER, TESSA, WITH HER DAUGHTERS CLOVER (LEFT) AND SOPHIE (RIGHT), 1989.

SOPHIE DAHL

> "I'd rather be treated like any other model—being booked because a client likes the look of me, not because I'm size 16 with big tits. There's nothing sexual about models' typical androgynous skinniness."
> SOPHIE DAHL

It's not unusual for female descendants of the rich and famous to end up as models. Sophie Dahl's modeling career kicked off in 1996 following a chance encounter with *Vogue* fashion expert Isabella Blow—who is also credited with discovering Alexander McQueen and Stella Tennant. When Blow found Sophie, she was crying on the steps outside her mother's house after an argument. Sophie offered to help Blow carry her bags to her apartment where Blow—who later described Sophie as a "blow-up doll with brains"—asked her if she wanted to be a model. Sophie said "yes," and before long was blazing a trail as a plus-size supermodel. Since then, however, Dahl has exercised off much of her abundance and is now a regular supermodel size 8.

{ dahl family tree }

A LITTLE NONSENSE NOW AND THEN IS RELISHED BY THE WISEST MEN.
ROALD DAHL

ROALD DAHL
1916–90

A paradoxical and difficult man, Roald was one of the most popular writers of the 20th century, particularly for his children's books and macabre short stories. As a child his nickname was "Apple," as he was the apple of his mother's eye. After enduring the nastiness of an English boarding school, he joined the Shell company, which posted him to Africa. He was a fighter pilot in World War II, then worked for British Intelligence in Washington. He began to publish short stories before the end of the war. In 1951, he married the actress Patricia Neal. They had five children but the marriage was marked by medical emergencies. He nursed her through a series of strokes, then later left her for her best friend.

HARALD DAHL 1865–1920

He lost his left forearm in a boyhood accident but still managed to emigrate from his small town near Oslo, Norway, to become a successful Welsh ship-broker. His first wife, Marie, died leaving him with two young children. Four years later he married Sofie, who bore him four daughters and a son, Roald. His daughter Astri died from appendicitis at the age of 7, and Harald followed her 2 months later from pneumonia, though the story was that he actually died of a broken heart.

SOFIE HESSELBERG 1885–1967

Her mother, Ellen Wallace, was a Norwegian who claimed to be descended from the Scottish patriot, Sir William Wallace, while her father once edited the Norwegian *Nature* magazine. Sofie married Harald in 1911. When he died, she was left with two step-children and four of her own. Although she was Norwegian, she stayed in England to fulfill her husband's wish that his children be educated in English schools, which he thought were the best in the world.

1ST WIFE

PATRICIA NEAL 1926–

Patricia took up with Dahl on the rebound from an affair with the married Gary Cooper, which had ended in him convincing her to abort a pregnancy. She won an Best Actress Oscar in 1963 for *Hud*, but the rest of the 1960s were tragic: a daughter died, her son was brain-damaged and she had a series of paralyzing strokes, which took years of rehabilitation. She recovered to gain another Best Actress Oscar nomination for *The Subject Was Roses* in 1968, but her career has been uneven since then. She divorced Roald in 1983.

2ND WIFE

FELICITY CROSLAND 1938–

This fashion executive was a close friend of Patricia Neal, until it was revealed that she'd long been having an affair with Roald behind Patricia's back. When it finally came out into the open, Dahl divorced Neal and married Crosland. He remained with her until his death.

ACTRESS PATRICIA NEAL RECOVERING AT HOME AFTER A STROKE, WITH HER HUSBAND, AUTHOR ROALD DAHL, AND THEIR THREE CHILDREN, THEO (LEFT), BABY OPHELIA AND TESSA, GREAT MISSENDEN, ENGLAND, 1965.

OLIVIA TWENTY DAHL 1955–62

Born April 20, 1955, she died of measles encephalitis. After her death, Roald went to his old Repton School Headmaster, Geoffrey Fisher, who became the Archbishop of Canterbury to ask whether Olivia could have dogs to keep her company in the afterlife and got angry when Fisher told him there was no place for animals in heaven.

TESSA DAHL 1957–

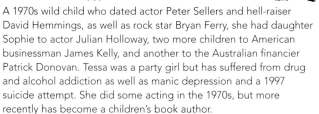

A 1970s wild child who dated actor Peter Sellers and hell-raiser David Hemmings, as well as rock star Bryan Ferry, she had daughter Sophie to actor Julian Holloway, two more children to American businessman James Kelly, and another to the Australian financier Patrick Donovan. Tessa was a party girl but has suffered from drug and alcohol addiction as well as manic depression and a 1997 suicide attempt. She did some acting in the 1970s, but more recently has become a children's book author.

SOPHIE DAHL 1977–

She became the world's first and most well-known plus-size supermodel. She has acted in a number of films and published an adult fairy tale, *The Boy with the Dancing Eyes*. Sophie inspired her grandfather's hugely popular *BFG* (*The Big Friendly Giant*), and she hit the Fleet Street headlines when she had an affair with model-loving Mick Jagger.

JULIAN HOLLOWAY 1944–

A British actor who has played in many TV shows and films, but who is perhaps most memorable for his roles in the *Carry On* films.

CLOVER DAHL 1981–

Another curvy glamour girl, she impressed Mick Jagger with her singing at a party and has studied acting in New York.

JAMES KELLY 1939–

THEO DAHL 1960–

Four-month-old Theo was being pushed in his pram by his nanny when a taxi cab crashed into him. Theo was badly injured and developed hydrocephalus (water on the brain). With Theo's doctor, Kenneth Till, and a hydraulic engineer friend, Stanley Wade, Roald designed an improved valve for the shunt used to drain off the excess fluid on Theo's brain. It was a success and Theo lived to marry, while the shunt was inserted into thousands of other patients, until replaced by superior technology.

LUKE KELLY 1986–

Clover's brother is an assistant photographer at *Vogue*, a hobby his grandfather was also interested in—especially at school where he used the dark room as a haven for smoking illicit cigarettes.

SOPHIE DAHL STARTED OUT AS A PLUS-SIZE MODEL, BUT HAS SINCE SLIMMED DOWN TO A SIZE 8.

OPHELIA DAHL 1964–

While her father enjoyed his adventures in Africa working for an oil company, Ophelia is a well-known health activist in the developing world. She is the Executive Director of Partners in Health, which in 2005 received the Conrad N. Hilton Humanitarian Prize—the world's richest—for the its work in Haiti, Rwanda and other countries.

LUCY DAHL 1965–

The youngest daughter of Roald and Patricia is a scriptwriter whose screenplay, *Wild Child*, a comedy about a badly behaved girl who gets sent to a boarding school, is currently in production. Lucy was expelled from her boarding school for setting fire to the kitchen.

IF THERE'S EVER BEEN EVIDENCE FOR A SCIENTIST GENE, THE DARWIN FAMILY IS IT. THEY ARE PERHAPS THE PREMIER SCIENTIFIC FAMILY OF ALL TIME, PRODUCING THREE UNDISPUTED SCIENTIFIC GENIUSES IN ERASMUS AND CHARLES DARWIN AND FRANCIS GALTON, AS WELL AS A HOST OF OTHER SCIENTISTS AND SURGEONS WHO HAD TO BE CONTENT WITH BEING LEADERS IN THEIR FIELD.

THE DARWINS

PORTRAIT OF DARWIN BY OULESS, C.1880.

HOW THEY RATE

WEALTH ★ ★ ★
The Wedgwood fortune has helped the family, but they have always seemed more interested in ideas than money and were probably happier because of it.

HEALTH ★ ★ ★
Varied. At times it's hard to think of the Darwins in terms of survival of the fittest. Although their longevity is reasonable, many Darwins died when young and others, such as Charles, had chronic illnesses, as often as not acquired during their adventures abroad.

HAPPINESS ★ ★ ★
For high-achievers they are remarkably sane and seemingly happy, though Charles Darwin, in particular, struggled with tragedy and his health.

FAME ★ ★ ★ ★ ★
It's hard to imagine anyone not knowing the name Charles Darwin.

SEXINESS ★
More in the theory than the practice, the non-conformist and Quaker origins of this family have perhaps instilled a lack of sexiness in the family. They can't even be considered the thinking person's hottie.

BLACK SHEEP FACTOR ★
Very little odd behavior at all. They seem to be a family that embodies a basic ethics.

ECCENTRICITY ★ ★ ★
Yes, the Darwins were famous for their non-conformist thinking and for questioning behavior that occurred because of stale habits. Darwin women, in particular, were unconventional and independent. But they seldom crossed over the mark that divides eccentricity and insanity.

INFLUENCE ★ ★ ★ ★ ★
Huge. The evolutionary theory became more accepted than the Biblical view of human origins, and is a cornerstone of modern biology. Other Darwins were deeply involved in ethical matters, such as the abolition of the slave trade, and made major contributions to all manner of knowledge fields.

The Darwins are most famous for their work in the natural sciences—in particular, evolution. Erasmus Darwin anticipated Charles's theory of the Origin of the Species, while often-overlooked cousin Francis Galton, as part of his extraordinary achievement, founded the field of eugenics.

Of course the wherewithal for much of this scientific activity was founded by the Wedgwood pottery dynasty, which pioneered the manufacture of reliable tableware and remains a quality product today. Without this fortune built on plates and cups, it's unlikely that Darwin would have been able to make that voyage on the HMS *Beagle* which inspired his later ideas. Interestingly there is more than one instance of inter-marriage between the two sides of this dynamic clan—a practice which was to trouble the evolutionary minded Charles.

In addition to science and ceramics, the Darwin–Wedgwoods have also prospered in artistic, political, academic and adventurous pursuits. A Darwin descendant was the first Briton to go as a Republican to the Spanish Civil War, while anthropologist Camilla Wedgwood pioneered the study of women in New Guinea and Oceania. The most conspicuous achiever in the arts is Ralph Vaughan Williams, acclaimed as one of Britain's greatest composers. Yet the family also includes a world-class wood engraver, a painter, two poets, any number of authors and most recently an actor, in the form of Skandar Keynes, who played the role of Edmund in the film *The Chronicles of Narnia: The Lion, the Witch, and the Wardrobe*. With considerable eccentricity but few hopeless failures, when you stack them up, the Darwin family's achievements are simply astonishing.

BUT IN THE NEXT WORLD I SHAN'T BE DOING MUSIC, WITH ALL THE STRIVING AND DISAPPOINTMENTS. I SHALL BE BEING IT.
RALPH VAUGHAN WILLIAMS

THE SHOWROOMS OF WEDGWOOD & BYERLEY, LONDON, 1809.

WEDGWOOD AND ABOLITION

IN 1787, JOSIAH WEDGWOOD, THOMAS CLARKSON AND GRANVILLE SHARP FORMED THE SOCIETY FOR THE ABOLITION OF THE SLAVE TRADE. WEDGWOOD WAS ON THE COMMITTEE AND ALSO PRODUCED THE ABOLITION SOCIETY'S SEAL, WHICH SHOWED A BLACK SLAVE IN CHAINS KNEELING, HIS HANDS LIFTED UP TO HEAVEN. THE MOTTO READ: "AM I NOT A MAN AND A BROTHER?" HE REPRODUCED THE DESIGN IN A CAMEO WITH THE BLACK FIGURE AGAINST A WHITE BACKGROUND AND DONATED HUNDREDS OF THEM TO THE SOCIETY FOR DISTRIBUTION. THOMAS CLARKSON WROTE THAT, "LADIES WORE THEM IN BRACELETS, AND OTHERS HAD THEM FITTED UP IN AN ORNAMENTAL MANNER AS PINS FOR THEIR HAIR ... AND THUS FASHION, WHICH USUALLY CONFINES ITSELF TO WORTHLESS THINGS, WAS SEEN FOR ONCE IN THE HONOURABLE OFFICE OF PROMOTING THE CAUSE OF JUSTICE, HUMANITY AND FREEDOM."

> TO KILL AN ERROR IS AS GOOD A SERVICE AS, AND SOMETIMES EVEN BETTER THAN, THE ESTABLISHING OF A NEW TRUTH OR FACT.
> CHARLES DARWIN

ERASMUS DARWIN'S EVOLUTIONARY POETRY

The poetry of Erasmus Darwin anticipated some of the ideas contained in his grandson Charles's *Origin of the Species*.

Organic life beneath the shoreless waves
Was born and nurs'd in ocean's pearly caves;
First forms minute, unseen by spheric glass,
Move on the mud, or pierce the watery mass;
These, as successive generations bloom,
New powers acquire and larger limbs assume;
Whence countless groups of vegetation spring,
And breathing realms of fin and feet and wing.

ERASMUS DARWIN,
THE TEMPLE OF NATURE, 1802

ERASMUS DARWIN.

LUNAR SOCIETY

THE LUNAR SOCIETY WAS A CLUB COMPRISED MAINLY OF SCIENTISTS AND INDUSTRIALISTS WHO MET AROUND BIRMINGHAM, ENGLAND, TO DISCUSS IDEAS AND EXPERIMENTS BETWEEN 1765 AND 1813. THE CLUB GOT ITS NAME FROM THE FACT THAT THEY USED TO MEET ON A FULL MOON—WHICH MADE IT EASIER TO RIDE HOME AFTERWARD, SINCE THERE WAS NO STREET LIGHTING AT THE TIME. ALTHOUGH ITS MEMBERS REFERRED TO THEMSELVES AS "LUNATICS," THEY WERE ANYTHING BUT. ITS CORE MEMBERS INCLUDED JOSIAH WEDGWOOD; ERASMUS DARWIN; JAMES WATT, THE INVENTOR OF THE STEAM ENGINE; MATTHEW BOLTON, A PIONEER OF THE MODERN FACTORY AND BUSINESS PARTNER OF WATT; JOSEPH PRIESTLY, WHO WAS THE FIRST TO ISOLATE OXYGEN; AND WILLIAM WITHERING, A DOCTOR WHO PIONEERED THE USE OF DIGITALIS AS A HEART MEDICINE AND WHO OWNED ONE OF THE FIRST WATER CLOSETS IN BRITAIN. OTHER LUMINARIES WHO CAME TO MEETINGS OF THE LUNAR SOCIETY INCLUDED THOMAS JEFFERSON, BENJAMIN FRANKLIN AND THE WYATT BROTHERS, WHO WERE BOTH FAMOUS ARCHITECTS.

THE LIBRARY–STUDY OF CHARLES DARWIN.

A TYPICAL DAY IN THE LIFE OF
CHARLES DARWIN

Like many great thinkers, Darwin was a creature of habit, even more so because he thought that alterations of his routine had an effect on his health. His son, Francis, who managed much of his father's literary estate, outlined a typical day in the life of his father as resembling the following:

Morning

	Charles Darwin got up early before sunrise to take a short walk outside.
7:45–8:00	Had a small breakfast by himself.
8:00–9:30	He did his best research during this time.
9:30–10:30	Read letters in the drawing room. Family letters were read aloud by his wife, Emma, while he relaxed on the couch. She would also read novels to him.
10:30–12:00	More research.

Afternoon

12:00–1:00	Took his dog, Polly, a white terrier, for a walk, stopping by the greenhouse to check up on how his plant experiments were doing.
1:00–1:30	Lunch.
1:30–2:00	Read the newspaper on the couch in the drawing room.
2:00–3:00	Sat down in his big chair in the study by the fireplace and wrote letters.
3:00–4:00	Rested in his bedroom on the couch while his wife read a novel to him.
4:00–4:30	Late afternoon stroll.
4:30–5:30	More research.
5:30–6:00	Chilled out.

Evening

6:00–7:30	Another rest with a novel read to him by his wife.
7:30–8:00	Dinner with wife and children.
8:00–8:30	Nightly two games of backgammon with Emma.
8:30–9:00	Read a scientific text in the drawing room or study.
9:00–9:30	Listened to wife playing the piano.
9:30–10:00	Emma read more from a novel while Darwin relaxed in the drawing room.
10:00–10:30	Went upstairs to get ready for bed.
10:30	Bed.

CHARLES DARWIN KEY PUBLICATIONS

1839 *JOURNAL AND REMARKS*
(THE VOYAGE OF THE BEAGLE)

1859 *ON THE ORIGIN OF SPECIES BY MEANS OF NATURAL SELECTION, OR THE PRESERVATION OF FAVOURED RACES IN THE STRUGGLE FOR LIFE*

1871 *THE DESCENT OF MAN AND SELECTION IN RELATION TO SEX*

1958 *AUTOBIOGRAPHY OF CHARLES DARWIN*

CHARLES DARWIN & GOD

In Darwin's time many naturalists were members of the clergy since it gave them a comfortable living and time to investigate the wonder of God's creation. However Darwin's evolutionary theory would do more to destroy the orthodoxy of Biblical creation than anything else. It was something Darwin himself was profoundly uncomfortable with. For many years, even while he was developing his theories, he subscribed to William Paley's argument, which basically claimed that the complexity of the world was proof that it had to have been created by an intelligent mind and that therefore God exists. It's an argument that can bridge both creation and evolution. (It has recently had a reprisal in the "intelligent design" theory that's been causing controversy in schools.) Darwin, however, came to have doubts concerning Paley's beneficent God on the *Beagle* voyage. Confronted by sights such as wasps paralyzing caterpillars as live food for their eggs, he began to think that nature was an amoral entity. When his 10-year-old daughter, Annie, died in 1851 from tuberculosis, he lost any residual faith in a benevolent God. Nonetheless, he left the defense of his ideas against attacks from the Anglican establishment to supporters such as biologist, Thomas Huxley, who became known as "Darwin's bulldog." One of the problems for the reception of evolutionary theory was that it eroded the distinction between man and beast, which was critical to the Biblical world view. As such Darwin was often depicted by the cartoonists of the day as a "Monkey Man." When Samuel Wilberforce, Bishop of Oxford and an evolution skeptic, asked Huxley if he was descended from apes on his father's or mother's side, Huxley apparently retorted "I'd rather be descended from an ape than a bishop."

A TREE OF LIFE DIAGRAM IN CHARLES DARWIN'S FAMOUS "B" NOTEBOOK.

Shortly after Darwin's death, temperance campaigner and evangelist Lady Elizabeth Hope claimed she visited him at his deathbed, and witnessed a renunciation of his scientific views in favor of God. Her story was printed in a Boston newspaper and subsequently spread, though it seems it was Christian propoganda. Darwin's daughter Henrietta stated, "I was present at his deathbed ... He never recanted any of his scientific views, either then or earlier."

GALTON AND EUGENICS

NAZI JOSEF MENGELE, A MAN WHO HAD A KEEN INTEREST IN EUGENICS.

Ever since the days of Adolf Hitler and his beloved Aryan race, eugenics has acquired a nasty taint. However, when Francis Galton coined the idea in 1865, it was really meant to be a logical extension of his cousin's evolutionary theory. As Galton himself wrote in the introduction to his 1869 book *Hereditary Genius*, "... a man's natural abilities are derived by inheritance, under exactly the same limitations as are the form and physical features of the whole organic world. Consequently, as it is easy, notwithstanding those limitations, to obtain by careful selection a permanent breed of dogs or horses gifted with peculiar powers of running, or of doing anything else, so it would be quite practicable to produce a highly-gifted race of men by judicious marriages during several consecutive generations."

As Francis Galton saw it, eugenics was simply a philosophy of selective breeding, designed to improve the human race and counteract a marked tendency in society toward reproductive mediocrity, whereby the less intelligent (in his reckoning) out-reproduced the intelligent. It turned out to be a popular philosophy that had a considerable effect—for better or worse—on social policy in the early part of the 20th century and attracted many of the best minds of the time as its adherents.

Nazi Germany, with its euthanization of the disabled, a breeding program designed to produce Aryan supremacy and the clinical efficiency of the Holocaust, brought out the ugly potential of eugenics. More recently, however, with the completion of the Human Genome Project, eugenics has again become a hot topic in science, with debates as to whether what kinds of pre-natal, and in some cases pre-marital, genetic screening are ethical.

SIR FRANCIS GALTON, FOUNDER OF THE THEORY OF EUGENICS.

DARWIN'S EVOLUTIONARY THEORY HAS BEEN DESCRIBED AS...
"THE MOST POWERFUL AND THE MOST COMPREHENSIVE IDEA THAT HAS EVER ARISEN ON EARTH. IT HELPS US UNDERSTAND OUR ORIGINS ...
WE ARE PART OF A TOTAL PROCESS, MADE OF THE SAME MATTER AND OPERATING BY THE SAME ENERGY AS THE REST OF THE COSMOS, MAINTAINING AND REPRODUCING BY THE SAME TYPE OF MECHANISM AS THE REST OF LIFE ..."
JULIAN HUXLEY, GRANDSON OF THOMAS HUXLEY, **EVOLUTIONARY HUMANISM**

TY-ONE-YEAR-OLD BRITISH COMPOSER, RALPH VAUGHAN WILLIAMS, PICTURED WITH CONDUCTOR MALCOLM SARGENT, 1958.

HEY: CHILD ······▶ **ADOPTED CHILD** ······▶ **MARRIED** ────── **DIVORCED** ━ ━ ━ **DE FACTO** ━·━·━ **SPLIT UP** ─ ─ ─ ─

CELEBRITY FAMILY TREES **64**

{darwin family tree

JOSIAH WEDGWOOD 1730–95
The thirteenth and youngest son of a potter, he followed in his father's footsteps. Because of a smallpox-damaged (later amputated) leg, he was unable to use the potter's wheel and became, through necessity, a designer of pottery and glazes. In this sense his success was founded on compensating for his weakness, an interesting story given his grandson would coin the phrase "survival of the fittest."

JOSIAH WEDGWOOD II 1769–1843
He took over the family business from his father and began Wedgwood's manufacture of bone china. He was also the Member for Stoke on Trent in the English Commons. He and his brother Tom granted Samuel Taylor Coleridge an annuity of £150 per annum, so he could create poetry without having to worry about how to earn a crust.

THOMAS WEDGWOOD 1771–1805
Together with Sir Humphey Davey, he published a paper, "An account of a method of copying paintings upon glass and of making profiles by the agency of light upon nitrate of silver." Their work was very nearly a breakthrough in photography, however, the chemicals were insufficiently sensitive to fix the images.

SARAH WEDGWOOD 1734–1815
She was a cousin of Josiah who had to make a certain amount of money before her father would consent to her marriage. Her husband placed great trust in her judgment and she had veto power over his designs.

SUSANNAH WEDGWOOD 1765–1817

ERASMUS DARWIN 1731–1802
Something of a renaissance man, he was one of the leading English intellectuals of the 18th century, and a respected physician, poet, philosopher, botanist and naturalist. King George III (the mad one) invited him to be royal physician but he declined. His scientific work included inquiries that formed a precursor to the evolutionary theory of Lamarck, and later his grandson, Charles. He also published work on zoology, the formation of clouds, and his experiments into galvanism were one of the inspirations for Mary Shelley's *Frankenstein*. Darwin's poetry, which reflected his scientific interests, was admired by poets Wordsworth and Coleridge and contained anticipations not just of evolutionary theory, but also the Big Bang theory of the origins of the universe. His personal life bordered on the chaotic. His first wife, Mary, gave him five children before she died of alcohol- related liver failure at the age of 31. He had another two children, extra-maritally, to a Miss Parker, and another eight to his second wife, Elizabeth, whose Colonel husband fortunately died soon after Erasmus became smitten with her.

ROBERT DARWIN 1766–1848
A noted physician from Shrewsbury, and also a canny businessman engaged in the dawn of capitalism, the combination of his income as a socially connected physician, and inheritance and investments, enabled him to fund his son Charles's less lucrative activities. He married Susannah Wedgwood, daughter of Josiah Wedgwood. Physically, he was an imposing figure, standing 6 feet 2 inches tall. When he reached 24 stone, he gave up weighing himself proving that, while he survived, he was probably not of the fittest. He made his coachman test the floorboards for him before he entered a new patient's house.

VIOLETTA GALTON (NEE DARWIN) 1783–1874
The daughter of Erasmus by his second wife Elizabeth, she published her own book, *Advice for Young Women Upon Their First Going out into Service*, and had seven children with her husband, Samuel Tertius.

SAMUEL "JOHN" GALTON 1753–1832
An unusual combination of ironmonger, arms manufacturer and Quaker, he was chiefly responsible for building his family's fortune. He was also an amateur scientist who published a three-volume book, *On the Life of Birds*, and was a prominent member of the Lunar Society.

SAMUEL TERTIUS GALTON 1783–1844
He inherited his father's business and, while he converted from Quakerism to the Church of England, it was he who took the family business out of the armanents game. He married Violetta Darwin, the daughter of his father's Lunar Society friend Erasmus.

CAROLINE SARAH DARWIN 1800–88

JOSIAH WEDGWOOD III 1795–1880

FRANCIS WEDGWOOD 1800–80

EMMA WEDGWOOD 1808–96

MARGARET SUSAN WEDGWOOD 1843–1937

SON RALPH VAUGHAN WILLIAMS NEXT PAGE

ARTHUR VAUGHAN WILLIAMS 1834–75

CLEMENT FRANCIS WEDGWOOD 1840–89

SON JOSIAH WEDGWOOD NEXT PAGE

CHARLES ROBERT DARWIN 1809–82

The young Charles Darwin showed little sign of being a great scholar. In fact his father removed him from boarding school because of his bad grades and laziness. It was decided that he would follow in the family tradition by becoming a doctor, and he enrolled at Edinburgh University. The gore of surgery put him off, however, so his father enrolled him in a Cambridge theology course, along with the army—a traditional career path for sons of the well-to-do. Although he preferred rising and shooting to studying at Cambridge, it was here that he became interested in natural history via the collection of beetles, and then the classes of the Reverend John Henslow, who would later be a strong rebutter of Darwin's *The Origin of Species.*

GEORGE HOWARD DARWIN 1845–1912

The second son and fifth child of Charles and Emma. George Howard was an astronomer and mathematician. He was Plumian professor of astronomy and experimental philosophy at Cambridge University, and specialized in cosmogony (the study of the origins of the universe).

3 CHILDREN NEXT PAGE

FRANCIS DARWIN 1848–1925

He followed his father, Charles, into botany and co-authored *The Power of Movement in Plants* with him. He was elected a Fellow of the Royal Society in the year his father died. He also edited his father's autobiography and correspondence.

2 CHILDREN NEXT PAGE

LEONARD DARWIN 1850–1943

The fourth son and eighth child of Charles. An army officer, member of parliament and Chairman of the British Eugenics Society (1911–28). He was also a close friend and backer of Ronald Fisher, who is considered the second great evolutionary biologist. Curiously, despite having two wives, he was another leading eugenicist who failed to reproduce.

SIR FRANCIS GALTON
1822–1911

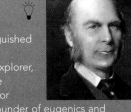

Another scientist in this distinguished family, Galton was a genuine polymath. He was an African explorer, meteorologist (he invented the weather map), as well as a major pioneer in statistics, and the founder of eugenics and differential psychology. In founding eugenics, he applied the theories of his half-cousin, Charles Darwin, to improving humanity via selective breeding. He married Louisa Jane Butler in 1853, but unfortunately they had no children. So despite his formidable genius, he was unable to add to the stock of the species.

HORACE DARWIN 1851–1928

The youngest of the children to survive, Horace was a civil engineer who founded the Cambridge Scientific Instrument company and later became Mayor of Cambridge.

DAUGHTER NORA BARLOW NEXT PAGE

> "The publication in 1859 of **The Origin of Species** by Charles Darwin made a marked epoch in my own mental development, as it did in that of human thought generally."
> SIR FRANCIS GALTON

SON OF MARGARET SUSAN WEDGWOOD &
ARTHUR VAUGHAN WILLIAMS

RALPH VAUGHAN WILLIAMS
1872–1958

One of Britain's greatest classical composers, his maternal grandmother, Caroline Sarah Darwin, was Charles Darwin's older sister, and his maternal grandfather, Josiah Wedgwood III, was the older brother of Darwin's wife Emma.

{ "LISTENING TO THE FIFTH SYMPHONY OF RALPH VAUGHAN WILLIAMS IS LIKE STARING AT A COW FOR FORTY-FIVE MINUTES." AARON COPLAND }

SON OF CLEMENT FRANCIS WEDGWOOD

JOSIAH WEDGWOOD, 1ST BARON WEDGWOOD **1872–1943**

The great great grandson of Josiah Wedgwood I, he was initially a Liberal and subsequently a Labour member of parliament, and served in the military during the Second Boer War and World War I. He was raised to the peerage in 1942.

CHILDREN OF GEORGE HOWARD DARWIN

CHARLES GALTON DARWIN **1887–1962**

He was a physicist who was Director of the National Physics Laboratory during World War II. After his retirement he became Chairman of the Eugenics Society 1953–59.

GWEN RAVERAT (NEE DARWIN) **1885–1957**

She was a Bloomsbury artist who became famous for her wood engravings. She married the French artist Jacques Raverat in 1911, whose suffering from multiple sclerosis she eventually ended by suffocating him with a pillow.

ELIZABETH KEYNES (NEE) DARWIN **1890–1974**

GEOFFREY KEYNES
1887–1982

Geoffrey was the brother of famous economist John Maynard Keynes. A noted surgeon (specializing in blood transfusion) he was also a literary scholar and the executor of his friend, poet Rupert Brooke's, literary estate.

CHILDREN OF FRANCIS DARWIN

BERNARD DARWIN **1876–1961**

He recovered from the death of his mother 4 days after his birth to become a golf writer.

FRANCES CORNFORD (NEE DARWIN) **1886–1960**

She was an English poet of some renown.

DAUGHTER OF HORACE DARWIN

NORA BARLOW (NEE DARWIN) **1885–1989**

The daughter of Horace Darwin, she studied genetics at Cambridge and edited *The Autobiography of Charles Darwin*. Her husband, Alan Barlow, was a civil servant and noted collector of Chinese and Islamic Art.

'PROPAGANDA IS THAT BRANCH OF THE ART OF LYING WHICH CONSISTS IN NEARLY DECEIVING YOUR FRIENDS WITHOUT QUITE DECEIVING YOUR ENEMIES. FRANCES CORNFORD'

CAMILLA WEDGWOOD 1901–55

Despite public opinion, this upper-class anthropologist and daughter of Josiah Wedgwood braved the highlands of New Guinea and the islands of Nauru in her ground-breaking research into the cultures of Oceania.

'MAGNIFICENTLY UNPREPARED FOR THE LONG LITTLENESS OF LIFE.
FRANCES CORNFORD'

RANDAL KEYNES 1948–

Randal is the author of the critically acclaimed Darwin biography, *Annie's Box*, which concerned the relationship between Charles and his daughter Annie, whose early death affected his views on religion and humanity greatly.

SKANDAR KEYNES 1991–

Randal's son, Skandar, is a child actor who most famously played Edmund in the 2005 film *The Chronicles of Narnia*.

RICHARD KEYNES 1919–

A former Cambridge University physiologist who cashed in on his famous family by editing Charles Darwin's account of his *Beagle* voyage in 1979 (*The Beagle Record*) and John Maynard Keynes's letters to his wife Lydia.

QUENTIN KEYNES 1921–2003

Quentin explored Africa and the sub-equatorial islands of the Atlantic and Indian Ocean. He was also a noted bibliophile with an extensive collection of books specializing in the great explorers of the 19th century, but also had titles covering travel, natural history and modern literature.

ROBIN DARWIN 1910–74

A painter and Principal of the Royal College of Art, his portrait of relative Ralph Vaughan Williams hangs in the National Portrait Gallery in London.

JOHN CORNFORD 1915–1936

Like his mother, Frances, he was a poet. He became a communist at university and was the first Briton to enlist on the Republican side in the Spanish Civil War. He was killed just outside of Madrid.

HORACE BARLOW 1921–

Like his cousin, Richard Keynes, Horace Barlow was a noted physiologist, though he specialized in visual neuroscience.

A DARWIN IN NARNIA
THE LAST IN A LONG LINE OF DARWINS TO ACHIEVE FAME IS TEENAGE ACTOR SKANDAR KEYNES, WHO PLAYED EDMUND IN THE FILM ADAPTATION OF C. S. LEWIS'S *THE CHRONICLES OF NARNIA*. IRONICALLY, C. S. LEWIS, A LEADING 20TH-CENTURY CHRISTIAN APOLOGIST, WAS HIGHLY CRITICAL OF THE WAY SCIENTIFIC EVOLUTION HAD BECOME THE PROGRESSIVE IDEOLOGY OF "EVOLUTIONISM," OTHERWISE KNOWN AS SOCIAL DARWINISM. *THE CHRONICLES OF NARNIA* IS RENOWNED FOR BEING AN ALLEGORY OF CHRISTIANITY.

THE DU PONTS

ON NEW YEAR'S DAY 1952, 632 MEMBERS OF THE DU PONTS HAD A FAMILY REUNION.

From a family with a history of watchmaking, the Du Ponts were important members of the French political elite during the tumultuous years at the turn of the 19th century. However, when their house was ransacked by a mob, the patriarch, Pierre, decided to emigrate to the United States, where the family was already acquainted with luminaries such as Thomas Jefferson. Their excellent connections did not guarantee an easy life, though. Pierre lived profligately and the elder son, Victor, was more of a diplomat than a businessman. It was the gunpowder-making brother, E. I., who was to start the first successful business on the banks of the Brandywine River in Delaware, thus bringing the DuPont dynasty into being. Even then it was not that easy, with hazards, such as frequent explosions, eating into profits. But E. I. Du Pont de Nemours and Company—as it was officially called—eventually began to prosper from the 19th century's propensity for war.

By the end of the 19th century, the Du Ponts were one of the richest families in America. The beginning of the 20th century saw their wealth and influence expand astronomically. By the declaration of World War I, DuPont owned 75 percent of America's gunpowder and explosives production and almost all of its smokeless powder. Until America entered the war, the Du Ponts made a fortune supplying both sides.

After the war, under the leadership of Pierre S. Du Pont, the company began to diversify, moving into man-made fiber and plastics, for which they are perhaps most famous today. However, as this was happening, the family influence in the company was being diluted, and the Du Ponts became more renowned for their wealth, philanthropy and inbred eccentricities than their work. Since Pierre S., the Du Ponts, who now number over 2000 have, with the occasional exception, largely vanished from the company and into unremarkable high society.

HOW THEY RATE

WEALTH ★★★★★
At various stages probably the richest family in America.

HEALTH ★★
Reasonable longevity, but a propensity toward madness, chronic disease and, in the early years, getting blown up.

HAPPINESS ★★
Even in their most successful years, there's a grimness to their ambition—perhaps the karma from having profited from so many deaths.

FAME ★★★
They've never really sought it, but the DuPont company's innovations have ensured they remain a household name.

SEXINESS ★★
French haughtiness, incest, gunpowder and a death in a brothel—this is stuff strictly for the perverse.

BLACK SHEEP FACTOR ★★★
The madness of John E. Du Pont wins the prize, but the family also has a history of ostracizing its members for minor deeds.

ECCENTRICITY ★★★★★
Insular, inbred, stubborn and rich—few families offer such fertile soil for the production of eccentricity.

INFLUENCE ★★★★★
Big time—when you consider the Confederates might have won the Civil War if not for the Du Ponts.

JUST BEFORE THE END OF WORLD WAR I, THE DUPONT COMPANY HAD SOLD THE US GOVERNMENT AND ITS ALLIES NEARLY 1,500,000,000 POUNDS OF EXPLOSIVES.

THE DU PONTS AND THE BONAPARTES

Pierre Du Pont, although he considered Napoleon a vile little Corsican, was a crucial player in American–French relations during the Napoleonic era, through his friendship with the great diplomat Talleyrand. It was Pierre who suggested the Louisiana Purchase as a way of preventing a war between America and France over the former Spanish territory. He also used a letter signed by Joséphine Bonaparte privileging him to enter the Tuileries in Paris without an appointment, in order to secure investors into his family's American business schemes. The Bonapartes, however, were not always helpful to the Du Ponts' business. When Napoleon's younger brother, Lucien, ran away to America and married the heiress Elizabeth Patterson against his brother's wishes, his line of credit was cut. He asked Victor Du Pont to help. He ended up lending Lucien $140,000 when the business was in a make-or-break phase. When Lucien eventually returned to the family fold, Napoleon refused to honor the debt, arguing that it had been given to sustain behavior he hadn't approved of in the first place.

PIERRE DU PONT'S SON VICTOR-MARIE (1767–1827) WAS APPOINTED ATTACHE TO THE FIRST FRENCH LEGATION TO THE UNITED STATES OF AMERICA IN 1787.

MARY DU PONT, WHO MARRIED HER COUSIN WILLIAM DU PONT.

MODEL WEARING A DUPONT RAYON DRESS.

PRODUCTS DUPONT INVENTED

1. **Soda powder** Gun powder based on sodium nitrate. instead of potassium nitrate
2. **Creosote** A type of tar.
3. **Nylon** The first synthetic material.
4. **Freon** The gas used in fridges until it put holes in the ozone layer.
5. **Dacron** A polyester-type material.
6. **Teflon** Used for the building of the first atomic bomb as well as non-stick frying pans.
7. **Lycra** The stretchy stuff in swimming costumes.
8. **Kevlar** Full circle from gunpowder to this bullet-proof body armour.

INSIDERS

IT WAS QUITE COMMON FOR MALE DU PONTS TO MARRY THEIR FEMALE COUSINS. HOWEVER, MANY OF THE MARRIAGES WOULD PROVE UNHAPPY, EXACERBATED BY THE ISOLATIONIST ATTITUDE THE FAMILY HAD TOWARD THE REST OF THE WORLD. WHEN GENERAL HENRY SAW THE PROBLEMS THESE MARRIAGES WERE CAUSING TO FAMILY UNITY, HE TRIED TO BAN THEM, ONLY TO BE DISOBEYED SOON AFTER BY HIS SON WILLIAM. DURING THE PERIOD OF MODERNIZATION UNDER PIERRE S., DU PONT, WOMEN (ALONG WITH THEIR INHERITANCES) WERE OFFERED TO PROMISING YOUNG EXECUTIVES TO BIND THEM TO THE FIRM.

PIERRE DU PONT AND JOHN J. RASKOB WERE CHARGED WITH TAX EVASION IN 1937.

CHAIN OF COMMAND

The chain of ownership of DuPont has been complicated and contested for much of its existence. When founder, E. I. Du Pont died, the company was divided between his seven children, with major decisions to be made by a family council, presided over by a senior partner. The first senior partner was Alfred, eldest son of E. I. However, the council eventually came to the conclusion he was not up to the task and his younger brother, Henry, took over. Henry ruled the company with an iron fist until his death in 1889, when his nephew Eugene was appointed. By then the family was split and Eugene, a compromise candidate, lacked the force of character to bring it together. When he died, it was decided to sell DuPont to their main competitor. However three of the younger cousins, Alfred I., T. Coleman and Pierre S. Du Pont, put in a counter-offer which was eventually accepted by the family. They managed to modernize the company and it profited spectacularly, particularly during America's period of neutrality in World War I—during which time they charged both sides double the price they charged the American government for gunpowder. However, this prosperity also caused tensions between the three cousins. Coleman, who had never lived in Delaware, was bored with gunpowder and offered to sell his shares back to the company. Pierre S. effectively hoodwinked his cousin Alfred I., and bought the shares for himself and two younger brothers, thus gaining control of the company. The ensuing lawsuit, which Pierre S. won against Alfred I., destroyed forever the chance of family unity. Pierre S. was nonetheless a consummate businessman. He realized the need for DuPont to escape from being a gunpowder manufacturer, dependent for its profits on war, and facilitated the company's move into chemical and polymer products. He also made DuPont the owner of up to 37 percent of General Motors. When GM looked like it was going to go bankrupt in 1920, Pierre S. became its chairman and turned it into the biggest corporation in the world, making his relatives billions of dollars in the process. He remained chairman of DuPont until 1940—the last in the family to exert control over the company.

POPPED FOR PATERNITY

ON MAY 16, 1893 THE LOUISVILLE *COURIER JOURNAL* REPORTED THAT FRED DU PONT HAD DIED FROM A HEART ATTACK ON THE SIDEWALK OUTSIDE THE GALT HOTEL. THE REAL STORY, HOWEVER, WAS THAT HE WAS VISITING MAGGIE PAYNE, THE MADAM OF LOUISVILLE'S TOP BROTHEL. SHE'D JUST HAD A CHILD, WAS CONVINCED THAT FRED WAS THE FATHER AND WAS DEMANDING FINANCIAL SUPPORT. IN THE DAYS BEFORE PATERNITY TESTS, HER CLAIM COULD NOT BE PROVED EITHER WAY. FRED DECIDED ON THIS BASIS THAT, DESPITE BEING THE WEALTHIEST MAN IN LOUISVILLE, HE WASN'T GOING TO PAY. HE ENDED UP PAYING WITH HIS LIFE. HE AND MAGGIE ARGUED UNTIL SHE PULLED OUT A GUN AND SHOT FRED DU PONT DEAD. APPARENTLY THE *COURIER JOURNAL* LIED ABOUT THE STORY BECAUSE ITS OWNER WAS HEAVILY IN DEBT TO FRED, AND THIS WAS HIS WAY OF PAYING THE DEBT OFF. THE CHARADE ONLY LASTED 2 DAYS, HOWEVER, BEFORE THE REAL STORY CAME OUT IN A RIVAL NEWSPAPER.

A WORKER AT THE DUPONT COMB PLANT IN LEOMINSTER, MASSACHUSETTS, C.1950, SHOWING OFF AN AVERAGE DAY'S PRODUCTION OF COMBS FOR JUST ONE MAN, USING THE DUPONT FACTORY'S MODERN MOLDING MACHINES. THE DUPONT COMPANY BEGAN MANUFACTURING PLASTICS AS A BY-PRODUCT OF ITS EXPLOSIVE PRODUCTS IN 1904.

ETHEL DU PONT

ETHEL DU PONT (DAUGHTER OF EUGENE DU PONT JR), AND HER FIANCE, FRANKLIN ROOSEVELT JR (SON OF THE PRESIDENT), PICTURED ON THE COVER OF *TIME* MAGAZINE, JUNE 1937. THE FAMOUS COUPLE WERE MARRIED IN 1930 BUT LATER DIVORCED IN 1949. ETHEL REMARRIED LAWYER BENJAMIN S. WARREN SR IN 1950, AND IN 1965, AGED 49, SHE COMMITTED SUICIDE.

JOHN E. DU PONT, AS WELL AS BEING AN ORNITHOLOGIST AND MURDERER, WAS A KEEN PHILATELIST. AT AN AUCTION IN 1980 HE ANONYMOUSLY PAID AROUND $1 MILLION FOR THE BRITISH GUIANA 1856 "PENNY MAGENTA"—ONE OF THE RAREST STAMPS IN THE WORLD.

THE SAD STORY OF LOUIS DU PONT

With their mother in a lunatic asylum and their father, Irénée, newly dead from tuberculosis, the children of Swamp Hall, Alfred I., Anne, Marguerite, Maurice and Louis Du Pont faced, being split up and spread around their relatives. With Alfred I. armed with a shotgun and the others with axes, clubs and knives, they met with Uncle Fred who persuaded General Henry to change his mind and let the children stay together. On the surface, the kids were pretty successful in being their own parents.

Years later, things were looking good for Louis Du Pont. He was studying at Yale and had fallen in love with Bessie Gardner, a southern beauty from quality Virginian stock. Wanting to do things properly, he kept his plan to propose to her to himself, until after his graduation. Still, he was proud to introduce her to his beloved elder brother Alfred. He got the shock of his life soon after, though, when Alfred proposed to Bessie and she accepted. Although he put a brave face on it, Louis was heartbroken. He hit the booze, dropped out of Yale, then dropped out of Harvard law school before moving to New York and becoming a trust fund bum, rarely going back to Delaware because it hurt him that his brother—now with two daughters—had the house, job and wife he'd wanted for himself. His torture ended when he shot himself in the head in the exclusive Wilmington Club, where he stayed when in Delaware, instead of having to face the mirror image of his lost happiness back at Swamp Hall.

With Louis's suicide, the torture for Alfred I. had only just begun. His marriage eventually soured, ending in an affair and bitter divorce. After fighting so hard to keep his own siblings together, he wasn't to see his children for over 20 years.

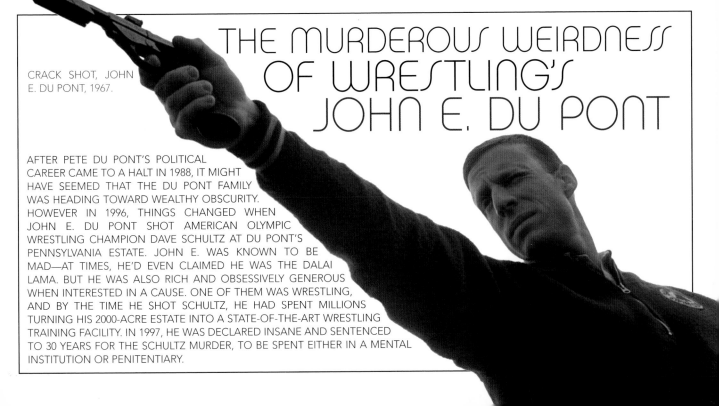

CRACK SHOT, JOHN E. DU PONT, 1967.

THE MURDEROUS WEIRDNESS OF WRESTLING'S JOHN E. DU PONT

AFTER PETE DU PONT'S POLITICAL CAREER CAME TO A HALT IN 1988, IT MIGHT HAVE SEEMED THAT THE DU PONT FAMILY WAS HEADING TOWARD WEALTHY OBSCURITY. HOWEVER IN 1996, THINGS CHANGED WHEN JOHN E. DU PONT SHOT AMERICAN OLYMPIC WRESTLING CHAMPION DAVE SCHULTZ AT DU PONT'S PENNSYLVANIA ESTATE. JOHN E. WAS KNOWN TO BE MAD—AT TIMES, HE'D EVEN CLAIMED HE WAS THE DALAI LAMA. BUT HE WAS ALSO RICH AND OBSESSIVELY GENEROUS WHEN INTERESTED IN A CAUSE. ONE OF THEM WAS WRESTLING, AND BY THE TIME HE SHOT SCHULTZ, HE HAD SPENT MILLIONS TURNING HIS 2000-ACRE ESTATE INTO A STATE-OF-THE-ART WRESTLING TRAINING FACILITY. IN 1997, HE WAS DECLARED INSANE AND SENTENCED TO 30 YEARS FOR THE SCHULTZ MURDER, TO BE SPENT EITHER IN A MENTAL INSTITUTION OR PENITENTIARY.

{ du pont family tree }

PIERRE SAMUEL DU PONT DE NEMOURS 1739–1817

The son of a French watchmaker and minor nobleman, he defied his father's wish that he join him in the trade, and became part of a liberal intellectual set at the court of Louis XV. His writings on economy were praised by Voltaire and Turgot, while his book, *Physiocracy*, which argued for free trade between nations, influenced the thinking of Scottish philosopher Adam Smith. As a liberal, whose publications were often suppressed, and who had been sacked for criticizing the spending habits of Marie Antoinette, he was initially in favor of the French Revolution. He hoped for a constitutional monarchy, and was President of the National Constituent Assembly. But after physically defending the former king and queen against a mob riot in 1792, he was sentenced to the guillotine—a fate which he escaped when Robespierre, the former leader of the Reign of Terror, lost his own head. When his family's home was trashed by a mob in 1797, he decided in 1799 to emigrate with his family to America. He was already a friend of Thomas Jefferson, since he had helped in the negotiations that led to the Treaty of Paris, which ended the American War of Independence. He came up with the idea for the Louisiana Purchase, in his role as informal liaison between France and USA during the Napoleonic era, but he caused his family considerable problems with his extravagance and unrealistic business dealings.

VICTOR MARIE DU PONT 1767–1827

He spent 8 years as a French diplomat to the United States, and his contacts were instrumental in the family's decision to emigrate. On arriving in America, he was involved in a number of failed business ventures before founding Du Pont, Bauday & Co., a wool manufacturer, across the Brandywine Creek from his brother's gunpowder mills. Never really much of a businessman, he was better in matters of state, and became a member of the Delaware General Assembly.

ELEUTHERE IRENEE DU PONT 1771–1834

The founder of the DuPont Corporation was the scientist of the family. At age 14 he wrote a paper on the manufacture of gunpowder and, with his father's assistance, gained a position at France's central powder agency, where he studied advanced explosives production techniques with the famous chemist Antoine Lavoisier.

DU PONT WEALTH

WHEN E. I. DU PONT ARRIVED IN THE UNITED STATES, HE NOTICED THE STANDARD OF AMERICAN GUNPOWDER WAS VERY POOR. SO, AFTER A RETURN TO FRANCE IN 1801, TO FIND INVESTMENT BACKING AND BUY EQUIPMENT IN 1802 HE SET UP THE ELEUTHERIAN MILLS POWDER WORKS ON THE BRANDYWINE RIVER IN DELAWARE. IT WASN'T IMMEDIATELY SUCCESSFUL BUT, A DOUR, UNSPECTACULAR MAN, HE WAS PERSISTENT. HE REWARDED HIS WORKERS FOR THEIR LOYALTY— SOMETHING WHICH BROUGHT HIM INTO CONFLICT WITH HIS ORIGINAL PARTNER—THE FORMER SANTO DOMINGO SLAVE-OWNER, PETER BAUDUY. FOR THE 32 YEARS OF HIS LEADERSHIP E.I. CARRIED SUBSTANTIAL DEBT, INCLUDING LOANS, SO HE COULD PROVIDE PENSIONS TO THE FAMILIES OF THE THIRTY-THREE WORKERS KILLED IN A MAJOR FACTORY EXPLOSION IN 1818. BY 1827, HOWEVER, HE EMPLOYED OVER 140 MEN AND, WHEN HE DIED IN 1834, THE ANNUAL PRODUCTION OF GUNPOWDER WAS WORTH OVER $1.8 MILLION.

CHARLES IRENEE DU PONT 1797–1869

He worked for his father and became the head of Du Pont, Bauday & Co when his father died in 1827 and stayed there until retiring in 1856. He was also one of the organizers of the Delaware Railroad, President of the Farmers' Bank of Delaware and served in the Delaware senate.

SAMUEL FRANCIS DU PONT 1803–65

With his father's business not generating sufficient income for his education, he joined the US navy at the age of 12 and rose to the rank of Rear Admiral. He commanded attacks during the Mexican–American War and the American Civil War with mixed success, and was influential in the modernization of the US Navy, particularly regarding ironclad and steam-powered ships.

GREEN-FINGERED DU PONTS

WHEN THEY WEREN'T BUSY MAKING GUNPOWDER, THE DU PONT CLAN WERE KNOWN FOR THEIR GREEN THUMBS. DURING THE 19TH CENTURY THE DU PONT RESIDENCES ON THE BRANDYWINE RIVER WERE OFTEN FILLED WITH FLOWERS. AT LEAST THREE DU PONT HOUSES AND GARDENS HAVE NOW BEEN PRESERVED AS MUSEUMS AND OPENED TO THE PUBLIC. ONE OF THEM, MONTPELIER IN VIRGINIA (ABOVE), BOUGHT BY GENERAL HENRY'S ERRANT SON, WILLIAM, WAS ALSO THE HOME OF US PRESIDENT JAMES MADISON.

ALFRED VICTOR PHILADELPHE DU PONT 1798–1856

More of a boffin than a businessman, he was the eldest son of E. I. Du Pont and the first to take over the company. He worked on guncotton for the navy and modernized the powder works. But after being traumatized by a major explosion, he resigned under pressure from his family, who thought he wasn't paying sufficient attention to the bottom line.

4 CHILDREN NEXT PAGE

HENRY DU PONT 1812–89

Known as the General, he was a West Point graduate who took over from his older brother in 1850 and was senior partner until his death in 1889. He abandoned some of the capitalist idealism of his father and turned the business toward the pure pursuit of profit, most notably when he chose to sell gunpowder to both sides in the Crimean War. His autocratic leadership has been credited with consolidating Du Pont as a business family dynasty. Yet he also provoked fierce family disputes and his inflexibility caused younger, more talented, Du Ponts to abandon the company for greener pastures.

2 CHILDREN NEXT PAGE

ALEXIS IRENEE DU PONT 1816–57

The youngest son of the founder, he was another Du Pont who was more at home with the powdermen than high society. He died tragically trying to prevent a massive explosion from devastating the entire powderworks.

SON EUGENE NEXT PAGE

AMERICAN CIVIL WAR ADMIRAL SAMUEL DU PONT (CENTER), PICTURED WITH ADMIRAL SIDNEY S. LEE (LEFT) AND ADMIRAL DAVID DIXON PORTER (RIGHT), C.1865.

4 CHILDREN OF ALFRED VICTOR PHILADELPHE

2 CHILDREN OF HENRY 1812

HENRY ALGERNON DU PONT 1838–1926

During the American Civil War he achieved the rank of Lieutenant Colonel and was awarded the Medal of Honor for his role in the Battle of Cedar Creek. He stayed in the US Army for 10 years after the war, then returned to Delaware. He was President and General Manager of the Wilmington & Western Railroad Company from 1879 until 1899. He was elected to the US Senate in 1906 and served until 1917.

WILLIAM DU PONT 1855–1928

When his father issued an edict against Du Ponts marrying other Du Ponts, he went ahead and married his cousin Mary anyway. He caused a further scandal when the marriage soured and ended in divorce. Henry made William a partner, but he was a lightweight in terms of the business.

SON OF ALEXIS IRENEE

EUGENE DU PONT 1840–1902

When Henry died, Eugene was his reluctant successor as senior partner of DuPont, but while he modernized the company he lacked his uncle's iron will.

ALFRED VICTOR DU PONT 1833–93

Known as Fred, with his brother, Bidermann, he escaped the strictures of the family company under Uncle Henry to become a successful banker in Louisville, Kentucky. An eccentric bachelor, known for his frugality, he lived for years in a shabby hotel room, giving the mansion he built to his brother. Life-long stinginess would prove his undoing. He was shot in the heart by the madam of a brothel he frequented for failing to provide financial support for a child she argued was his.

ELEUTHERE IRENEE DU PONT II 1829–77

He joined the company and became a partner in DuPont when his father retired. Henry always kept a close eye on him. His life was badly damaged by the insanity of his wife, Charlotte. One of the reasons for her madness was the way she was treated by her mother-in-law who needled her constantly for being a southerner. As such, Irénée refused to speak to his mother for the last 12 years of his life.

LAMMOT DU PONT 1831–84

He joined the company after graduating in chemistry from the University of Pennsylvania and became a DuPont partner in 1857 under his uncle Henry who, worried by his abilities, sent him on missions which put his life at risk. He overcame Henry's resistance to making dynamite to found the Repauno Chemical Company in New Jersey and resigned from DuPont to work on it. He was killed there in an explosion in 1884. Lammot also caused a family scandal because he chose a wife with Jewish heritage.

ANTOINE BIDERMANN DU PONT 1837–1923

He moved to Kentucky with his brother Alfred and built up a successful paper business. His son, Coleman, would return to Delaware and play an important role in DuPont.

PICTURED HERE, PIERRE S. DU PONT (THIRD FROM RIGHT) AND OTHER FAMILY MEMBERS VIEW A MEMORIAL OF THEIR FOUNDING ANCESTOR ON NEW YEAR'S DAY, 1952.

ALFRED IRENEE DU PONT
1864–1935
One of the crucial Du Ponts in the inter-generational takeover battle. The last of the hands-on Du Pont powdermen breed, he joined with two cousins to mount a successful bid for the company in 1902. His personal life, however, was disastrous and caused serious ructions in the family, which made him bitter and vulnerable to the machinations of his more strategic cousin, Pierre S. Du Pont.

LOUIS DU PONT   1868–92
Shot himself in the head while sitting in an armchair at the exclusive Wilmington Club.

PIERRE S. "GRAVEYARD" DU PONT   1870–1954

The final and most successful member in the triumvirate of cousins who took over DuPont in 1902. A quiet achiever, Pierre was a cautious businessman and ruthless strategist, who couldn't rest until he had gained control for himself. In the process of doing so he ignited a bitter feud with his cousin Alfred. Pierre S. was the last Du Pont to rule the company, though his hold on the family was more tenuous. Still, he made them millions by buying into the General Motors company, becoming its chairman and turning it into the world's biggest corporation, of which up to one-third was owned by DuPont.

THOMAS COLEMAN DU PONT   1863–1930
Raised in Louisville, Kentucky, Coleman was a successful banker, manufacturer and prototypical corporate raider, whose capital Alfred I. sought out to help fund the younger generation's takeover. He became Chairman and embarked on a buying spree which put DuPont in the powerful position of owning 75 percent of America's gunpowder and explosives and nearly all of its smokeless gunpowder capacity. He got bored with the gunpowder business, however, and sold out controversially to Pierre S., before going on to become a successful New York City skyscraper builder and US Senator.

VICTIMS OF THE FAMILY PRODUCT
IN THE NYE COMMISSION OF THE 1930s, THE DU PONT COMPANY EARNED THE NICKNAME "MERCHANTS OF DEATH."

LAMMOT DU PONT   1880–1952
Along with his brother Irénée, he was trained up by big brother Pierre S. to have an executive role in the company and rose as far as Vice President. When Pierre S. mounted his push against Alfred I., both Lammot and Irénée profited on his coattails.

PIERRE S. DU PONT III   1911–
He spent time working for the family company and was a noted collector of maps and other printed matter from the age of exploration.

PETE DU PONT   1935–
After graduating as a lawyer, he worked for DuPont between 1963 and 1970. His political career began in 1968 in the Delaware House of Representatives and, in 1970, he became a Republican member of the US House of Representatives. He was elected Governor of Delaware in 1976 and served two terms until 1985. He ran unsuccessfully as an independent for President in 1988

THE DU PONT BROTHERS AT THE WORLD'S FAIR, APRIL 1939. FROM LEFT TO RIGHT: RENEE DU PONT, HENRY B. DU PONT, R. M. CARPENTER, WILLIAM DU PONT AND LAMMOT DU PONT.

THE FARROWS

In the end, the Farrows are one of the odder family assemblages imaginable. It started with John, a womanizing, Australian director, who was also a devout Catholic, and his scantily clad, jungle-inhabiting, upper-crust Irish wife, Maureen, who was also a devout Catholic. They had seven children. One of them died tragically and, of the remaining six, only Mia escaped from the shadow cast by her famous parents. The first notable thing Mia did was to marry Frank Sinatra. Then she embarked on a movie career. After this there was a second marriage to musical genius André Previn, before beginning her third major relationship with Woody Allen, who she never lived with, but had one biological and two adopted children with, as well as appearing in thirteen of his films over a 12-year period.

But just as remarkable is the way Mia collects children in the same old way as some mad old ladies collect cats. At last count, she had thirteen children—three biological and ten adopted—often rescuing them from appallling conditions in countries such as Vietnam, Korea and India, as well as places closer to home. The children that come to her have often been seriously disabled. While this must be lauded, it has a certain aura of the pathological about it. Her biological son with Allen, Satchell, looks like he could be a genius, but some of her other children have faced serious life difficulties.

The artistic careers of both Farrow and Allen were transcended by scandal when it was discovered Allen was having an affair with one of Farrow's adopted daughters. Neither of their careers has recovered since. The next generation are yet to stand up and be counted but, considering their sheer numeracy, it's hard to imagine that at least one of them won't make serious waves.

HOW THEY RATE

WEALTH ★★
In Hollywood terms, fairly unspectacular.

HEALTH ★★
Neuroses, hypochondria and Mia's collection of disabled souls means health is not a forte for the Farrows.

HAPPINESS ★★
Not a priority here.

FAME ★★★
In some ways, this family is not as famous as its collective achievements.

SEXINESS ★★★★
Mia's pop was a hard-living casanova, mom was Tarzan's onscreen love interest, while Mia not only has her own looks but married one of the great crooners. Meanwhile Woody, for someone so geeky, seems to have done very well, laughing women into bed.

BLACK SHEEP FACTOR ★★★
Soon-Yi has been ostracized from her family for marrying Woody, while Woody's kids won't speak to him. Impressive.

ECCENTRICITY ★★★★★
Yes. They're all completely mad.

INFLUENCE ★★
They're a significant entertainment family, yet Mia has tended to latch onto men whose influence is more powerful than that of anyone in her own immediate family.

MAUREEN O'SULLIVAN WITH HUSBAND JOHN FARROW, PICTURED WITH SIX OF THEIR SEVEN CHILDREN, C.1950. MIA IS STANDING AT THE FAR LEFT.

> I'M SUCH A GOOD LOVER BECAUSE I PRACTICE A LOT ON MY OWN.
> WOODY ALLEN

MIA FARROW HAVING HER BLONDE HAIR CUT INTO ITS TRADEMARK SHORT CROP BY STYLIST VIDAL SASSOON, CALIFORNIA, 1967.

JOHN CARRYING MIA FROM HOSPITAL, 1954.

JOHN FARROW

Novelist, screenwriter, film director and naval officer John Farrow succeeded at pretty much everything he put his hand to. Born in Sydney, Australia, he later went to the British Royal Naval Academy. During his 4-year stint in the navy, he wrote short stories and plays. He also wrote an acclaimed English-Tahitian dictionary. He went to Hollywood in the late 1920s as a technical consultant for high seas movies and stayed on to become a screenwriter. He was a Hemingwayesque character—a ferocious philanderer, drinker, adventurer and reader. He married Maureen O'Sullivan in 1936—the same year that the movie *Tarzan Escapes*, on which they'd both worked, was released. Despite John's tendency to stray, the couple had seven children and remained married until his death. Also in 1936, Farrow began his movie directing career with *The Magic Spectacles*.

During World War II John rejoined the British Navy and was injured while serving as a Lieutenant Commander. The experience was influential in his subsequent conversion to Catholicism. He marked his conversion with a biography of English saints, and a history of the papacy—*Pageant of the Popes*. In 1956 he won an Oscar for his screenwriting on the movie adaptation of *Around the World in Eighty Days*. He was also nominated for a director's Oscar for *Wake Island* (1942), and his other films, such as the western *Hondo*, starring John Wayne, have become classics.

> EDGAR RICE BURROUGHS, THE AUTHOR OF THE **TARZAN** BOOKS CALLED MAUREEN "MY PERFECT JANE," WHILE JOHNNY WEISSMULLER, THE OLYMPIC SWIMMING CHAMPION WHO PLAYED TARZAN, CALLED HER MAGGIE BECAUSE HE THOUGHT MAUREEN SOUNDED TOO SNOOTY.

MAUREEN O'SULLIVAN

From a privileged Irish background, which included education at London's Convent of the Sacred Heart, Roehampton—where Vivien Leigh was also a student—and finishing school in Paris, Maureen is most famous for shacking up with a savage (Johnny Weissmuller) in the *Tarzan* series. She was spotted by Hollywood director Frank Borzage at a dinner dance for the Dublin Horse Show and was invited to screen test in Hollywood. She went there with her mother and, after a short and unsuccessful career at Fox studios, she signed with MGM in 1932. While Tarzan's Jane was her defining role, she acted in more than sixty films. For most of the 1940s she abandoned making movies to raise her seven children and returned to the job in the 1950s where she acted mainly for stage and TV. She appeared in her husband's last film, *John Paul Jones*, as did two of her children. She also appeared as Mia's mother in Woody Allen's 1986 *Hannah and her Sisters*, a role which brought her critical acclaim. Her second marriage was to a retired construction executive.

MAUREEN IN *DAVID COPPERFIELD*, 1935.

IRISH-BORN MAUREEN O'SULLIVAN IN HER HEYDAY, 1935. EVER SINCE HER SCHOOL-DAYS MAUREEN HAD HAD HER HEART SET ON BECOMING A MOVIE STAR.

MIA AS ALLISON IN PEYTON PLACE, 1965.

IT'S ALL ABOUT MIA

HER FRAIL LOOKS CONCEAL A WILL OF IRON AND A NEUROTIC DETERMINATION TO MOTHER THE WHOLE WORLD. AT LAST COUNT SHE HAS 13 CHILDREN—FOUR BIOLOGICAL AND THE REST RESCUED FROM ABANDONMENT OR EQUALLY DIABOLICAL CIRCUMSTANCES IN PLACES AS FAR-FLUNG AS KOREA AND VIETNAM.

BORN INTO HOLLYWOOD PRIVILEGE, MIA'S CHILDHOOD NONETHELESS HAD ITS MOMENTS OF ADVERSITY, MOST NOTABLY WHEN SHE CONTRACTED POLIO AT THE AGE OF 9. AFTER HAVING TO SPEND TIME IN AN IRON LUNG, SHE RECOVERED AFTER A LONG STINT IN HOSPITAL. AFTER THIS HER PARENTS SENT HER TO BOARDING SCHOOL IN ENGLAND. IN 1958 THE WHOLE FAMILY WAS ROCKED BY TRAGEDY WHEN MIA'S ELDEST BROTHER WAS KILLED IN A PLANE CRASH. MIA'S FATHER, JOHN, DIED WHEN SHE WAS 18—THIS MIGHT HAVE BEEN AN INFLUENCE ON HER FIRST MARRIAGE TO FRANK SINATRA WHEN SHE WAS JUST 20 AND HE 50. THE MARRIAGE LASTED FOR ONLY 2 YEARS, ALTHOUGH THE TWO REMAINED FRIENDS.

MIA IS A TALENTED, DIFFICULT WOMAN WHO SPECIALIZES IN THE TALENTED AND DIFFICULT. ALL OF HER LONG-TERM PARTNERS HAVE BEEN OSCAR WINNERS. AFTER FRANK SHE MARRIED COMPOSER, ANDRE PREVIN, AFTER BEFRIENDING HIS WIFE. HER LAST MAJOR RELATIONSHIP TO COMEDIAN AND FILM-MAKER, WOODY ALLEN, SAW THEM BECOME MANHATTAN'S MONARCHS OF NEUROSIS—A POSITION HELD UNTIL MIA DISCOVERED THAT WOODY HAD BEEN MAKING WHOOPEE WITH HER ADOPTED DAUGHTER SOON-YI.

MIA FIRST ACHIEVED FAME WHEN SHE PLAYED THE ROLE OF ALLISON MCKENZIE IN THE TELEVISION SERIES *PEYTON PLACE*. APART FROM THE *GREAT GATSBY* AND *ROSEMARY'S BABY*, MUCH OF HER MOVIE SUCCESS HAS COME FROM ACTING IN WOODY ALLEN FILMS, INCLUDING *THE PURPLE ROSE OF CAIRO*, *HANNAH AND HER SISTERS* AND *ZELIG*.

MIA'S MEN

Also known as Old Blue Eyes, Sinatra (pictured above with Mia on their wedding day in 1966) was arguably the singer of his generation and part of the famous Rat Pack with Dean Martin, Sammy Davis Jr, Peter Lawford and Joey Bishop. Mia was the third of his four wives. An early marriage to Nancy Barbato was followed by the glamour match to Ava Gardner. He stayed married to Mia for 2 years between 1966 and 1968, while his final wife, Barbara Marx, was formerly married to the youngest of the Marx Brothers,

Zeppo. According to Mia's biography, *What Falls Away*, Frank offered to have Woody's legs broken when he was busted having an affair with Mia's adopted daughter Soon-Yi Previn.

The family of Mia's second husband, André Previn (pictured below right with Mia), escaped the Nazis just in time, settling in the US in 1938. When he left his second wife, singer/songwriter Dory Previn, for Mia, Dory ended up in an asylum getting doses of electric shock therapy. André was married to Mia between 1970 and 1979, but their friendship survived the divorce. Previn has been married five times, with his latest wife being German violin virtuoso Anne-Sophie Mutter. Previn's career has been just as eclectic—he has been a jazz pianist, a concert pianist, a composer and an orchestra conductor. Amazingly he has excelled at them all and, at four Oscars, is the most Academy-Awarded in this entire Farrow clan.

Third man, Woody Allen, started out at 15, writing one-liners for gossip columns, and did time as a stand-up comedian before he landed a job writing the screenplay for *What's New Pussycat?* Since then he has produced a major comic cinematic opus. His neurotic New York comedies have attracted a world-wide audience and have seen him nominated for more

Best Original Screenplay Oscars than any other Hollywood writer.

His first wife was a philosophy student, Harlen Rosen, who he married in 1956 and divorced in 1962. He set a pattern with second wife, Louise Lasser—his co-star in *Bananas*—for sleeping with his leading ladies, which went on to include Diane Keaton as well as Mia Farrow—although Woody married neither of them. His relationship with Mia was unorthodox. While they had children together, they never actually lived together. However, their apartments were in view of each other, separated by Central Park.

Woody's choice of third wife, Mia's adopted daughter Soon-Yi, caused an enormous scandal, resulting in claims of child abuse and serious damage to his career.

{ "IN THE BEGINNING, I TRIED TO REACH OUT TO HER ... BUT I DECIDED IT WOULD BE BEST FOR ME AND THE REST OF THE CHILDREN TO JUST CLOSE RANKS AND PROTECT OURSELVES. I'LL PROBABLY NEVER SEE HER AGAIN." MIA FARROW ON DAUGHTER SOON-YI }

> *There were three of us in the relationship: Woody, his shrink and me. No decisions were ever made without her. He didn't even buy sheets without talking to her. I know that part of several sessions went into his switch from polyester-satin to cotton.* MIA ON WOODY

MIA'S BEST WOODY FIVE
1. *Zelig* (1983)
2. *Broadway Danny Rose* (1984)
3. *The Purple Rose of Cairo* (1985)
4. *Hannah and her Sisters* (1986)
5. *Husbands and Wives* (1992)

MIA'S BEST NON-WOODY FIVE
1. *Rosemary's Baby* (1968)
2. *Secret Ceremony* (1968)
3. *The Great Gatsby* (1974)
4. *Death on the Nile* (1978)
5. *Widow's Peak* (1994)

ROMAN POLANSKI DIRECTING MIA IN A SCENE FROM *ROSEMARY'S BABY*, 1968.

"My children are a continuous joy. The latest is Soon-Yi (aged 6, 7 or 8—we're saying 7). She's from Korea—was found abandoned in the streets of Seoul—with rickets, malnutrition—even her finger nails had fallen off, she had lice and sores everywhere. Now she speaks English and is learning to read, write, play piano, dance ballet & ride a horse. She is also learning that people can be believed in and even loved. These are golden times and I am aware of that every single second."
MIA IN A LETTER TO NANCY SINATRA AFTER THE ADOPTION OF SOON-YI

WOODY AND SOON-YI

GOLDEN TIMES NEVER LAST FOREVER BUT MIA CAN'T HAVE EXPECTED IT TO END IN QUITE THE WAY IT DID. "IT WOULD TAKE A DIRTY MIND TO THINK THAT," SAID MIA'S MOTHER, MAUREEN, WHEN ASKED IF WOODY—LIKE HIS CHARACTER IN HANNAH AND HER SISTERS—HAD EVER MADE A PLAY FOR ANY OF MIA'S SISTERS. LITTLE DID SHE KNOW THAT 5 YEARS LATER, HE'D BE FOUND GETTING IT ON WITH 17-YEAR-OLD SOON-YI PREVIN, ONE OF MIA'S ADOPTED DAUGHTERS. THE REVELATION CAME WHEN MIA FOUND NUDE POLAROID PICTURES OF HER DAUGHTER IN ALLEN'S APARTMENT. THE DISCOVERY SENT STRONG SHOCKWAVES THROUGH THE FAMILY AND MADE THEM THE SUBJECT OF TABLOID SPECULATION. IT WASN'T HELPED WHEN MIA SUED FOR CUSTODY OF THE THREE CHILDREN THEY SHARED, ALLEGING WOODY HAD ABUSED HIS DAUGHTER DYLAN. WHILE THE ABUSE WAS NOT PROVEN, THE JUDGE DID END UP IDENTIFYING THE NOTORIOUSLY SELF-ABSORBED ALLEN AS A LESS-THAN-IDEAL PARENT, WHILE MIA—WITH HER HISTORY OF ADOPTING THE KIDS OTHER PEOPLE HAD THROWN OUT—HAD SUPERIOR MORAL WEIGHT. SINCE THE SCANDAL, WOODY'S KIDS HAVEN'T SPOKEN TO HIM, WHILE MIA HASN'T SPOKEN TO SOON-YI. IN 1996, 4 YEARS AFTER THE SCANDAL, WOODY AND SOON-YI WERE MARRIED AND THEY ARE NOW THEMSELVES THE PARENTS OF TWO ADOPTED CHILDREN.

CELEBRITY FAMILY TREES 82

{ farrow family tree }

DANIEL O'SULLIVAN
dates unknown

He became Lord Mayor of Cork, Ireland, in 1881 and was later knighted by Queen Victoria.

MAUREEN O'SULLIVAN
1911–1998

Born in Boyle, Roscommon County, Ireland to an Irish Major in the British Army, this lithe beauty began playing ingenue roles while still in her teens, but found major fame as Tarzan's consort Jane. Yet her filmography shows a diverse, if not always unerring talent and her career, despite its respites, was one of remarkable longevity, especially considering she also managed to mother seven children.

MICHAEL FARROW   1940–1958

Michael was killed in a plane crash while taking flying lessons in 1958.

PATRICK FARROW   1943–

He made a couple of insignificant film appearances.

MIA FARROW
1945–

While most of her siblings dabbled in acting, Mia was the only one to have a degree of success to rival her parents. However, her acting career has been overshadowed to some extent by her relationship with Woody Allen, who cast her in many of his movies, and the calamitous events surrounding their break-up.

CHARLES JOSEPH O'SULLIVAN
c.1887–1950

He was an officer in the British Army who retired wounded from the Army in World War I, aged 28.

JOHN FARROW
1904–1963

This Australian-born sailor, screenwriter and film director won an Oscar, wrote books of Catholic history, and was a notorious Hollywood pantsman while staying married to Tarzan's Jane for 27 years, a rare Hollywood marriage which kept to the promise of "Until death us do part."

MARY FRAZER
dates unknown

When Maureen was growing up, her mother was having a series of nervous breakdowns.

JOHN CHARLES FARROW   1946–

He made a few more equally insignificant appearances in the movies than his older brother Patrick.

PRUDENCE FARROW   1948–

She did some work in film production, but is most famous as the addressee in the Beatles' song *Dear Prudence*. She was at the ashram when the Beatles visited India. For most of their time there, she stayed in her room. John Lennon, who was worried that she was depressed, rather than meditating, wrote the song.

STEPHANIE FARROW   1949–

She has appeared in two Woody films: *Zelig* and *The Purple Rose of Cairo*.

THE CAST FROM THE 1939–42 *TARZAN* FILM SERIES: CHEETA THE CHIMPANZEE, JOHNNY SHEFFIELD AS BOY, JOHNNY WEISSMULLER AS TARZAN, AND MAUREEN O'SULLIVAN AS JANE.

THERESA "TISA" FARROW   1951–

She appeared in a number of 1970s movies, including Woody's *Manhattan* and Z-grade cult film *Zombie Flesheaters* before disappearing to Vermont where she became a nurse.

FRANK SINATRA
1915–1998

One of America's most popular singers, Sinatra also acted in films and was the leading figure in the hard-living Rat Pack. His tough guy image was helped by his association with the Mafia. Mia Farrow was his third wife.

ANDRE PREVIN   1929–

Born in Germany, he came to the US in 1938 when his parents escaped the Nazis. A musical prodigy of the highest order, he is a noted concert pianist and has conducted most of the world's best orchestras. He is also a prolific composer and his movie scores have won Oscars. Mia Farrow was his second of five wives.

WOODY ALLEN   1935–

Born Allen Stewart Konigsberg in New York City, he came to attention first as a comedian then as a writer, director and actor in his own comedy films, which often starred his real-life lovers. His status as a representative of brains over brawn in the sexiness stakes took a beating, however, in 1992 when he started sleeping with Soon-Yi Previn, the adopted Korean daughter of his partner, Mia Farrow. The scandal occurred around the same time that he made a number of mediocre movies and his popularity has never fully recovered.

MALONE FARROW   1985–

She was adopted in 1985 after Mia and Woody had tried for 2 years to have a baby, and became the meat in the sandwich during the Soon Yi affair.

SATCHEL O'SULLIVAN FARROW   1987–

Woody and Mia's only biological child is a prodigy. He began college at the age of 11 and was accepted into Yale's law school aged 16. He has worked as the UN Spokesperson for Youth in Nigeria, Angola and Sudan.

BECHET ALLEN   dates unknown

MANZIE TIO ALLEN   dates unknown

MATTHEW PHINEAS PREVIN
1970–

He became an attorney.

SASCHA VILLIERS PREVIN   1970–

He became an accountant who married Carrie Englander, a social worker who moonlights in stand-up comedy.

FLETCHER PREVIN   1974–

With ambitions to go into the movies, at the age of 32 he has little to show for it.

SOON-YI PREVIN   1971–

Adopted at the age of 7, she was found abandoned in a shocking state in the streets of Seoul, South Korea. Mia Farrow had the adoption laws changed to permit the adoption of a third child. Soon-Yi went on to marry Woody Allen.

LARK SONG PREVIN   1974–

An orphan from Vietnam, she was the first child Mia adopted. She has two young daughters. According to some reports, Lark contracted HIV from a dirty tattoo needle and her children, born after the incident, are HIV positive too.

SUMMER SONG "DAISY" PREVIN   1975–

Her plane crashed while taking orphans out of Vietnam. She weighed just 6 pounds when she arrived in America at the age of 7 months. She married the brother of Lark's husband.

MOSES PREVIN   1979–

Adopted by Mia in 1980, he'd been abandoned in a phone booth in Korea, and was suffering from cerebral palsy. When Woody's affair was uncovered, he wrote to him "You have done a horrible, unforgivable, ugly, stupid thing. I hope you get so humiliated you commit suicide." He now has a master's degree in marriage and family therapy.

ISAIAH FARROW
1991–

In February 1992 Mia, having just learnt of Woody Allen's affair with her daughter Soon-Yi, was called by an adoption agency and asked if she would take an African–American baby who was addicted to crack-cocaine.

TAM FARROW
1980–99

She arrived at almost the same time as Isaiah after a long adoption process. She was a blind Vietnamese orphan and had never been to school. She died of a heart condition aged 19.

QUINCY FARROW
1995–

A healthy African–American except for the fact she was unable to move her arms.

THADDEUS FARROW   1990–

Abandoned at a Indian train station, he is a polio victim. Mia initially called him Gabriel Wilk, after the judge who ruled in her favor in her custody battle against Woody Allen.

MINH FARROW
1991–

Called Frankie-Minh after Frank Sinatra. She's a blind Vietnamese orphan who Mia adopted when she was 3 years old.

THE FONDAS

THE FONDA FAMILY IS BEST KNOWN FOR ITS ACTING PROWESS, BUT IT HAS ACCOMPLISHED FAR MORE THAN JUST THREE FAMOUS OSCARS. AMONG OTHER THINGS, IT HAS PRODUCED THREE SUICIDES, SEVEN DIVORCES—BETWEEN HENRY AND JANE AND THEIR SPOUSES ALONE— TWO CULT MOVIES, AND AN AEROBICS VIDEO.

JANE WITH THE POSTAGE STAMP CREATED IN HONOR OF HER FATHER, HENRY, IN 2005.

HOW THEY RATE

WEALTH ★★★
Getting rich seems to have been a by-product of other ambitions.

HEALTH ★★★
Physical longevity, though prone to neurosis and narcissism.

HAPPINESS ★
Many suicides, divorces, and damaged parent–child relationships.

FAME ★★★★★
Hollywood aristocracy.

SEXINESS ★★★★
Henry and Peter's all-American looks; Bridget and Jane both pin-ups; Jane's son Troy once voted one of America's most beautiful people.

BLACK SHEEP FACTOR ★★
Hard to tell in a world where notoriety is as valuable as good works.

ECCENTRICITY ★★★★
Seventy years in Hollywood is enough to make any family weird.

The Fonda name can be traced to the Adriatic Coast of Italy in the 14th century, but it was from Amsterdam in Holland to New Amsterdam (New York) that Jellis Douwes Fonda sailed with his cousin-wife Hester Janse and their children in 1650, to become the first American Fondas. The Fondas had significant roles to play in both the War of Independence and American Civil War and there is still today in New York state a town named after Douw "The Patriot" Fonda. The Fonda family later spread throughout the country, but the most famous Fondas were to emerge from Omaha Nebraska.

It was in the Omaha Community Playhouse in 1925 where the Fonda acting dynasty began. Henry Fonda, to become one of Hollywood's greatest actors, but at that time a 20-year-old college dropout, was persuaded by his mother to help her friend Dorothy Brando (Marlon's mom) fill the roles in Phillip Barry's *You and I.* Henry went on to play the lead in many Hollywood hits such as *Grapes of Wrath* before winning his Oscar for *On Golden Pond* in 1981, the year before his death. His personal life was arguably less of a success than his acting career. Henry went through five wives and his children felt damaged by his remoteness. Still, of his three children, Jane and Peter both became successful actors. From her sex symbol status Jane branched out into more serious roles, winning Oscars for *Klute* (1971) and *Coming Home* (1978), as well as five other nominations. Outside of acting, Jane's life seems to have changed according to the husband she was with at the time—erotic starlet with Roger Vadim, social activist with Tom Hayden, and liberal-cause capitalist with Ted Turner.

While Peter's career has not been as stellar as his sister's, he starred in the iconic sixties film *Easy Rider.* All of Jane's and Peter's children have dabbled in the film industry, but only Peter's daughter Bridget has remotely approached anything like the success of her forebears.

{ **"I WOULD HAVE GIVEN UP ACTING IN A MINUTE. I DIDN'T LIKE HOW IT SET ME APART FROM OTHER PEOPLE."** JANE FONDA }

JANE FONDA IN *LOVE'S CAGE,* 1963.

FOUNDING FONDAS

PETER AND SUSAN FONDA WITH THEIR CHILDREN JUSTIN AND BRIDGET, 1970.

The first Fondas in America were the married cousins Jellis Douwes (1614–59) and Hester (1615–90). Perhaps starting a long line of multiple-marriage Fondas, when Jellis died, Hester married Barent Gerritse. It didn't last long, though. In 1663 he was killed in the Escopus Indian War. Hester and her daughter, Sarah, were then captured by the Indians. Only Hester returned.

Douw "The Patriot" Fonda moved his family from Schenectady to Caughnawaga (now called Fonda). In 1780, during the American Revolution, British loyalist Sir John Johnston, son of Douw's neighbor Sir William Johnston—the explorer with whom he was on good terms—led a raiding party peopled with Mohawk soldiers. At the age of 79 Douw was tomahawked and scalped by a Mohawk called One-Armed Peter, who Douw was also on good terms with and had often entertained in his house. When asked why he'd killed a man he was friendly with, One-Armed Peter replied it might as well have been him who earned the bounty as anyone else.

Ten Eyck Hilton Fonda was Henry's grandfather and responsible for moving this branch of the Fondas to Nebraska. His biggest brush with fame came when he was responsible for giving the telegram from Secretary of War, Edwin Stanton, warning the Union Army of the approach of Confederate General Lee at Gettysburg and commanding General George Meade to take up the offensive. Described by an Omaha newspaper as "the agent that began the conflict," Fonda himself wrote, "I had orders to spare nothing, horseflesh and money was of no account if I would only deliver the message."

REMBRANDT'S PUPIL

HESTER DOUWEDR JANSE (1615–90), COUSIN AND WIFE OF JELLIS DOUWES FONDA (1614–59), WAS ALSO THE SISTER OF DUTCH PAINTER GERRIT (GERARD) DOU (1613–75). DOU STUDIED UNDER REMBRANDT AND IS BEST KNOWN FOR HIS PAINTINGS OF DOMESTIC INTERIORS WHICH SOLD EXCEEDINGLY WELL AND MADE HIM A VERY SUCCESSFUL ARTIST. DOU WAS SAID TO HAVE HAD AN OBSESSIVE LOATHING OF DUST AND WAS OVERLY FASTIDIOUS ABOUT THE CLEANLINESS OF HIS TOOLS AND WORKING CONDITIONS. DOU WENT ON TO HAVE HIS OWN WORKSHOP OF PUPILS WHO CARRIED ON HIS PARTICULAR STYLE.

FONDA FILMS
select filmography

HENRY
Grapes of Wrath (1940)
Mister Roberts (1955)
War and Peace (1956)
12 Angry Men (1957)
Fail-Safe (1964)
On Golden Pond (Oscar) (1981)

JANE
Barbarella (1968)
Klute (Oscar) (1971)
Coming Home (Oscar) (1978)
The China Syndrome (1979)
The Morning After (1986)
Monster in Law (2005)

PETER
Easy Rider (1969)
Dirty Mary Crazy Larry (1974)
Ulee's Gold (1997)

BRIDGET
Single White Female (1992)
Jackie Brown (1997)
A Simple Plan (1998)

★

A DIFFICULT RELATIONSHIP

HENRY STARRED IN *12 ANGRY MEN* AND BY ALL ACCOUNTS HE WAS ONE HIMSELF. HE LEFT HIS CHILDREN FEELING UNSURE AS TO WHETHER HE LOVED THEM. HE WAS A BIT MIFFED WHEN JANE WON AN OSCAR BEFORE HIM.

INLAWS AND OUTLAWS

Roger Vadim
(married to Jane 1965–73)
Corresponded to Jane's naughty phase. Vadim was one of the late 20th century's most successful pantsmen. He also married the sex goddess Brigitte Bardot and bedded Catherine Deneuve among countless others. Jane met him while she was studying at the Sorbonne in Paris. He shared his wife by casting her as the erotic lead in his film *Barbarella* and by inviting hookers into their marital bed for threesomes.

Tom Hayden
(married to Jane 1973–90)
Corresponded to Jane's social activist/ Hanoi Jane phase. Hayden was a member of the Chicago Seven arrested for protesting at the 1968 Democratic Convention. He was also an ardent supporter of the Black Panthers. He was with Jane on the Vietnam trip which earned her the sobriquet "Hanoi Jane." They split up around the time she started making millions through her aerobics videos.

Ted Turner
(married to Jane 1991–2000)
After spending the eighties in lycra, Jane celebrated the nineties by marrying billionaire Ted Turner. She had given up acting and was dedicating herself to less revolutionary causes. According to Jane, Ted is overly needy. She once said: "Ted needs someone to be there 100% of the time. He thinks that's love. It's not love—it's babysitting." One of the reasons they split up in 2000 was because Jane announced that she had become a Christian.

JANE FONDA TIMELINE

1937	Born.
1950	Mother suicides.
1952	First appearance of bulimia.
1954	Debuted with Dad in Omaha Community Theatre Play.
1960	Screen debut in *Tall Story*.
1965	Married Roger Vadim.
1968	*Barbarella*.
1968	Daughter Vanessa born.
1971	First Oscar (for *Klute*).
1972	Hanoi Jane.
1973	Divorced Roger; married Tom Hayden (did she cheat on Roger in Nam?).
1973	Son Troy born to Tom (July: yes, she did cheat on Roger in Nam).
1978	Second Oscar (for *Coming Home*).
1981	*Jane Fonda's Workout Book* published.
1982	In *On Golden Pond* with Henry.
1990	Divorced Tom; Ted asked her on a date the same day.
1991	Married Ted; retired from acting.
2000	Became a Christian and divorced Ted.
2005	Starred in *Monster in Law*.
2005	Released her memoirs *My Life So Far*.

CAPTAIN AMERICA Peter Fonda

Peter has lived in the shadow of his more famous relatives; first his father, then his sister, and more lately his daughter, Bridget. After his mother Frances committed suicide, Peter nearly followed suit by shooting himself accidentally in the stomach at the age of 10. Maybe it wasn't an accident? His comment to John Lennon that he knew what it was like to be dead, when they were both on acid at a party, inspired the Beatles song *She Said She Said*. Fonda thought John Lennon hated him and he was also insecure about his father. A long campaign of drugs and booze didn't help, and Fonda has remained in the background since his main moment with *Easy Rider* in the sixties.

"I DIG MY FATHER. I WISH HE COULD OPEN HIS EYES AND DIG ME."

PETER FONDA

THE FIVE WIVES OF HENRY FONDA

A man with five wives is generally considered to be something of a restless soul. Perhaps it's a flow-on effect from a job that consists of pretending to be other people. Although he didn't much like the social circuit, Henry's wives were often high-society dames with a number of husband notches on their belts—the boy from Nebraska proving his worth? They also had a tendency to be psychologically disturbed.

THE FONDA FAMILY AT THEIR HOME, 1948. HENRY IS STANDING BY THE TREE NEXT TO PETER. IN FRONT OF HIM IS JANE. AT THE FAR LEFT IS HIS WIFE (AND PETER AND JANE'S MOTHER) FRANCES SEYMOUR BROKAW, AND SEATED IN THE CENTER IS FRANCES'S DAUGHTER FROM A PREVIOUS MARRIAGE, FRANCES BROKAW.

WIFE NO. 1
MARGARET SULLAVAN
(married to Henry 1931–32)

Married on Christmas Day, it was all over a few months later. The daughter of a wealthy stockbroker and heiress, Margaret was a movie star in her own right. She was less successful in love, going through three more husbands, including director William Wyler and agent Leland Hayward, before she took a barbiturate overdose aged 49.

WIFE NO. 2
FRANCES SEYMOUR BROKAW
(married to Henry 1936–50)

This was a longer marriage that produced Peter and Jane before ending in madness and tragedy. Frances was another high-society lady with American ancestry including Samuel Adams, one of the hosts of the Boston Tea Party. Her first husband, stockbroker George Tuttle Brokaw, died in 1936 leaving her a daughter, Frances, and an estate of over $5 million. Already destabilized by childhood abuse, Henry's affairs pushed her over the edge and she voluntarily entered an asylum where she committed suicide by slashing her throat with a carving knife in 1950. Jane was told her mother had died of heart failure but discovered the truth while reading a magazine some months later.

WIFE NO. 3
SUSAN BLANCHARD
(married to Henry 1950–56)

The grieving period didn't last long before Henry married again. This stepdaughter of Oscar Hammerstein II was only 10 years older than Jane, but was popular with her and Peter, who called her "Mom 2." Susan and Henry adopted a child and called her Amy. But Henry got restless and divorced Susan in 1956.

WIFE NO. 4
AFDERA FRANCHETTI
(married to Henry 1957–61)

Henry and Afdera (pictured right) met in Italy when Henry was filming *War and Peace*. This Italian countess was part of the Rothschild family—yet another high-society Fonda wife. Her father was an explorer and envoy of Mussolini whose plane was shot down when she was 3, and her brother, Baron Raimondo Nanuk Franchetti, was a hunting buddy of Ernest Hemingway. She survived marriage to be jailed for smuggling drugs and write her memoirs.

WIFE NO. 5
SHIRLEE MAE ADAMS
(married to Henry 1965–82)

The longest-married and last of Henry's wives. The closest Shirlee came to high society was in her former career as a flight attendant.

KEY: CHILD ·······▶ ADOPTED CHILD ·······▶ MARRIED ━━━━ DIVORCED ━ ━ ━ DE FACTO ━·━·━ SPLIT UP ━ ━ ━

fonda family tree

JELLIS DOUWES FONDA 1614–59

This Dutchman was the first Fonda in America, where he worked in the whaling industry and as a brandy distiller. He came with his wife, Hester, who also happened to be his cousin. The Fonda artistic gene, which would come through so strongly in later generations, can be detected in the fact that Hester was the sister of the famous Dutch painter of domestic interiors, Gerrit Dou (1613–75), who studied under Rembrandt.

HESTER DOUWEDR JANSE 1615–90

She was captured by the native Americans in the Escopus Indian War.

> I've been close to Bette Davis for thirty-eight years—and I have the cigarette burns to prove it.
> HENRY FONDA

DOUW JELLIS FONDA 1641–1700

JELLIS ADAM FONDA 1670–1737

DOUW FONDA 1700–80

He was the Fonda who had a town named after him in New York State. Douw was tomahawked at the age of 79 by a Mohawk, who sold his scalp to the British for approximately $8.

ADAM DOUW FONDA 1736–1808

Adam was captured with his brother, John, by the British in the same raid that killed their father (1780) during the War of Independence. Adam later became a Tryon Country judge and New York State assemblyman.

DOUW ADAM FONDA 1774–1855

GARRET T. B. FONDA 1808–79

TEN EYCK HILTON FONDA 1838–1913

In the American Civil War this Fonda delivered the telegram that warned the Union Army of the approach of Confederate General Lee at Gettysburg.

WILLIAM BRACE FONDA 1879–1935

He once ran an advertising business with his brother and also worked as an oil salesman. He was the proprietor of a printing press when his son, Henry, was born.

HERBERTA LAMPHEAR JAYNES 1879–1934

She was heavily involved in the Omaha Community Playhouse where all her children also acted. She was also a good friend of Dodie Brando (Marlon Brando's mother).

HENRY FONDA 1905–82

Henry was born in Grand Island, Nebraska. He studied journalism at college but dropped out. His first acting role was the juvenile lead in Phillip Barry's *You and I* at the Omaha Community Playhouse in 1925. He moved to New York to act on Broadway, and played his first Hollywood role in *A Farmer Takes a Wife*. His penetrating blue eyes became synonymous with the roles of the honest and decent (if contrary) men he became famous for playing. Henry was renowned for his seemingly effortless acting. He won an Academy Award for *On Golden Pond*, the year before he died.

1ST WIFE

FRANCES SEYMOUR BROKAW 1908–50 ☠

A socialite with a pedigree as far back as the Boston Tea Party, she married Henry in 1936. She committed suicide by cutting her throat on her 42nd birthday.

2ND WIFE

MARGARET SULLAVAN 1911–60 ☠

Only married to Henry for a few months, she had a Broadway career herself. She was found dead from an overdose in a hotel room.

3RD WIFE

SUSAN BLANCHARD 1928–99

This stepdaughter of Oscar Hammerstein II was apparently popular with Jane and Peter who called her "Mom 2." They married in 1950 and divorced in 1956.

4TH WIFE

AFDERA FRANCHETTI 1933–

This naughty Italian countess, with links to the Rothschilds, married Henry in 1957 when she was 23 and he was 53. She was once arrested for smuggling drugs.

5TH WIFE

SHIRLEE MAE ADAMS 1932–

This former flight attendant was the last of Henry's five wives. She married him in 1965 and stayed with him until his death in 1982.

HARRIET MCNEILL FONDA 1907–98

The sister of Henry who forged the way for the later Fondas with her close involvement with the Omaha Community Playhouse.

JAYNE FONDA 1909–58

JANE FONDA 1937–

From naughty schoolgirl, to erotic starlet, then anti-Vietnam war campaigner, Oscar-winning actress, cause junkie, aerobics tycoon, wife of a media tycoon, now newborn liberal Christian feminist. In her 2005 memoirs, *My Life So Far*, she talks of an "internalized misogyny," she said that contributed to her lifelong habit of quickly conforming to the habits, desires and ambitions of the men in her life at the expense of her own character. She was married three times and has two children.

VANESSA VADIM 1968–

Emerged from the licentious union of her parents and inherited her mother's social conscience to make worthy documentaries such as *The Quiltmakers of Gee's Bend*.

TROY GARITY 1973–

A Hollywood actor with a sideline in worthy causes. When he was 16 he dropped out of school to run after a circus performer he was in love with. However, the highlight of his career is perhaps being voted as one of *People* magazine's 50 Most Beautiful People in 1998.

ROGER VADIM 1928–2000

Being Jane's first husband, he used this intimate knowledge to cast her cleavage in the main role of his, now cult classic, film *Barbarella*. He had four children to four different women, including Jane, and a love child to Catherine Deneuve.

TOM HAYDEN 1939–

This 1960s revolutionary and accumulator of trendy left-wing political causes was also once the leader of a Berkeley Commune. After divorcing Jane, he became an assemblyman in the California State congress.

> I'M AFRAID OF MAKING A MISTAKE.
> I'M NOT TOTALLY NEUROTIC, BUT
> I'M PRETTY NEUROTIC ABOUT IT. I'M
> AS CLOSE TO TOTALLY NEUROTIC
> AS YOU CAN GET WITHOUT BEING
> TOTALLY NEUROTIC.
> BRIDGET FONDA

TED TURNER 1939–

Like Jane's mother, Ted Turner's dad committed suicide. Ted then took over the family billboard business and turned it into the socially conscious CNN empire. He has owned baseball teams, skippered the winning boat in the America's Cup yacht race, invented World Championship Wrestling, and is the largest private landowner in the United States.

BRIDGET FONDA 1964–

Goddaughter of Larry Hagman, at 18 she enrolled at New York University and spent 4 years there and at the Lee Strasberg Theater Institute. Following a period honing her stage craft, she has played the lead in a number of films. After relationships with Dwight Yoakam and Eric Stolz, she married composer Danny Elfman. She turned down the TV role of Ally McBeal because she was afraid she'd like it too much. She has one son, Oliver.

PETER FONDA 1940–

Born in New York City, Peter studied at the University of Omaha and got involved with the Omaha Community Playhouse where he was mentored by his aunt, Harriet. He recovered from breaking his back twice to take acid with John Lennon and to star in iconic counter-culture films such as *The Trip*, and *Easy Rider*, which he co-wrote and for which he received an Oscar nomination for Best Original Screenplay.

DANNY ELFMAN 1964–

One of the most famous composers in Hollywood, his credits include the theme to *The Simpsons*, *Batman*, *Edward Scissorhands* and *Charlie and the Chocolate Factory*.

SUSAN BREWER 1941–

PORTIA REBECCA (BECKY) CROCKETT 1942–

According to some, she is a descendant of Davy Crockett.

JUSTIN FONDA 1966–

Although often described as an actor, his film career seems to have been limited to playing a child in a commune in *Easy Rider* (1969), an airline attendant in *Big Eden* (2000) and himself in two TV documentaries about his family.

AMY FONDA 1953–

THE FREUDS

THE FATHER OF PSYCHOANALYSIS, SIGMUND FREUD AT HIS DESK IN HIS STUDY, VIENNA, AUSTRIA, 1935.

In the current generation of Freuds there are three novelists, an architect of Tony Blair's New Labour government and a celebrated London fashion designer. It should also be noted here that perhaps one of the secrets to the success of the Freuds is their longevity. It's rare that a Freud doesn't reach 80.

The Freud fame began with Sigmund, founder of psychoanalysis, one of the three great shaping ideas that emerged, along with Marxism and Darwinism out of the second half of the 19th century. While belief in the effectiveness of psychoanalysis, sometimes known as "the talking cure," as a tool for psychiatric healing has waned over the years, it remains central to the way we understand ourselves and imagine the invisible regions of our minds and personalities. Terms such as the "ego" and the "id," or the idea that someone is oral or anal, now make instinctive sense to us, whether the research they are based upon has been scientifically proven or not.

Sigmund's psychiatric work, carried on by his youngest daughter and one of his grandsons, would be enough for most families to down tools and rest on their laurels for a century or two. Not with the Freuds, however. In America, Sigmund's nephew by blood and marriage, Edward Bernays, was responsible for applying the knowledge gained by his uncle in matters of managing the public sphere. In essence, Bernays was the first of the spin doctors: "If we understand the mechanism and motives of the group mind, it is now possible to control and regiment the masses according to our will without their knowing it," he argued, a technique he described as "the engineering of consent." Whether you think this kind of logic is evil or not, with the rising significance of spin in all areas of society, there is no doubting its influence. And Bernays is not the only powerful spin doctor in the Freud clan. Matthew Freud, great grandson of Sigmund, is a powerful player on the English PR scene and happens to employ a number of his younger relatives.

WITH THE FATHER OF PSYCHOANALYSIS, THE FOUNDER OF PUBLIC RELATIONS, A MEMBER OF THE HOUSE OF COMMONS AND ONE OF THE WORLD'S MOST RENOWNED CONTEMPORARY PAINTERS, THE FREUD FAMILY HAS ARGUABLY HAD A GREATER IMPACT ON WESTERN CULTURE OVER THE COURSE OF THE 20TH CENTURY THAN ANY OTHER. AND IT IS NOT DONE YET.

HOW THEY RATE

WEALTH ★★★
Very comfortably off rather than filthy rich.

HEALTH ★★★★★
Fantastic. If you're a Freud and you didn't make it to 80, you'd feel cheated.

HAPPINESS ★★
There's too much thinking going on in this family for true happiness

FAME ★★★★
Sigmund of course, though, with the exception perhaps of Lucian, the fame of subsequent Freuds tends to be concentrated in Great Britain.

SEXINESS ★★★★★
Freud was into sex, conceptually at least, while Lucian, who has been attributed with powerful sexual charisma, still manages to squire 20-somethings, even though he's into his 80s. Some of his daughters are renowned for their looks too.

BLACK SHEEP FACTOR ★★★
Although Sigmund was very much a moralistic Jewish patriarch, Lucian was once banned from every race track in Britain for failing to pay his gambling debts and has lived an existence almost entirely devoid of traditional morality.

ECCENTRICITY ★★★★★
Having been born in Germany, Clement Freud has nonetheless almost mastered the art of being an entertaining English eccentric. Lucian's children meanwhile tend to have published novels about their wacky upbringings in the sixties.

INFLUENCE ★★★★
Freud's theories are on the wane, but he's in the everyday way we think about ourselves, while Lucian is a bona-fide art star of great orginality. Edward Bernays, as the founder of Public Relations in America, is arguably the most influential Freud of them all. It will be interesting to see if subsequent generations can pull off anything comparable to these heavy-hitters.

SIGMUND FREUD, AGED 16, PICTURED WITH HIS MOTHER AMALIE. FREUD WAS EXTREMELY CLOSE TO HIS MOTHER, AND HE WAS HER CLEAR FAVORITE. FREUD'S FATHER, JACOB, HAD ALREADY BEEN MARRIED TWICE BEFORE, SO THE AGE GAP BETWEEN FREUD AND HIS MOTHER WAS LESS THAN BETWEEN AMALIE AND JACOB.

> WE ARE NEVER SO DEFENSELESS AGAINST SUFFERING AS WHEN WE LOVE, NEVER SO FORLORNLY UNHAPPY AS WHEN WE HAVE LOST OUR LOVE OBJECT OR ITS LOVE.
> SIGMUND FREUD

THE FATHER OF PUBLIC RELATIONS

"The conscious and intelligent manipulation of the organized habits and opinions of the masses is an important element in democratic society. Those who manipulate this unseen mechanism of society constitute an invisible government which is the true ruling power of our country ... We are governed, our minds molded, our tastes formed, our ideas suggested, largely by men we have never heard of. This is a logical result of the way in which our democratic society is organized..."
Edward Bernays, the opening to *Propoganda* (1928)

PR COUPS OF THE FREUDS

On behalf of bully-boy banana company United Foods, Bernays engineered a CIA-sponsored coup against a moderate Guatemalan government which was trying to regulate the quasi-slavery conditions of its agricultural workers, by creating the impression in the American press that it was infiltrated with communists who, following the domino theory, posed a risk to the United States.

With American tobacco as a client, he engineered (with the help of feminists) the end of the taboo against women smoking by getting ten debutantes to smoke as a Torch of Freedom protest as they walked down Broadway during the 1929 parade.

Matthew Freud worked for the British Labour Party which, with themes like New Labour and the "third way," made its way back to power in 1997, ending 18 years in the political wilderness. He is married to a daughter of Rupert Murdoch.

The only Freud to hold actual political office has been Clement Freud, who was a Liberal member of parliament in the English House of Commons for 14 years. Many of the successes of the Freud family, however, have been in the arts. Clement's brother, artist Lucian Freud, is perhaps the most celebrated portrait painter of his time. His works routinely sell for millions of dollars. Between them, these two brothers—although they no longer speak to each other—have produced three novelists, a TV presenter and high-level script editor, one of London's leading couturiers, as well as Matthew of PR fame.

BRITISH MEMBER OF PARLIAMENT, CHEF AND HUMORIST, CLEMENT FREUD, 1973.

NOVEL FREUDS

British writer J. G. Ballard once described Sigmund Freud as the great novelist of the 20th Century. Perhaps then it's not surprising how many of his descendants have either written novels or chosen to sleep with people who do.

★ **ROSE BOYT** (pictured above) One of Lucian's daughters to have turned her hand to fiction. Rose's two novels are *Sexual Intercourse* and *Rose: A Novel*, although she hasn't published anything since 1991. Both her novels have leaned heavily on autobiographical elements derived from her unorthodox childhood.

★ **SUSIE BOYT** The younger and more prolific sister of Rose. Her novels include *Only Human*, *Normal Man*, *The Last Hope of Girls* and *The Characters of Love* and have a reputation for their exploration of the intimate realms of life. Susie Boyt is also a journalist and has recently written a column on shopping for the *Financial Times*.

★ **ESTHER FREUD** More renowned perhaps than her half sisters, Esther originally trained as an actress (including an appearance in the British cult TV *Dr Who* episode "Attack of the Cybermen"). She fell into writing by accident. Her novels include *Hideous Kinky* which was made into a film starring Kate Winslet, *Peerless Flats*, *Gaglow*, *The Wild* and *The Sea House*. She has also come to attention for her work on the scripts of famous British comedies such as *Notting Hill* and *Bridget Jones's Diary*.

★ **LADY CAROLINE BLACKWOOD** An underrated writer with a reputation for black humor, her novel *Great Granny Webster*, about the horrors of her Northern Ireland upbringing, was nominated for the Booker Prize in 1977. Her third marriage was to famous American poet Robert Lowell, who died in a taxi clutching *Girl in Bed*—a Lucian Freud portait of his wife. At the time, Lowell had left Blackwood and London to return to his former life. Caroline Blackwood was also a notorious alcoholic.

★ **ROBERT FOX** Sixteen years older than his partner Bella Freud, Fox fits into Bella's pattern of falling for older men. One wonders what Sigmund would have said about this in relation to the absence of her father for some of her formative years. Robert Fox is most famous for his 1983 bestseller, *White Mischief*, while his relatives are also of impressive stock, and include Nancy Astor, Britain's first female member of parliament.

FREUD IN HIS CONSULTING ROOM, VIENNA, 1925.

WORKS OF SIGMUND

STUDIES ON HYSTERIA (WITH JOSEF BREUER), 1895

THE INTERPRETATION OF DREAMS, 1899

THE PSYCHOPATHOLOGY OF EVERYDAY LIFE, 1901

THREE ESSAYS ON THE THEORY OF SEXUALITY, 1905

TOTEM AND TABOO, 1913

ON NARCISSISM, 1914

BEYOND THE PLEASURE PRINCIPLE, 1920

THE EGO AND THE ID, 1923

THE FUTURE OF AN ILLUSION, 1927

CIVILIZATION AND ITS DISCONTENTS, 1929

MOSES AND MONOTHEISM, 1939

AN OUTLINE OF PSYCHO-ANALYSIS, 1940

> "MOST PEOPLE DO NOT REALLY WANT FREEDOM, BECAUSE FREEDOM INVOLVES RESPONSIBILITY, AND MOST PEOPLE ARE FRIGHTENED OF RESPONSIBILITY." SIGMUND FREUD

LUCIAN FREUD PICTURED HERE IN DUBLIN, IRELAND, 1952.

LUCIAN'S PAINTING CAREER

LUCIAN FREUD IS ONE OF THE WORLD'S TEN MOST EXPENSIVE LIVING ARTISTS. HIS PAINTINGS SELL FOR BETWEEN $2 AND $5 MILLION AT AUCTION AND IT IS ESTIMATED THAT PRIVATE SALES HAVE SEEN HIS WORKS CHANGE HANDS FOR BETWEEN $6 AND $9 MILLION. HE BEGAN TO WORK FULL TIME AS AN ARTIST AFTER BEING INVALIDED OUT OF THE MERCHANT NAVY IN 1942. LUCIAN FREUD SPECIALIZES IN PORTRAITS AND NUDES, AND THE ART CRITIC ROBERT HUGHES ONCE DESCRIBED HIM AS "THE BEST REALIST PAINTER ALIVE." HIS MODELS ARE FREQUENTLY HIS WIVES, LOVERS AND EVEN HIS DAUGHTERS. HIS TEXTURING OF THE PAINT, HOWEVER, AT TIMES GIVES HIS SUBJECTS AN ALMOST UGLY YET THOROUGHLY HUMAN INTENSITY.

FASHION DESIGNER BELLA FREUD PICTURED HERE (RIGHT) WITH JEMIMA KHAN, 2006.

To promote her 1999 collection, but not on the catwalk, Bella Freud collaborated with John Malkovich to make two short videos, **Strap Hanging**, a bizarre series of events set on a train, and **Lady Behave**, which takes place in a charm school.

{ freud family tree }

JACOB FREUD 1815–96

Sigmund's father was a textile salesman trading primarily in wool. He was married twice before marrying Amalie, Sigmund's mother, by which time he had children who were already older than her. One of the early shocks of Sigmund's life was when his father's business failed and they were forced to leave the slow pace of life in Freiburg, Moravia (now a part of the Czech Republic), and move to bustling Vienna, the cosmopolitan center of the Habsburg Empire.

AMALIE NATHANSON 1835–1930

Amalie was the embodiment of the doting mother and was crucial to Sigmund's success. She gave him clear preference over his other siblings. It's not surprising that she felt so close to Sigmund. There was the same age difference between them as there was between her and her husband.

MOTHER LOVE
FREUD, WHO WAS CONTINUALLY WORRIED ABOUT HIS POOR HEALTH, FEARED THAT HE WOULD DIE BEFORE HIS MOTHER. HE COULD NOT BEAR THE THOUGHT THE EMOTIONAL STRAIN THAT WOULD RESULT FROM HER HAVING TO BE TOLD THAT HE HAD DIED.

EMANUEL FREUD 1833–1914

Emanuel and Phillip, Sigmund's half brothers, both migrated to Manchester in England. They were also slightly older than Sigmund's mother and consequently prone to flirting with their father's new bride.

PHILLIP FREUD 1834–1911

‘ A man who has been the indisputable favorite of his mother keeps for life the feeling of a conqueror.
SIGMUND FREUD ’

JULIUS FREUD 1857–58
Died from illness at the age of 1.

ANNA FREUD 1858–1955
Married Ely Bernays, a grain broker. Ely was the big brother of Freud's wife, Martha. Therefore their children were both Sigmund's blood relatives as well as nephews and nieces in law.

ELY BERNAYS 1850–1923

ROSA (REGINE DEBORAH) FREUD 1860–1942
She was gassed at Treblinka, a Nazi extermination camp.

MITZI (MARIE) FREUD 1860–1942
She was also gassed at the Treblinka death camp in Poland. Her family tended toward the theater. Eldest daughter, Margerete (1887–1984), was a playwright who married then divorced a playwright while another, Lilly (1888–1970), was an actress who stayed married to the same actor for 52 years.

DOLFI FREUD 1862–1942
She died in Theresienstadt, a Nazi concentration camp, from which Jewish prisoners were mostly re-routed to the death camps further east.

PAULA FREUD 1864–1942
Like two of her sisters, she was also gassed at Treblinka.

ALEXANDER EPHRAIM GOTTHOLD FREUD 1866–1943
He was a professor at an Export Academy in Vienna.

SIGMUND FREUD
1856–1939

Along with Darwin and Marx, Freud was one of the three most influential thinkers of the late 19th century. Even though his theories have become increasingly discounted in recent years, with terms such as the "subconscious," the "ego," the "id" and the "Oedipus complex," they remain embedded in the ways we imagine ourselves and our emotional connections to others. Originally named Sigismund Schlomo Freud, he changed his name to Sigmund on reaching the age of 21.

MATHILDE FREUD   1887–1978
The eldest of their children, she married a book salesman and emigrated to England.

JEAN MARTIN FREUD   1889–1967
He was a lawyer who also emigrated to England.

OLIVER FREUD   1891–1969
He was a civil engineer who married painter and teacher Henny Fuchs in Berlin before emigrating to Massachusetts, USA.

2 CHILDREN: ERNST & SOPHIE NEXT PAGE

MARTHA BERNAYS   1861–1951
She was a friend of Sigmund's sisters and came to Freud's attention when she came home with them to play. He was immediately smitten, but they did not immediately marry because he was too poor to propose to her. Accordingly, he gave up poorly paid scientific research in favor of the more lucrative option of becoming a doctor. In 9 years of marriage, Martha gave birth to six children and played the role of the classic Jewish mother and wife of the patriarch.

> "I was always looking outside myself for strength and confidence but it comes from within. It is there all the time."
> ANNA FREUD

EDWARD BERNAYS   1891–1994
The only son out of Ely and Anna Bernays is considered to be the father of public relations in America. A charismatic, if morally dubious man, he lived to the age of 104 and was an advisor to US presidents and American corporations. In many ways his skill was being able to apply his uncle's theories of the operations of the subconscious into the fields of marketing and public relations.

ANNA FREUD   1895–1982
The youngest of Sigmund and Martha's children was also the only one to follow in her father's footsteps. In her working life she became a pioneer of child psychoanalysis. She also showed some of her father's stubborn feistiness. Her theoretical dispute with fellow pioneer, Melanie Klein, was so brutal it threatened at times to split the British psychoanalytical society. When she wasn't theorizing, Anna was active in setting up and working in children's homes and shelters.

TRAGEDY AT TREBLINKA
AMALIE FREUD (CENTER) PICTURED WITH HER TWO DAUGHTERS (LEFT DOLFI AND RIGHT MITZI). TREBLINKA WAS THE NAZI DEATH CAMP 60 MILES NORTHEAST OF WARSAW IN POLAND WHERE THREE OF FREUD'S SISTERS: MITZI, PAULA AND ROSA (ALL IN THEIR SEVENTIES AND EIGHTIES AT THE TIME) WERE MURDERED. ESTIMATES OF THE NUMBER OF PEOPLE KILLED AT TREBLINKA VARY BETWEEN 700,000 AND 1,400,000. IN THE BEGINNING, VICTIMS WERE BURIED IN MASS GRAVES, AND THE STENCH FROM THE DECOMPOSING BODIES COULD BE SMELLED UP TO 6 MILES AWAY, THE PEOPLE (MAINLY JEWS) WHO WERE WAITING IN THE TRAINS, WERE AWARE OF THEIR DESTINY AND MANY COMMITTED SUICIDE. WHEN THE NAZIS BUILT NEW GAS CHAMBERS IN SEPTEMBER 1942, THEY WERE ABLE TO MURDER 3000 PEOPLE EVERY 2 HOURS.

CHILDREN OF SIGMUND & MARTHA

ERNST LUDWIG FREUD 1892–1970

The youngest son of Sigmund and Martha, Ernst Ludwig was a successful architect who, along with many of his siblings, was assisted by his father's influential friends to emigrate from Austria and Germany when the Nazi's attitude toward the Jewish people became clear.

LUCIE BRASCH 1896–1989

She and Ernst married in 1920. She was the daughter of a prosperous grain merchant. Between the death of her husband and her own death she suffered a long depression, which was partly alleviated by the hundreds of sittings she did for Lucian, her famous painter son.

SOPHIE FREUD 1893–1920

Unusually for the generally long-lived Freud family, Sophie didn't enjoy a long life. Nonetheless, she married early to Max Halberstam and had two children. One of them died at the age of 5 while the other, Ernst, was the only grandchild of Sigmund Freud to become a psychoanalyst.

ERNST FREUD 1914–

The only grandchild of Sigmund to become a shrink, he also changed his name from his father's Halberstam to the career-progressing Freud. He also married a psychoanalyst.

STEPHAN FREUD 1921–

The eldest and least conspicuous of these three Freud brothers, Stephan chose a career in publishing and has married twice.

LUCIAN FREUD
1922–

There is no denying that Freud's grandson Lucian is one of the 20th century's greatest painters—critic Robert Hughes called him "the best realist painter alive." He is particularly famous for his ingenious approach to the genre of portrait painting. He has also lived a life of conspicuous bohemianism. At times, he has been reprimanded for his dissolute behavior, such as being warned off all British racecourses for failing to pay a $35,000 debt to a bookmaker or enjoying the London demi-monde in association with people as varied as fellow painter Francis Bacon and London gangsters, the Kray brothers. He has also sired at least fourteen children by a variety of women, including his two wives.

CLEMENT FREUD 1924–

The youngest member of the family, Clement was a Liberal member of the British House of Commons between 1973 and 1987. When he left parliament he received a knighthood. He has also been a TV chef, a nightclub owner and journalist. Like his brother, he is known as something of a bon vivant. A crucial difference, however, is that he has been married to actress Jill Freud for over 50 years. Although they were close as children, he hasn't spoken to brother Lucian for over 50 years.

> *If you resolve to give up smoking, drinking and loving, you don't actually live longer; it just seems longer.*
> CLEMENT FREUD

JUNE FLEWETT 1927–

Actress Jill Freud was born June Flewett. As a child during World War II, she was sent to live with C. S. Lewis, author of the Narnia books. In fact, it is thought she may have been the inspiration for the character of Lucy.

EMMA FREUD 1962–

Emma is a British broadcaster and cultural commentator. She has been a television broadcaster, BBC radio announcer and script editor for movies, such as *Bridget Jones's Diary* and she also plays the saxophone. She is married to famous British scriptwriter and producer Richard Curtis, whose successes include the films *Four Weddings and a Funeral* and *Love Actually*. Curtis and Freud have four children.

MATTHEW FREUD 1963–

Matthew Freud, born into the famous Jewish family, is head of Freud Communications Limited, and is the great grandson of Sigmund Freud and the son of British writer Clement Freud. In August 2001 he married Elisabeth Murdoch, daughter of international media magnate and billionaire Rupert Murdoch.

KATHLEEN EPSTEIN 1926–

Also known as Kitty Garman, she is the daughter of sculptor Jacob Epstein. She was married to Lucian 1948–53 and they have two daughters together, Annie and Annabel.

LADY CAROLINE BLACKWOOD
1931–96

An heiress to the Guinness fortune and noted beauty and wit who was married to Lucian from 1952 to 1956 before his gambling habits and her drinking habits came between them. She later had three daughters from her marriage to composer Israel Citkowitz and a son from her marriage with poet Robert Lowell.

BERNADINE COVERLEY 1941–

A sixties hippy she moved in with Freud when he was 40 and she was 21. It didn't last and she took her kids off to Morocco to escape the stigma of being a single mom.

SUZY BOYT c.1939–

She met Lucian when she was studying and he teaching at the Slade School of Fine Art.

> I've stopped caring about skeptics, but if they libel or defame me they will end up in court.
> URI GELLER

FREUD OR FRAUD?
URI GELLER-FREUD (1946–)

BEST KNOWN FOR HIS CELEBRITY SPOON-BENDING, THIS FAMOUS AND CONTROVERSIAL ISRAELI PARANORMALIST ALSO CLAIMS TO BE RELATED TO SIGMUND FREUD. SOLOMON FREUD—HIS MOTHER, MARGARET FREUD'S PATERNAL GRANDFATHER—WAS, ACCORDING TO VARYING ACCOUNTS, EITHER A NEPHEW, SECOND COUSIN OR THIRD COUSIN OF SIGMUND. THEN AGAIN WITH URI GELLER, A MASTER ILLUSIONIST, THINGS ARE NOT ALWAYS WHAT THEY SEEM. STILL, IT CAN BE SAID THAT GELLER, ALONG WITH THE IRISH BAND CLANNAD, WAS ONE OF MATTHEW FREUD'S FIRST TWO CLIENTS WHEN HE SET UP HIS PR COMPANY IN 1985. APPARENTLY, FREUD WAS TO RECEIVE A 10 PERCENT COMMISSION OF THE SPOILS IF GELLER MANAGED TO DIVINE GOLD ON A TROPICAL ISLAND, WHICH WOULD HAVE MADE HIM RICH. UNFORTUNATELY GELLER DIDN'T.

> EVER SINCE I WAS LITTLE I REALLY LOVED BOYISH CLOTHES—I HAD A REAL OBSESSION WITH STRICT CLOTHES, LIKE UNIFORMS. THEY REALLY GOT ME GOING.
> BELLA FREUD

BELLA FREUD 1961–

Bella is a top London fashion designer and woman about town, who has designed for celebrities and off-the-rack items for labels such as Jaeger and Kangol. She even managed to get her father, Lucian, to sketch their pet dog, Pluto, for a T-shirt belonging to the label of the same name. She once lived with Prince Dado Ruspoli, the Italian playboy who Federico Fellini based the Marcello Mastroianni character in *La Dolce Vita* on. She is now married with a child to novelist Robert Fox.

ESTHER FREUD 1963–

She started out as an actor but has since become better known for her novels after the break-through success of *Hideous Kinky*, the semi-autobiographical tale of a mother and her two young daughters living the hippie life in Morrocco in the 1970s after being dumped by their famous artist father. It has since been made into a film, starring Kate Winslet as the mother. Esther has also published another four novels to critical acclaim.

ROSE BOYT 1959–

Rose is the second of five children from the relationship between Lucian and Suzy. When she was 7, her mother took all her children on an 18-month cargo ship jaunt around the ports of Europe. This experience gave Rose the basis for her semi-autobiographical novel, *Sexual Intercourse*, about a young girl being abused by a sea captain.

SUSIE BOYT 1968–

The youngest of the five children, she is also a novelist, having published four novels to critical acclaim. She also works as a newspaper columnist and is married with a daughter to film producer Tom Astor, of the famous American high-society family.

THE GETTYS

In times of rapid change, experience could be your worst enemy. **J. PAUL GETTY**

AMERICAN MILLIONAIRE J. PAUL GETTY (AKA "BIG PAUL") HAVING A SIMPLE LITTLE DINNER PARTY AT HOME WITH A FEW FRIENDS, 1960.

The Getty story is an excessive tale of incredible wealth, massive eccentricity and tragedy. One of the things about money is that it is the ultimate shape-shifter. Take a few million dollars and one day it's a painting, the next a private jet, the following day a beach house. There are limits, however, to the forms that money can adopt, and the Getty family history shows what can happen when rich people become so deluded by the power of money they think it can take the shape of human affection. While Big Paul Getty once said that money was the only certain aphrodisiac, he was an emotional cripple—an autistic business genius who watched and sometimes even laughed while his family suffered around him. The legacy he left for his children and grandchildren was a double-edged sword. Millions and millions of dollars of oil money came with critically low self-esteem, addiction and dangerous obsessions, which only fueled the tragic circumstances that seemed to hover over the Gettys. It was a long way from the sober and deeply religious sense felt by Big Paul's parents that striking oil was a Calvinist sign of God's favor. Indeed with a family history that includes heroin addictions, overdoses, suicides, AIDS and ears sliced off by kidnappers, it seems God might have changed his mind. Yet, as with all families, there have also been the successes. In business, the latest is the Getty Images phenomenon. However, the Gettys have also done well in fields including Hollywood acting, opera composition, economic theory, African eco-tourism and, of course, philanthropy.

HOW THEY RATE

WEALTH ★★★★★
Big Paul Getty was once the richest American in the world and, even when the fortune was split four ways, Little Paul became the sixth-richest man in Britain overnight. This family, with the odd unfortunate exception, has shown itself to have the Midas Touch.

HEALTH ★★
Drugs, alcohol, overdoses, AIDS and the psychological cost of being a Getty is high. Still, Big Paul womanized into his eighties and, for those Gettys who manage to escape addiction, the chances are fairly good for a long life.

HAPPINESS ★
A contradiction in terms for this family.

FAME ★★★
Not in the limelight as much as they once were, though considering what usually got them into it, that's not a bad thing.

SEXINESS ★★★★
If Big Paul is right and money is the only true aphrodisiac then, yes. It seemed to work for him and his descendants in spite of their borderline personality disorders. Granddaughter Aileen, for instance, has had AIDS for 20 years but recently married for the third time, to the son of a famous Italian playboy, 20 years her junior.

BLACK SHEEP FACTOR ★★★★
This is the kind of family where the white sheep stand out.

ECCENTRICITY ★★★★★
Father George's heavy religion, Big Paul's meanness, Little Paul's bibliophilia and late-life cricket fanaticism, Gordon's opera composing—as they English might say, they are all barking mad.

INFLUENCE: ★★★
In terms of philanthropy the Getty Museum in Los Angeles and Little Paul's donations to British culture have been significant but, while in business terms they've made the most of opportunities, they've rarely changed the world.

THE MEANEST MAN IN THE WORLD

IN MANY WAYS IT'S HARD TO THINK OF A MORE MISERLY CHARACTER THAN J. PAUL GETTY (BIG PAUL). NOT ONLY WAS HE THE RICHEST MAN IN THE WORLD, HE WAS ALSO ONE OF THE MEANEST. HIS MEANNESS, FURTHERMORE WAS SOMETHING FROM WHICH HE OFTEN SEEMED TO DERIVE GREAT PLEASURE. HERE ARE JUST SOME EXAMPLES OF A MAN WHO PUTS EBENEEZER SCROOGE TO SHAME:

★ FAILURE TO PAY THE RANSOM FOR HIS KIDNAPPED GRANDSON JOHN PAUL GETTY III, UNTIL HIS GRANDSON'S EAR WAS SLICED OFF—AND EVEN THEN BIG PAUL ONLY AGREED TO PAY THE TAX-DEDUCTIBLE PART.

★ AT HIS HOME IN SUTTON PLACE HE INSTALLED A PAYPHONE FOR THE USE OF STAFF AND GUESTS OUT OF FEAR THEY WERE ABUSING HIS HOUSE PHONES BY MAKING LONG-DISTANCE CALLS.

★ WHEN BIG PAUL'S SON GORDON WAS BASED IN SAUDI ARABIA, GORDON PROTECTED A FEMALE EMPLOYEE FROM BEING STONED FOR ADULTERY BY HELPING HER LEAVE THE COUNTRY. BIG PAUL WAS ANGRY SINCE HE THOUGHT THE WOMAN HAD KNOWN THE RISKS AND THAT GORDON SHOULD HAVE LET HER PAY THE PRICE RATHER THAN JEOPARDIZE BUSINESS. GORDON WAS REPLACED IN THE COMPANY SOON AFTER.

★ HIS FAILURE TO ALLOW HIS SON RONALD MORE THAN $3000 FROM THE TRUST, WHILE HIS BROTHERS HAD FULL SHARES. THOUGH BIG PAUL DANGLED INCLUSION AS A CARROT TO RONALD, HE NEVER REWROTE THE TERMS, AND THIS TEASING TREATMENT CAME CLOSE TO RUINING RONALD'S LIFE.

★ WHEN HE DIED WITH $1 BILLION TO HIS NAME, HE LEFT HIS SECRETARY OF 20 YEARS $5000, WHILE HIS LONG-STANDING BUTLER GOT 6 MONTHS' NOTICE AND THE GARDENERS 3 MONTHS NOTICE.

JOLLY GOOD SHOW, LITTLE PAUL

The transition of John Paul Getty II from a heroin-addicted hermit to a knighted British citizen and philanthropist—who counted among his friends Mick Jagger, Margaret Thatcher and the Queen Mother—is one of the more fascinating tales in the Getty family. After the splitting up of the Sarah C. Getty Trust, where Big Paul had stashed most of the company oil profits in order to protect them from the taxman, Little Paul suddenly became the owner of £750 million, making him the sixth- wealthiest man in Britain. The ensuing philanthropy binge, which was to last until his death, began with his rescuing of the history of British cinema via a £20 million donation. As a reclusive addict with odd sleeping patterns, one of Getty's major hobbies was watching old movies, and this donation helped the transference of the British film archive onto non-perishable stock.

Getty's next great act of charity came when he gifted the National Gallery a cool £50 million. At the time he was living in the London Clinic trying to get off drugs. This didn't stop Margaret Thatcher from coming to thank him in person. Being generous must also have been a pleasant way for Little Paul to differentiate himself from his father. Its reward was also an acceptance by the English upper classes that his father had coveted but never received. Giving was something to which, like heroin, he became addicted.

Aside from art and book collecting, Getty's other great British hobby came when Rolling Stone Mick Jagger, who'd been a friend of Getty since the sixties, dropped round one day while Little Paul was watching TV and suggested he switch the channel to the Test Cricket—at 5 days per game, the world's longest and most intricate live sport. Getty became such a fan that by the end of his life he was chairman of the Surrey Cricket Club, had donated millions to build a new stand at Lords—the home of cricket—and was the owner of Wisden, whose annual almanac is the cricket Bible. This stood him in good stead in English society as well.

JOHN PAUL GETTY JR (LITTLE PAUL) AT A PEACE DEMONSTRATION IN ROME, 1969.

GETTY TRAGEDY CHRONOLOGY

1890 George and Sarah Getty's only child, Gertrude, died in the typhoid epidemic that swept through Minnesota, USA, that winter.

1958 Tim Getty, J. Paul's fifth son, died during an operation to perform cosmetic surgery on his head, since an earlier operation to remove a brain tumor had disfigured him.

1971 Having cured herself of her drug addictions and becoming Rudolph Nuyerev's only female lover, Talitha Pol Getty (pictured right), daughter of artist Willem Pol, and step granddaughter of British artist Augustus John, phoned Paul Getty in Rome to ask for a divorce. He persuaded her to come to Rome to talk it over. She never returned. After an argument the first night, she went back to his apartment to continue the discussion on the second night. Talitha stayed the night, but when Paul woke up the next morning, she was dead, probably due to a combination of alcohol and barbiturates. Her death in turn precipitated a heart attack in her her father from which he never fully recovered.

1972 Throughout his life George Getty suffered from low self-esteem caused primarily by his father. Although he rose to become vice president of the family business—an achievement that would have crowned life for many an ambitious man—George probably lacked the talent for the job and his pop never ceased to remind him. He turned to drink, and when that proved no solution, he locked himself in his bedroom, took an overdose of Nembutal and tried to stab himself to death with a barbecue fork. He failed, managing only to fall into a coma. When his friends discovered him they decided it would be too embarrassing to take him to the casualty department of the nearby public hospital, so drove instead to a private hospital 20 minutes further away. In that 20 minutes the Nembutal took hold and George died.

1973 No one story embodies the Gettys as a bunch of rich screw-ups than the July 10 kidnap of John Paul Getty III (right) in Rome by members of the Calabrian Mafia. When they first confirmed the kidnapping, the initial ransom request was for $17 million. Only Big Paul Getty had access to that kind of money. However, he wasn't speaking to Little Paul (John Paul II) and, although he was aware of the kidnapping, he refused to take calls from John Paul III's mother, Gail. He disapproved of his grandson's hippie ways and blamed him for getting himself kidnapped. As the demands of the kidnappers became more shrill, Big Paul became more and more adamant, defending his miserliness by arguing that to pay would put his other granchildren at risk. In his autobiography he also tried to justify himself philosophically, claiming: "The second reason for my refusal was much broader-based. I contend that acceding to the demands of criminals and terrorists merely guarantees the continuing increase and spread of lawlessness, violence and such outrages as terror-bombings, 'skyjackings' and the slaughter of hostages that plague our present-day world." Meanwhile the kidnappers had sold John Paul III up the chain to a more professional and ruthless bunch of Mafioisi, who played Russian roulette against his 16-year-old head. The worst came soon after when, on the pretence of cutting his hair, they sliced off his right ear. The ear was put in the mail as a warning of things to come if the ransom wasn't paid. Italy, however, was in the grip of a postal strike and it languished in a warehouse for 3 weeks. After 4 months, John Paul's health had got to the point where if he wasn't rescued soon he would die, an outcome to no-one's advantage. By this time the ransom had been reduced to $3.2 million. John Paul's other grandfather eventually persuaded Big Paul to cough up, but in typical style, Big Paul agreed only to pay the portion of the ransom that was tax-deductible ($2.2 million) leaving the rest to be drawn in regular instalments from John Paul II's trust income at an interest rate of 4 percent. The ransom was inevitably paid and John Paul III was freed on December 14. The next day was his grandfather's birthday. Gail suggested John Paul III ring his grandfather to thank him. When asked by his assistant if he wanted to speak to his grandson, Big Paul said no.

1981 Sadly the tragedy of John Paul III's life didn't end with his kidnapping. The psychological scars were immense and he became an alcoholic as a way of seeking reprieve from the anxiety and nightmares that besieged him. After more than 5 years of hard-core drinking, however, things started to look up when he started to get involved in acting. He was cast in a prominent role in the Wim Wenders movie *The State of Things*, and discovering that he couldn't both act and drink, he decided to give the latter up. But it was to prove his undoing. In order to help him sleep and calm his nerves during the withdrawal, his doctors prescribed him a cocktail of drugs, including valium and methadone. This caused his alcoholic's liver to fail and he slipped into a coma from which he emerged 6 weeks later a virtual quadriplegic whose capacity for speech but not his intellect was damaged. He has lived with a full-time nursing staff ever since.

1985 The year started well for Aileen Getty with the birth of her first son Andrew, but went downhill soon after. Her mother-in-law, Elizabeth Taylor, had become an AIDS activist and the constant talk reminded Aileen of the risks she had taken during the past. When she went for a test,

she turned out to be HIV-positive and, despite the support of Liz (right), the depression and shame sent her into a cocaine-fueled tail-spin that ended with divorce, the loss of custody of her children and being clinically dead until she became clean almost 10 years later, for 9 of which she has had AIDS. Although she has had AIDS for over 20 years, she recently married Bartolomeo Ruspoli, the son of Dado, a celebrated Italian playboy. Neither of her children has caught the disease.

THE OPENING OF THE GETTY MUSEUM TO THE PUBLIC.

THE ARTISTS IN THE OIL

While the Gettys have been defined by their enormous amounts of money, there have been numerous attempts to break into the arts. Mostly it has involved the philanthropy of the Getty Museum or Little Paul's British activities. In fact sometimes these two strands of the family have competed to purchase the same artworks. However, there have been a number of Getty attempts to create art rather than wealth, some of them more successful than others. After all, when the problem of having to earn a living has never existed, what is there to give a life the kinds of challenges that make it feel worthwhile living?

> Formula for success: Rise early, work hard, strike oil.
> **J. PAUL GETTY**

★

The meek shall inherit the Earth, but not its mineral rights.
J. PAUL GETTY

CLASSICAL COMPOSER GORDON GETTY AT HIS PIANO, 1985.

PLUMPJACK

Perhaps the most successful member of the family in terms of artistic achievement has been Little Paul's musical brother, Gordon, whose classical compositions and operas have been performed (albeit to mixed critical reaction) around the world. His opera *Plumpjack*, based on Shakespeare's character Falstaff, was also the inspiration for a chain of food and wine enterprises begun by Gavin Newsom—the son of Little Paul and Gordon's childhood friend, Bill Newsom—and one of Gordon's sons. The businesses have prospered while Gavin is currently the Mayor of San Francisco.

GETTYS AT THE MOVIES

At various times, quite a few Gettys have attempted to make an impact on Hollywood. Big Paul's unlucky son Ronald was perhaps the first with his production of a number of B-grade flops in the early 1970s. John Paul III was embarking on a movie career when it was cut short by his coma. Other members have made cameo Hollywood appearances, but the most successful member of the family in this respect is Balthazar Getty, who continues to have an acting career today that seems based on talent rather than the family fortune. Other Gettys, such as Aileen, who describes herself as an artist, have married into Hollywood aristocracy.

BALTHAZAR GETTY PICTURED WITH FRIEND DREW BARRYMORE, 1990.

Money is like manure. Spread it around or it smells.
J. PAUL GETTY

JEAN PAUL GETTY HAVING A PRETEND BOXING BOUT WITH FORMER US HEAVYWEIGHT CHAMPION, JACK DEMPSEY, 1967.

{ getty family tree }

GEORGE FRANKLIN GETTY 1855–1930

He was a Minneapolis insurance lawyer who got lucky in 1903 when he bought an Oklahoma oil lease on impulse for $500. It took 2 years for that lease to make his Minnehoma Oil Company a fortune and the family moved to California. He lent his son money to invest in the oil game and he was soon a millionaire, too. Ever since the death of his first child, George was deeply religious and he disapproved of his son waving his womanizing ways under his nose. When he died he left his estate worth around $15 million to his wife in the form of a trust which gave her the controlling interest.

SARAH RISHER 1852–1941

She made her younger husband change his plans to become a teacher in favor of law and was a driving force behind his subsequent success. She was stubborn and increasingly deaf as a consequence of the same typhoid that killed her daughter. Although religious, she indulged her only son's dalliances with the opposite sex, allowing J. Paul to turn his room in their Los Angeles home into a virtual flophouse, while preventing George Sr from taking punitive action. When her husband died, however, he left her in control of the Trust which had the controlling interest in the family oil company and J. Paul had to work around his mother to achieve some of his initial big schemes.

JEAN PAUL GETTY 1892–1976

For some time the richest American, "Big Paul" was also the stingiest, seemingly substituting money for affection in the way he dealt with his family. He expanded his father's oil fortune dramatically, with his greatest success being the petroleum rights he gained in Saudi Arabia and the line of supertankers he built to ship this oil back to the US. Although he had five children with four different wives, his attitude toward fatherhood was bizarrely callous and, other than making money, his life was an oddly detached manifestation of sex mania, miserliness, misanthropy and paranoia. Believing that in a past life he had been the Roman Emperor Hadrian, he decided to recreate in California the seaside estate where Hadrian had stayed in luxury, but too frightened to fly, he never left his late-life London base to visit it. The Getty Museum—as it became known—nonetheless was bequeathed most of his personal fortune in his will.

1ST WIFE
JEANETTE TREMONT 1906–

She married Getty in 1923 in a secret Mexican ceremony, when he was 30 and she was a 17-year-old high-school beauty. But when she got pregnant, Big Paul returned to his night-life habits and other girls. The marriage lasted 4 years during which Paul beat Jeanette and slept around, before it ended in divorce.

2ND WIFE
ALLENE ASHBY 1909–

She met Big Paul when he was studying at the University of Mexico, in between hunting down oil concessions in the gulf. He was having an affair simultaneously with Allene and her more beautiful sister, Belene, but chose to marry Allene because she was only 17. Their marriage made Getty a bigamist as his divorce still hadn't come through. The marriage lasted a year.

3RD WIFE
ADOLPHINE "FINI" HEMLE 1911–

The third of Getty's 17-year-old brides, she was a German girl staying with her family in the same hotel as Getty. Then 36, Paul seduced her, then persuaded her to elope with him to Cuba to escape her father's strong objections. They had a son, Ronald, but Big Paul was soon bored with married life and they were headed for divorce, when the threat of a large damages suit made Big Paul attempt a reconciliation that ultimately failed.

4TH WIFE
ANN RORK 1909–86

Anne was 23 when they married, but Big Paul first attempted to woo her when she was only 14. He started seeing her when she was 21 and they had a child out of wedlock during his messy divorce from Fini. After the usual Mexican marriage, Getty bought his first family home in Malibu but, by the birth of their second son, the couple weren't on speaking terms. She was stronger than her predecessors and got a decent divorce settlement before going on to marry another three times herself.

5TH WIFE
THEODORA "TEDDY" LYNCH 1913–

A niece of the high-society financier Bernard Baruch, she was a 23-year-old cabaret singer with plans of a career in opera when she met and became engaged to Big Paul. Three years later, they were married by the Mayor of Rome, then headed to separate continents after lunch. Their separate lives meant the marriage lasted almost 20 years.

GEORGE GETTY 1924–73

He was the eldest of the Getty sons, and the only son from Big Paul's first marriage to Jeanette Tremont. He spent most of his adult life working for the family business, where his father's unpaternal attitudes exacerbated the problems he had with his self-esteem. George once quipped that his father was the President for Success, while he was the Vice President for Failure. Despite having all the external trappings of the rich, his interior life was a shambles and ruled by a jealous quest for his father's love. He died from a drug overdose in 1973 while CEO of Getty Oil.

1ST WIFE

GLORIA GORDON 1931–

They married in 1951 and had three daughters before she sued for divorce in 1967 on the grounds that he was "aloof, cold, indifferent and insulting."

2ND WIFE

JACQUELINE RIORDAN unknown–c.1992

Her first husband left 30 million dubiously-earned dollars to her when he was buried in a mudslide. She married George in 1971 and, after he died, she married again and became known for her thoroughbred breeding of horses.

GORDON PETER 1933–

Tall and with a reputation for being absent-minded, Gordon is the only son of of Big Paul to have lived his life in relative happiness. Freed from the need to earn a living, he has composed operas and published economic theories. At the same time he managed to double the value of the Getty trust from $2 to $4 billion, something he achieved by selling Getty Oil to Texaco. With his wife, Ann, a leading American socialite, they have four children, and have enjoyed a life insulated from the tragedies that have afflicted other branches of the family. He caused a stir, however, when it was revealed in 1999 that he had had a secret second family with three daughters to Los Angeles woman Cynthia Beck.

ANN GILBERT 1938–

She has used her access to the Getty fortune to become one of San Francisco's leading socialites and philanthropists. She and Gordon have four sons, who have gone into a variety of careers.

RONALD GETTY 1930–

He was the only child born from Big Paul's third marriage to German beauty Aldolphine "Fini" Hemle. As Getty was considerably older than his young, naive wife, her father had bitterly opposed the marriage. The divorce was also bitterly contested and Getty showed his displeasure by limiting Ronald to a fixed income of $3000 from the family trust while his half brothers got millions. This affected him deeply, estranging him from the family, and fueling a sense of inadequacy. His numerous attempts to make a compensatory fortune failed and he ended up living in South Africa, pretty much broke.

KARIN SEIBL 1943–

She was the daughter of a German appliance wholesaler who married Ronald in 1964.

CHRISTOPHER RONALD 1965–

Although Ronald was restricted to earning $3000 a year from the family trust, his children had the same entitlements as the other grandchildren. Son Christopher has proved to be a canny investor and expanded his inherited wealth via the stock exchange. It also helped him in his career when he married Pia Miller, the eldest of the three socialite daughters of the Duty Free Shopping billionaire Robert Miller, and in his marriage choice and wealth, Christopher has expunged the inferiority complex his father developed from his place in the Getty family. It's curious, however, that his parents didn't attend the wedding ceremony.

PIA MILLER 1966–

The oldest daughter of Duty Free billionaire, Robert Miller. her sisters are both married to European royalty. Pia and husband Ronald have a daughter, Isabel.

SON JOHN PAUL GETTY II NEXT PAGE

TIM GETTY 1946–58

The fifth son, and only child Big Paul had with his fifth and final wife, Theodora "Teddy" Lynch, Tim was diagnosed with a brain tumor at the age of 6 whose removal left him half blind and with a disfigured head. When he was 12, Timmy went in for cosmetic surgery to fix some of this. In the days leading up to the operation, he beseeched his father via the phone to come and visit him. But Big Paul said he was too busy with business and Timmy failed to survive the operation.

SON OF JEAN PAUL & ADOLPHINE

JOHN PAUL GETTY II 1932–2003

Little Paul, as he was known, was one of Big Paul's two children with Ann Rork. As a child he once wrote a letter to his absent father, who merely sent it back with the spelling mistakes corrected. As a young adult he joined Getty Oil, becoming head of its Italian operation, but he didn't have a head for business. After breaking up with first wife, Gail, the mother of his four kids, he married Talitha Pol, the beautiful step-granddaughter of British painter Augustus John. They became rich hippies who fraternized with the Rolling Stones and developed the same drug habits. Talitha died of an overdose, while John Paul disappeared into an oblivion of heroin, booze and books, only to re-emerge in his fifties as Britain's biggest cultural philanthropist, for which, having changed his citizenship, he received a knighthood.

1ST WIFE

GAIL HARRIS 1933–

The daughter of San Francisco's Federal Chief Judge George Harris. If there's a saint in the Getty family, Gail Harris is it. She looked after her husband long after he left her, looked after the child he had with second wife Talitha Pol, after her tragic drug-related death, and had the strength of character to finally force Big Paul to pay up to secure the release of her son. Her children have gone through all sorts of tragedy and she has been there for them every time—a marked contrast to her former husband and father-in-law.

2ND WIFE

TALITHA POL 1940–71

A sixties "it" girl, daughter of Dutch painter Willem Pol and step-daughter of Augustus John's daughter, Poppet. Her first years were spent in a Japanese prison camp in Java, which destroyed her mother's health. She and Little Paul led a drug-fueled hippie existence, mingling with likes of the Rolling Stones until she died of an overdose in Rome.

3RD WIFE

VICTORIA HOLDSWORTH 1949–

A former model and Nivea girl, their love affair began when he was still married to Talitha. He credited her with rescuing him from the self-destruction of his drug addiction. They finally married in 1994, by which time she had already been married three times, to Lionel Brook, the last white Rajah of Sarawak, an antiques dealer and a Saudi Arabian businessman.

AILEEN GETTY 1957–

Like her father and brother she was something of a wild child. Whereas her father's poison of choice was heroin, for Aileen it was cocaine. She contracted HIV from an affair and it ended her marriage to Christopher Wilding. However she has joined forces with her former mother-in-law, Elizabeth Taylor, in becoming an AIDS activist.

CHRISTOPHER WILDING 1955–

He's the son of Elizabeth Taylor and actor Michael Wilding, and has worked as a film editor and photographer.

BARTOLOMEO RUSPOLI 1978–

Twenty years younger than his wife, he is the son of Italian playboy Dado Ruspoli.

> If it hadn't been for HIV, I would still be a victim. Victimized by my parents, by my legacy, by life. I'd been in seven institutions, I'd had 12 shock treatments, I'd had seven miscarriages. I was anorexic, a self-mutilator. I'd been there and back. AILEEN GETTY

ARIADNE GETTY 1962–

The youngest of Little Paul's children with Gail Harris, she became an architectural photographer and married the actor Justin Williams in 1992 with whom she has two seasonally named children, Natalia and August.

JUSTIN WILLIAMS unknown–

He married Ariadne in 1992 and has acted in a number of films and television shows including *Star Trek: Voyager* and *The X-Files*.

JOHN PAUL GETTY III
1956–

The eldest grandson of Big Paul, he fell into his father's hippie ways in Rome, pretending to be a painter and living the bohemian life until he was kidnapped by Calabrian criminals and held for ransom. When his grandfather refused to pay the ransom, the kidnappers sliced off his right ear. Eventually the ransom was paid and Paul was released, but his troubles were only just beginning. He married a German woman Martine, but slid into alcoholism. When he started to find acclaim as an avant-garde actor in films by directors such as Wim Wenders, he decided to give up drinking but one night took an overdose of pills that put him in a coma from which he emerged a virtual quadriplegic some weeks later. Initially his father refused to fund his treatment, but there was a rapprochement and he lives in a specially designed house cared for by full-time nurses.

GISELA MARTINE ZACHER   1948–

She was 8 years older than John Paul and a divorced single mom when they started dating in 1973. After his release by the kidnappers, they stayed together and got married when she discovered she was pregnant with Balthazar. Even though they separated, she supported him after his overdose coma.

MARK GETTY   1960–

The white sheep of the family, he studied high finance, worked for a number of merchant banks, then was the driving force behind internet bonanza, Getty Images. He is married to Domitilla Harding, who is related to an old Roman family, reflecting Mark's fondness for the city where he and his siblings spent relatively happy years before their brother's kidnapping.

DOMITILLA HARDING   1960–

On her maternal side she belongs to an old Roman family whose ancestors include Pope Julius III.

TARA GABRIEL GALAXY GRAMOPHONE GETTY
1968–

For someone whose name embodies the worst excesses of the sixties, this only son of Little Paul and Talitha Pol spent his childhood with stepmom Gail and his half siblings after the death of his mother from a drug overdose in 1971. He has managed to avoid the limelight by spending most of his time in southern Africa where he has been a pioneer of eco-tourism and is the owner of exclusive game reserve lodges.

> WHEN HE WAS A CHILD BALTHAZAR WAS KNOWN BY HIS FAMILY AS "LITTLE BUDDHA," BECAUSE HE HAD A RED BIRTHMARK IN THE CENTER OF HIS FOREHEAD.

BALTHAZAR GETTY
1975–

The son of John Paul III, he has managed to create a career for himself as a Hollywood actor and has appeared in films such as *Ladder 49* and David Lynch's *Lost Highway*. Yet he has also been afflicted with the Getty addictive streak—like his grandfather, his poison of choice was heroin. After seeing his best friend die from an overdose he eventually kicked the habit and now has a child with children's fashion designer Rosetta Millington.

ROSETTA MILLINGTON   1970–

She's a funky children's clothes designer and a friend of Patricia Arquette, who introduced the couple to each other.

AILEEN GETTY WITH PRINCESS DIANA IN 1996, WHO WAS PATRON OF THE NATIONAL AIDS TRUST.

★

THE HEARSTS

WILLIAM RANDOLPH HEARST DURING A GAME OF CROQUET, 1935.

HOW THEY RATE

WEALTH ★ ★ ★ ★ ★
Impressive. The Hearst Corporation is valued at around $20 billion.

HEALTH ★ ★ ★ ★ ★
George Hearst crossed the Sierra Nevadas while suffering from cholera and his descendants seem to be made of the same hardy stuff. There doesn't seem to be as much evidence of the drug and alcohol problems that usually come with being super-rich either.

HAPPINESS ★ ★ ★
Despite the depiction of William Randolph Hearst in *Citizen Kane*, this family, on average, seems pretty well balanced for billionaires—or maybe they're just scared of their own headlines.

FAME ★ ★ ★
Not so famous, but they'll never be forgotten and the young "it" girl cousins are at least keeping the family's face on the map of contemporary culture

SEXINESS ★ ★ ★ ★
Not too bad. Handsome men and beautiful women, but again, with the exception of William Randolph Hearst, a lack of the starlet-chasing you often find with the American rich.

BLACK SHEEP FACTOR ★ ★ ★ ★ ★
Patty Hearst. Was she really brainwashed?

ECCENTRICITY ★ ★ ★
A man prepared to gamble newspapers, a fantasy castle on the coast of California and a terrorist, but also a fair bit of solidity.

INFLUENCE ★ ★ ★
Pivotal to the development of California, while William Randolph changed the nature of journalism and provided the inspiration for one of the world's greatest movies.

From the rough-and-tumble of the final days of the American Frontier, to Hollywood excess, acts of terrorism and high-class catwalk action, the Hearst family has enjoyed a rich and often controversial passage over the last 150 years. The dynasty was founded by mining magnate George, who walked 1000 miles from Missouri to participate in the California Gold Rush. Yet it was when he struck it lucky, winning the *San Francisco Examiner* in a poker game, that the most salient feature of the family began. George's son, William Randolph, took over the paper aged 24 and in doing so revolutionized journalism with his sensationalist tabloid style. William Randolph built America's first media conglomerate. Using land inherited from his father, he also finished Hearst Castle, where he and his mistress, Marion Davies, lavishly entertained the cream of Hollywood society. Unlike J. Paul Getty, Hearst liked to throw his money around.

Many subsequent Hearsts have worked for the family's extensive media interests and some are still involved in the business today, which has diversified into TV and the internet. However, the most famous Hearst moment in the second half of the 20th century came when William Randolph's granddaughter, Patty, was kidnapped by the Symbionese Liberation Army, and subsequently became a participant in some of its violent acts. Since then things have quietened down for the Hearsts, though they remain prominent in social and philanthropic circles, while five family members are on the thirteen-member board that controls Hearst Corporation. However, the latest flowering of talent appears to be on the catwalk with Patty's daughter, Lydia, and her niece, Amanda—part of current trend of heiresses becoming top-flight models.

FOR THE FAMILY WHICH OPERATED AMERICA'S FIRST MEDIA CONGLOMERATE, THE HEARSTS HAVEN'T ENJOYED THE MOST LAUDATORY DEPICTIONS ON THE SCREEN, ALTHOUGH THEY HAVE FEATURED IN A NUMBER OF HIGH-QUALITY (AND SOME LOW) MOVIES AND TV SHOWS.

ORSON WELLES AS CITZEN KANE, 1941.

HEARSTS ON SCREEN

★ **CITIZEN HEARST** The most famous depiction of William Randolph Hearst is in *Citizen Kane*, Orson Welles's film which many think is the greatest ever made. Welles had actually come to Hollywood to make a version of Joseph Conrad's novel *Heart of Darkness* (the inspiration for Coppola's *Apocalypse Now*) but ran over budget during pre-production. The idea for *Citizen Kane* came from the need to use the unusual gift of a no-strings attached half million dollar budget he'd received from RKO.

While Hearst began life as a liberal, he became a political reactionary in his later years. Hearst was anti-New Deal and pro-isolationist, while Welles was the opposite. He wrote the script in collaboration with Herman Mankiewicz, an ex-journalist who had been to the lavish parties Hearst and Marion Davies held at Hearst Castle. Hearst got wind of the unflattering portrait before the film was even finished and pulled out all stops to kill it. By threatening studios and cinemas not to publicize the movies and implying that the lives of Hollywood bosses would become fodder for his newspapers, Hearst succeeded in stopping the film's widespread release and RKO withdrew its distribution. Fortunately, the producer, George Schaefer, turned down an offer Hearst made through intermediaries to pay him to destroy the negative and prints.

★ **THE CAT'S MEOW** The fact that William Randolph Hearst was the owner of America's biggest rumor mill didn't save him from being the subject of rumor himself. In 1924, Thomas Harper Ince, a silent-film maker and pioneer of the western, died while on a weekend yacht trip with Hearst, Davies and other prominent Hollywood personalities. The official cause of death was heart attack but soon after, a rumor began to circulate that Hearst had shot Ince and used his connections to cover up the truth. Apparently Hearst was very possessive of his mistress, Marion Davies, who had already had an affair with Charlie Chaplin. In one version of the rumor, Hearst mistakenly thought Ince was Chaplin and shot him in a jealous rage. While the story was deemed possible but unlikely, in 2001 the movie *The Cat's Meow* was released, which related this particular version of events.

★ **DEADWOOD** George Hearst figures as a character in the historical fiction mini-series *Deadwood*. Set in the South Dakota town of the same name, the show features historical characters such as Wild Bill Hickock, who died in Deadwood, and his legendary girl-friend, the foul-mouthed, hard-drinking Calamity Jane. In the show, Hearst features as the hard-nosed mining entrepreneur who comes to town in 1877 and buys up all the small claims that together form the Homestake Mine—something he also did in real life.

HEARST CASTLE, SAN SIMEON, 1951.

★

> ❝ YOU MUST KEEP YOUR MIND ON THE OBJECTIVE, NOT ON THE OBSTACLE. ❞
> WILLIAM RANDOLPH HEARST

HOPELESSLY RICH

In 2004 George Randolph Hearst III sued over his depiction in the 2003 TV show *Hopelessly Rich*. In the show, actor George Pilgrim impersonated Hearst, portraying him as a lame-brained, womanizing, decadent man who used $1 bills to wipe his bum and also to bulk up the look of his crotch when he was on the prowl. Interestingly, Pilgrim has claims to being an illegitimate relative of the Hearst Family and thus entitled to a share of multi-billion dollar fortune. Hearst sued him and the movie company for $7.5 million.

WILLIAM RANDOLPH JR

William Randolph Hearst pictured with son William Randolph Jr, the second of five sons, who grew up to win the Pulitzer Prize for international reporting. During World War II he served as correspondent in Europe and Africa, and was reportedly told by his pop not to report on missions until he'd flown one.

WILLIAM RANDOLPH HEARST JR, WHILE WAR CORRESPONDENT IN ITALY, 1944.

LAST OF THE FRONTIER

GEORGE HEARST, FOUNDER OF THE HEARST FORTUNE, BELONGED TO THE LAST OF AMERICA'S FRONTIER GENERATIONS. UPON HEARING GOLD HAD BEEN DISCOVERED IN SUTTER'S MINE, CALIFORNIA, GEORGE LEFT HIS MISSOURI FARM AND MOTHER AND SISTER IN THE CARE OF A FAMILY FRIEND AND SET OFF ON A 1000-MILE HIKE TO CALIFORNIA. IN THE COURSE OF THE WALK HE CAUGHT CHOLERA AND MANY OF HIS COMRADES DIED. HEARST, HOWEVER, MANAGED TO GET HIMSELF OVER THE SIERRA NEVADA MOUNTAINS WHILE VERY SICK, WITH ONLY BRANDY FOR MEDICINE. HE WAS FAMOUS FOR HIS ABILITY TO READ THE CONTENTS OF ROCK AND IT SERVED HIM WELL. ALTHOUGH HIS INITIAL SUCCESSES WERE MODEST, HIS UNDERSTANDING OF ROCK LED HIM TO BUY BIG INTO CALIFORNIA'S COMSTOCK LODE AND LATER LUCRATIVE MINES IN NEVADA AND MONTANA. HOWEVER, HIS OLD-STYLE FRONTIER WAYS NEVER LEFT HIM. WHO THESE DAYS WOULD WIN A NEWSPAPER IN A GAME OF POKER?

STARLETS JEAN COLLERAN, PEGGY LLOYD AND BETTY JANE HESS MIMIC A STATUE AT THE HOME OF WILLIAM RANDOLPH HEARST, 1943.

{ hearst family tree }

GEORGE HEARST 1820–91 💰

While only semi-literate, this Missouri-born miner, with a taste for poker, bourbon and tobacco, had an immaculate sense of where to find riches beneath the ground. His father died when he was 14 and George looked after the family land for his mother and sister. However, when gold was discovered in Sutter's Mine in California and he heard of the money people were making there, he got a family friend to look after his farm, walked to California and became a successful prospector. He subsequently built upon his wealth by investing in mines and his holdings came to include stakes in the biggest mines in the United States, such as the Anaconda copper mine in Montana. When he returned to Missouri to nurse his dying mother, he met and married Phoebe Apperson who was less than half his age. He diversified out of mining, becoming a successful rancher and businessman, before turning to politics. When he died in 1891, he was a US senator for California (Democrat), but he had also been a genuine man of the American Frontier.

WILLIAM RANDOLPH HEARST 1863–1951 💋 💰

At 24 he became the proprietor of the *San Francisco Examiner*, which his father had been given as payment for a gambling debt. The aggressive reporting and unabashed sensationalism of his papers revolutionized journalism. At the peak of his media empire in the 1920s, he owned thirty-six newspapers and sixteen magazines, including *Cosmopolitan* and *Harper's Bazaar*. An exuberant spender, Hearst's over-extended empire suffered badly during the Great Depression. Although the papers recovered during the war, Hearst never returned to the same eminence. His Gatsbyesque ways inspired his unflattering portrait in Orson Welles's *Citizen Kane*, whose release he failed to prevent.

MILLICENT WILLSON 1882–1974

When she met her husband, she was a New York City vaudeville performer. They married in 1903 and had five sons, but the marriage foundered because of Hearst's affair with the actress Marion Davies, and Millicent moved back east where she established a new life as a New York socialite who, while technically still married, seldom impinged on her husband's Californian existence.

PHOEBE APPERSON 1842–1919

She proved an interesting spousal counterpoint to George, whom she married when she was only 19 and he was 42. Soon after their marriage, the Hearsts moved to San Francisco, where Phoebe gave birth to their only child, William Randolph Hearst in 1863. Her life's achievements began in earnest when she inherited her husband's money and started to give some of it away. She gave generously to the University of California, funding the construction of thirty buildings and six of its campuses. In 1897 she was appointed its first woman Regent and she remained a board member until her death. She was also instrumental in establishing the National Congress of Mothers, which later became the National Parent-Teacher Association. In addition to her philanthropy, Phoebe was also known for her adherence to the Baha'i Faith, which she converted to after a meeting with the son of its founder in Haifa (in modern-day Israel) in 1898.

MARION DAVIES 1897–1961 🍸

She started off as a Ziegfield Follies dancer before hitting the big screen, attracting the eye of William Randolph Hearst, whose promotion of his mistress made her one of the biggest stars of the silent screen. When Hearst's wife moved back east, Marion moved into Hearst Castle and the couple played host to the cream of Hollywood society. The inevitable decline in her career as she got older (mirrored by a decline in Hearst's finances) was hard for her, and she acquired an alcohol problem. When Hearst died, his family did not allow her to attend his funeral. She went into business, married at age 54, and was a noted philanthropist.

SON GEORGE RANDOLPH JR NEXT PAGE

GEORGE RANDOLPH HEARST   1904–72

The eldest son of William Randolph Hearst's five sons with Millicent, he rose to become Vice President of Hearst Corporation. On his father's death, he became one of the five family trustees of the thirteen-member trust established under his father's will to run the company. In the 1950s, he secured a position on the board for his son George Randolph Hearst Jr, who succeeded him as a trustee, and has since risen to become Chairman of the Hearst Corporation board.

DAVID WHITMIRE HEARST   1915–86

Like his twin, Randolph Apperson Hearst, he joined the family company and became a Hearst Corporation Vice President and director of the Hearst Corporation.

DAUGHTER MILLICENT NEXT PAGE

WILLIAM RANDOLPH HEARST JR   1908–93

William Randolph Hearst's second son. In 1956 he shared the Pulitzer Prize for international reporting for interviews with four Soviet politicians that predicted the ascendancy of Nikita Khrushchev to the top job. That same year he became Editor in Chief of Hearst newspapers. During the Cold War he was staunchly reactionary, and used his weekly column to support the McCarthy witch hunts. In 1991 he published *The Hearsts: Father and Son,* in which he acknowledged his failure to live up to his larger-than-life father.

SON WILLIAM RANDOLPH III NEXT PAGE

JOHN RANDOLPH HEARST   1910–58

He had the reputation of being the best businessman of the five brothers. However, it didn't mean his father did him any favors. According to Hearst's biographer, David Nasaw, when John lost his job at the *Los Angeles Examiner*, his father hired him at the *American Weekly*. John wasn't happy about his salary and asked for an extra allowance. William Randolph refused saying, "You are on your own—sink or swim in New York. If you don't like the job, don't take it. You are not an infant any longer, swinging on a pap bottle." He lost his chance to find out if he measured up to his hard task-master of a father when he died 7 years after John Randolph did, aged only 48, leaving behind four children.

WILL'S WILL

THE WILL OF WILLIAM RANDOLPH HEARST WAS AN INTERESTING ONE. TO BEGIN WITH IT SPECIFIED THAT ANYONE WHO CONTESTED THE WILL WOULD BE AUTOMATICALLY DISINHERITED. ITS SECOND INTRIGUING CODICIL WAS THAT THE STRUCTURE OF THE FAMILY TRUST HAD TO REMAIN IN PLACE UNTIL THE DEATH OF THE LAST GRANDCHILD, WHO WAS BORN BEFORE WILLIAM RANDOLPH DIED. AS SUCH, IT IS ESTIMATED THE TRUST WILL STAY IN PLACE UNTIL AROUND 2035.

RANDOLPH APPERSON HEARST   1915–2000

He and his twin brother, David Whitmire Hearst, were the youngest of the brothers. After graduating from Harvard (unlike his father) in 1938, he joined the Hearst Corporation, and worked for its newspapers in Atlanta and San Francisco, rising through the managerial ranks to become Chairman of Hearst Corporation from 1973–96. One of his life's defining moments came, however, when his 19-year-old daughter Patricia ("Patty") was kidnapped by the Symbionese Liberation Army (SLA) in 1974. He was married three times and had four other daughters; the second oldest, Virginia, inherited his seat on the family trust.

2 SONS: JOHN RANDOLPH JR & WILLIAM RANDOLPH II NEXT PAGE

2 DAUGHTERS: PATTY & ANNE NEXT PAGE

{ "THERE'S ONLY ONE THING THAT'S SURE ABOUT MY BOY," GEORGE WOULD SAY. "WHEN HE WANTS CAKE, HE WANTS CAKE, AND HE WANTS IT NOW. AND I NOTICE THAT, AFTER A WHILE, HE GETS THE CAKE."   FATHER GEORGE ON SON WILLIAM RANDOLPH }

SON OF GEORGE RANDOLPH

JOHN RANDOLPH HEARST JR 1934–

The eldest son of John Randolph Hearst, he represents his branch of the family on the board of the Hearst Trust and, like his grandfather, has been a noted art collector. Nicknamed "Bunky," in 2005 he hit New York's gossip pages when his wife of 15 years, Barbara, sued for divorce. Bunky was fairly infirm and needed nursing, but not so infirm that his nurse didn't provoke lascivious thoughts. Allegedly, Bunky asked one of his nurses "Why don't you give me a blowjob?" The nurse wrote it down for self-protection and Bunky was mortified to discover that patient confidentiality only applies when you are talking to a doctor.

2 SONS OF JOHN RANDOLPH

WILLIAM RANDOLPH HEARST II 1942–

The son of John Randolph Hearst, his preference for anonymity came to an end in 2000 when he sued the board of the Hearst Family Trust when they embarked on a takeover of a rival media company. William Randolph had set up the Trust because he didn't trust his family to run the business. He also put in a clause that anyone who disputed his will would be written out of it. His grandson, however, believed there was not enough disclosure and that the external appointees who had the numbers on the board were adopting the common senior management trait of serving themselves before the stakeholders: "The foxes have taken over the chicken coop and have relegated to a secondary position the interests of the owner-beneficiaries to whom they owe the highest fiduciary duty."

2 DAUGHTERS OF RANDOLPH APPERSON

GEORGE RANDOLPH HEARST JR 1927–

He has been Chairman of the Hearst Corporation board since 1996, succeeding his uncle Randolph Apperson Hearst, and has been a director of the company for over 40 years.

PATTY HEARST 1954–

Patty Hearst hit the headlines in 1974 when she was kidnapped by the Symbionese Liberation Army, an urban guerilla group. After Hearst paid a ransom of $6 million in food to the poor of San Francisco, Patty was still not released. Later that year, she was filmed taking part in an armed bank robbery with her kidnappers. She was arrested in 1975 and in her trial she claimed Stockholm syndrome—whereby the victim is brainwashed into identifying with their kidnappers—as a defense. However, she was found guilty and sent to jail. She spent over 2 years in prison before her sentence was commuted by President Carter. Following her release, she married her former bodyguard, had two daughters and appeared in small roles in films. She was pardoned by Bill Clinton in 2001.

> "I FINALLY FIGURED OUT WHAT MY CRIME WAS. I LIVED. BIG MISTAKE."
> PATTY HEARST

ANNE HEARST unknown–

The younger sister of Patty Hearst, she is also the mother of emerging supermodel Amanda Hearst. A known New York socialite, she has most recently hit the gossip pages for her romance with *Bright Lights Big City* author and renowned (albeit apparently reformed) party animal, Jay McInerney.

SON OF WILLIAM RANDOLPH

WILLIAM RANDOLPH HEARST III 1945–

The son of William Randolph Hearst Jr, he became President of the William Randolph Hearst Foundation in early 2003, and is also a director of Hearst Corporation, where he was editor and publisher of the *San Francisco Examiner*. He was shown in TV commercials having a conversation with his grandfather's portrait—his grandfather died before young William was able to talk.

MILLICENT HEARST BOUDJAKDJI 1939–2002

The daughter of David Hearst, she was prominent on the boards that administer the Hearst family's philanthropy, becoming President of the William Randolph Hearst Foundation in 2001. Her husband was an Algerian diplomat whom she met while she was covering the United Nations for the Hearst news service. She was renowned for her passion for philanthropy which, like her great grandmother, Phoebe's, concentrated on education and the young.

DAUGHTER OF DAVID WHITMIRE

GEORGE RANDOLPH HEARST III   1955–

He is the second child of George Randolph Hearst Jr and Mary Astrid Thompson and the great grandson of William Randolph Hearst. He is currently a vice president of the Hearst Corporation.

AMANDA HEARST
1984–

Once upon a time models used their beauty to snare a rich hubby. Nowadays, heiresses are combining their looks with the marketable allure of their family name to make even more money for themselves. The daughter of Patty Hearst's sister, Anne, Amanda is one of the billionaire babes, a new breed of models with pedigree, such as the Hilton sisters, Laura Bush, the daughter of Donald Trump (Ivanka) and Amanda's own cousin Lydia, and she has been described as America's next Paris Hilton. She works for the famous Ford Agency. She is also the face of the Lilly Pulitzer preppie fashion range, a line started by a former wife of one of Joseph Pulitzer's grandsons. Ironically, Joseph Pulitzer, who gave the Pulitzer prize its name, was a major inspiration on William Randolph Hearst's style of journalism.

LYDIA HEARST SHAW
1984–

Lydia is the modeling daughter of Patty Hearst. Together, she and her cousin Amanda have been written up as competition for the sister act of Paris and Nicky Hilton, although while coming from a tabloid-funded family, they are yet to show any talent for generating media controversy.

PATTY HEARST AND THE SLA

THE KIDNAP OF PATTY HEARST BY THE SYMBIONESE LIBERATION ARMY (SLA) ON FEBRUARY 4, 1974, WAS THE BEGINNING OF A SERIES OF EVENTS THAT WOULD KEEP THE HEARSTS ON THEIR OWN FRONT PAGES FOR SOME TIME. THE SLA WAS AN URBAN GUERILLA GROUP, WHO DREW THEIR NAME FROM THE BIOLOGICAL TERM "SYMBIOSIS," WHICH REFERS TO THE MUTUALLY BENEFICIAL CO-EXISTENCE OF DIFFERENT ORGANISMS WITHIN AN ECOSYSTEM. WHILE THEY ONLY EVER NUMBERED THIRTEEN PEOPLE, THEY KNEW HOW TO GRAB THE ATTENTION OF THE MEDIA AND THE NATION.

THE SLA FORMED IN MARCH 1973 WHEN DONALD DEFREEZE (AKA FIELD MARSHALL CINQUE) ESCAPED FROM PRISON. HIS GOAL WAS TO START A REVOLUTION OF THE UNDERPRIVILEGED BUT, LIKE MOST TERRORIST LEADERS, HE WAS PRIMARILY A SELF-AGGRANDIZING FASCIST SPIRIT. IN NOVEMBER 1973, THEY ASSASSINATED DR MARCUS FOSTER, THE POPULAR OAKLAND CALIFORNIA SUPERINTENDANT OF SCHOOLS. SOON AFTER, TWO OF THE SLA MEMBERS WERE ARRESTED AND JAILED FOR THE MURDER. THE SLA DECIDED TO KIDNAP A HIGH-PROFILE FIGURE WHO THEY COULD USE AS LEVERAGE FOR A PRISONER SWAP. IN FEBRUARY 1974, 19-YEAR-OLD PATTY HEARST BECAME THE ONE.

WHEN THE PRISONER SWAP REQUEST WAS DENIED, THE SLA ASKED THE HEARSTS TO DISTRIBUTE FREE FOOD TO THE POOR OF SAN FRANCISCO BY WAY OF PAYING A RANSOM. THE FIGURE RANGED UP TO $400 MILLION, BUT WHEN THE HEARSTS BEGAN TO DO THIS, THE HAND-OUTS WERE MARRED BY RIOTS.

AN INTERESTING TWIST IN THE PATTY HEARST STORY CAME ON APRIL 15, 1974 WHEN SHE WAS FILMED ON A SECURITY CAMERA WAVING A CARBINE RIFLE AND SHOUTING ORDERS AT CUSTOMERS DURING THE SLA'S ROBBERY OF THE HIBERNIA BANK IN SUNSET, SAN FRANCISCO. THE PUBLIC WERE SHOCKED TO FIND THAT AMERICA'S MOST PROMINENT KIDNAP VICTIM LOOKED LIKE SHE'D BECOME A TERRORIST HERSELF. SOON AFTER, THE FBI RECEIVED A TAPE WITH HEARST'S VOICE SPOUTING SLA PROPAGANDA AND CALLING HER DAD "PIG HEARST."

THE HEMINGWAYS

ONE OF THIS FAMILY'S SUCCESS STORIES, ACTRESS MARIEL HEMINGWAY IN 1983.

From a fairly conservative and religious background in Oak Park, Illinois, this family has become known for its love of the outdoor pursuits, its suicides, its alcoholism, but most of all, its writing. Although the original artistic impulse in the family was musical, many of its members have gone on to be writers, yet none of them has ever come close to matching the presence and influence of the Nobel Prize-winning Ernest, who remains one of the most important figures in 20th-century literature.

Overall, there have been moderate successes, more than a few failures and some rather eccentric activities undertaken by members of the Hemingway clan. There have been champion hunters and champions of the environment. Also, unlike most famous families, Hemingways have tended to live outside of America's big cities in places like Idaho, Montana and Florida.

Sadly one feature common in the family is a nasty strain of depression. Ernest committed suicide as did his father, two of his siblings and a granddaughter. Other Hemingways have approached their psychological problems with even more unconventional strategies, most notably the gender reassignment surgery of Ernest's son Gregory. This is a family with one genius and a whole lot of other talented people who have often been too consumed by the struggle to keep themselves going to fulfill their talents.

HOW THEY RATE

WEALTH ★★
The royalties must have been pretty decent over the years, but hardly enough to put them in the Fortune 500.

HEALTH ★
Some longevity but too much depression, alcoholism and suicide.

HAPPINESS ★
It's hard to imagine a family less talented in terms of achieving happiness

FAME ★★★
While Ernest ranks with the immortals, the striving after fame of other members of the family has sometimes resulted in tragedy

SEXINESS ★★★★
Yes, men who are men, and women who are beautiful, with enough intelligence and screwed-upness to hook you even more.

BLACK SHEEP FACTOR ★★★★
Hard to argue the distinction really works here, though the practice of rebelling against the values of parents, whether it be Oak Park politeness or acquired Spanish machismo, is well-entrenched.

ECCENTRICITY ★★★★★
Some serious problems here—gender reassignment surgery and micro-nation-founding not the least.

INFLUENCE ★★★
Ernest Hemingway remains a huge figure in literature and a man who achieved legendary status in his own lifetime. But no other members of the family have really stood up to the plate.

ERNEST HEMINGWAY ARTIFICIALLY POSED AT THE TYPEWRITER AT HIS HOME IN IDAHO. HEMINGWAY DISAPPROVED OF THIS PHOTOGRAPH, SAYING, "I DON'T WORK LIKE THIS."

> IF TWO PEOPLE LOVE EACH OTHER, THERE CAN BE NO HAPPY END TO IT.
> ERNEST HEMINGWAY

MEMOIR MANIA

One remarkable fact about the Hemingway family is the number of books that have been written about being a Hemingway. The following list of Hemingways who have written their memoirs is perhaps unrivaled by any celebrity family.

★ **VALERIE HEMINGWAY** *Running with the Bulls*
★ **GREGORY HEMINGWAY** *Papa: A Personal Memoir*
★ **JACK HEMINGWAY** *Misadventures of a Fly Fisherman: My Life with and without Papa*
★ **ERNEST HEMINGWAY** *A Moveable Feast*
★ **MARIEL HEMINGWAY** *Finding My Balance*
★ **MARY WELSH HEMINGWAY** *The Way it Was*
★ **MARCELLINE HEMINGWAY** *At the Hemingways: A Family Portrait*
★ **MADELAINE HEMINGWAY MILLER** *Ernie: Hemingway's Sister "Sunny" Remembers*
★ **LEICESTER HEMINGWAY** *My Brother Ernest Hemingway*
★ **HILARY HEMINGWAY** *Hunting with Hemingway, Hemingway in Cuba* (even though he died before she was born.)
★ **LORIAN HEMINGWAY** *Walk on Water*

MARGAUX HEMINGWAY AT STUDIO 54, 1977. THIS GRANDDAUGHTER OF ERNEST WAS NAMED FOR THE WINE, CHATEAU MARGAUX, THAT HER PARENTS WERE DRINKING THE NIGHT SHE WAS CONCEIVED.

COVER OF THE FIRST EDITION OF HEMINGWAY'S 1940 SPANISH CIVIL WAR NOVEL, *FOR WHOM THE BELL TOLLS.*

ERNEST HEMINGWAY

While some celebrity families are like a galaxy of stars, the Hemingway family is like a single star with a whole lot of lesser planets drawn into its gravitational field. That star is Ernest Hemingway, one of America's most revered writers, Nobel Prize Laureate and a character, who as an emblem of manhood, was always larger than life.

Beginning as a journalist, Hemingway is renowned for the beauty and economy of his writing and remains a powerful influence on writers today. His commitment to realism and powerful descriptive language meant he was also a pioneer for the kind of new journalism practiced by the likes of Tom Wolfe and Truman Capote

His subject matter reflected the macho interests which dominated his non-literary life: wars, several of which he took part in as a combatant, correspondent and ambulance driver; bullfighting; fishing; hunting; boxing and boozing. Yet an obsessive relationship with such aggressively masculine activities was not enough to conceal a propensity for depression which, combined with such a massive ego and the long-term effects of alcoholism, made him a difficult person to be around for much of the time. Nonetheless, by the time he committed suicide at 61, it was inarguably a case of a life richly, if not always happily, lived.

★

ERNEST HEMINGWAY'S YOUNGEST SON, GREG, HOLDING A CLUTCH OF DEAD DOVES AFTER A SHOOT AT THE HEMINGWAY HOME IN IDAHO, 1941.

'I never had it in my heart to be angry with Greg, except momentarily, for he suffered far more than anyone I have known. So much of life passed him by because he was wallowing in despair, soaring with destructive mania, or discontented with the essence of his being.
VALERIE HEMINGWAY,
RUNNING WITH THE BULLS '

GREG OR GLORIA

Of all the battles that members of the Hemingway family have fought with liquor, depression and articulating their own identities, none is as unusual as the bizarre life story of Ernest's youngest son, Gregory. By the time Greg arrived, Ernest, who already had two sons, was hoping for a daughter. Ironically, in the end he got one—posthumously, via gender reassignment surgery. However, Gregory showed a propensity to engage with his female aspect from an early age, particularly through cross-dressing, a practice which was a flashpoint in the father–son relationship.

As a boy, Greg inherited many of the rugged outdoor masculine talents that his father prided. Aged only 11, Greg tied equal first from 140 entrants in the Cuban pigeon shooting championships, much to his father's delight. He was also learning how to drink—something his father also helped out with, advising his 12-year-old son to drink a bloody mary as a way of dealing with a hangover.

As he got, older, however, Gregory's interest in tranvestism continued to develop. It freaked his father out and Ernest rang up his ex-wife Pauline to abuse her about it. Unfortunately Pauline had an undiagnosed tumor in her adrenal gland. The stress of Ernest's phone call caused a deadly surge of adrenaline and within hours she was dead from shock. Rather than accept the blame himself, Ernest blamed Gregory, which upset Greg so much that he never saw his father again. Greg became depressed and abandoned his medical studies and went to Africa, where he got drunk and shot lots of elephants.

When he returned from Africa he continued his studies, through which he learned about the medical condition responsible for his mother's death. Having discovered this he sent his father a bitter letter shifting the blame back onto him. When Hemingway shot himself the next year, Gregory again felt responsible.

After his father's death, Greg married Ernest's secretary, Valerie, with whom he had three children, and he also worked successfully as a doctor, until his marriage disintegrated in the 1980s and his license to practice medicine was suspended. From this point Greg's life took a series of desperate turns, marked by money problems and mania. This exacerbated his sexual identity crisis and, in 1995 at the age of 64, after already having a single breast implant done, he went for gender reassignment surgery and renamed himself Gloria. Oddly enough, he continued to co-habit with his fourth wife and drink (under the name Greg and in male clothing) at The Taurus Ale House, their neighborhood bar.

Greg's demise came in October 2001, when he was arrested for indecent exposure after police found him naked in a park, carrying a dress and pair of high heels in his hands. He was remanded in the Miami-Dade women's jail on the basis of his genitalia, where he died a few days later as a result of high blood pressure and heart failure, aged 69.

Leicester Hemingway
AND THE NEW ATLANTIS

On July 4, 1964, Ernest Hemingway's brother Leicester was the founder of New Atlantis, a micro-republic near Bluefields, 6 miles off the coast of Jamaica. Measuring 8 x 30 feet, and 50 feet deep, it was a bamboo raft, anchored by a railroad axle and an old Ford engine block. His reason for building it was to provide a head-quarters for the International Marine Research Society—an organization he had also founded—which was designed to raise funds for and further marine research, and thereby help protect Jamaica's fishing. The six original inhabitants of New Atlantis included Leicester, his wife Doris, their daughters Anne and Hilary (7 and 3 years old at the time), Washington international public relations specialist Edward K. Moss and his assistant Julia Cellini. Leicester was elected the first President in 1965. He funded this nation-building effort with the proceeds from his biography, *My Brother, Ernest Hemingway*. Unfortunately, Leicester's plans to extend the nation never happened. Living up to the unfortunate history of the mythical name, Atlantis, it was largely sunk by a storm before Mexican fisherman came and pilfered its remaining reusable materials, just a couple of years after its foundation.

HEMINGWAY AND HIS WIFE, JOURNALIST AND WAR CORRESPONDENT MARTHA GELLHORN, STANDING ON THE DECK OF A BOAT, C.1941.

> *ALL POLITICIANS ARE BORES AND LIARS AND FAKES. I TALK TO PEOPLE ...*
> MARTHA GELLHORN

MARTHA GELLHORN

MARTHA WAS THE ONLY ONE OF ERNEST HEMINGWAY'S FOUR WIVES TO LEAVE HIM, AND FOR MUCH OF THEIR SHORT MARRIAGE THEY FOUGHT LIKE CAT AND DOG. WHILE ERNEST WAS ATTRACTED TO INTELLIGENT AND INDEPENDENT WOMEN, HE COULDN'T LIVE WITH ONE, AND MARTHA WASN'T ABOUT TO GIVE UP HER OWN INTERESTS FOR ANYONE, SINCE SHE WAS A FEMINIST BEFORE HER TIME.

MARTHA WAS A WRITER OF BOTH FICTION AND JOURNALISM. WHILE SHE DIDN'T OUTDO HER FAMOUS HUSBAND IN THE FORMER, SHE DID IN THE LATTER, BEGINNING WITH THE SPANISH CIVIL WAR AND BECOMING ONE OF THE 20TH CENTURY'S GREAT WAR CORRESPONDENTS. IT WASN'T A FASHIONABLE THING TO DO, AND ERNEST AT ONE STAGE TRIED TO STOP HER BY TAKING HER CORRESPONDENT'S CREDENTIALS DURING WORLD WAR II. WHILE THE MARRIAGE DIDN'T LAST THE WAR, MARTHA'S CAREER DID. SHE REPORTED ON A NUMBER OF WARS INCLUDING THE SIX-DAY WAR IN THE MIDDLE EAST AND VIETNAM, WHERE HER ARTICLES WERE DEEMED TOO ANTI-AMERICAN TO BE PUBLISHED.

SHE REPORTED ON WARS FROM THE PERSPECTIVE OF THE PEOPLE, RATHER THAN FROM THAT OF THE POWERS WHO PERPETUATED THEM, AND SHE CONTINUED TO DO SO RIGHT UP TO THE WARS IN NICARAGUA AND PANAMA IN THE 1980S. GELLHORN UNDERTOOK HER LAST TRIP WHEN SHE WAS 85 TO REPORT ON THE FATE OF CHILDREN LIVING IN THE SLUMS OF BRAZIL.

> ❝ IT'S VERY DIFFICULT WHEN PEOPLE DON'T WANT YOU ANYMORE. SHE WAS JUST A GENTLE LOVING SOUL WHO GOT LOST IN FAME AND FORTUNE. ❞
>
> CAREN ELIN
> (FRIEND OF MARGAUX ON HER DEATH)

75 CENTS — JUNE 16, 1975

TIME

The New Beauties

Margaux Hemingway

How New York Went Broke

MARGAUX HEMINGWAY ON THE COVER OF THE JUNE 1975 ISSUE OF *TIME* MAGAZINE.

"GRAVELY WOUNDED BY NUMEROUS PIECES OF SHRAPNEL FROM AN ENEMY SHELL, WITH AN ADMIRABLE SPIRIT OF BROTHERHOOD, BEFORE TAKING CARE OF HIMSELF, HE RENDERED GENEROUS ASSISTANCE TO THE ITALIAN SOLDIERS MORE SERIOUSLY WOUNDED BY THE SAME EXPLOSION AND DID NOT ALLOW HIMSELF TO BE CARRIED ELSEWHERE UNTIL AFTER THEY HAD BEEN EVACUATED."
Citation on Ernest Hemingway's Italian Silver Medal for Valor, awarded when he was wounded as an ambulance driver in World War I.

ERNEST HEMINGWAY TIMELINE

1899 Born July 21 in Oak Park, Illinois.

1917 Graduates from school and works for the *Kansas City Star*.

1918 Becomes a World War I ambulance driver for the American Red Cross and is wounded on the Italian front.

1919 Begins filing stories for the *Toronto Star*.

1921 Marries Hadley Richardson.

1922 Moves to Paris with letters of introduction from Sherwood Anderson. Covers the Greco-Turkish War for the *Toronto Star*.

1923 *Three Stories and Ten Poems* published. Birth of son John.

1924 *In Our Time*, a collection of vignettes, published.

1925 *In Our Time* republished with fourteen short stories added to the earlier vignettes.

1926 *The Torrents of Spring* and *The Sun Also Rises* published.

1927 Publishes short story collection, *Men Without Women*. Marries Pauline Pfieffer after divorcing Hadley Richardson.

1928 Moves to Key West, Florida. His father commits suicide. Birth of son Patrick.

1929 *A Farewell to Arms* published.

1931 Birth of son Gregory.

1932 *Death in the Afternoon* published.

1933 Short story collection, *Winner Take Nothing*, published.

1935 *Green Hills of Africa* published.

1937 Travels as war correspondent to the Spanish Civil War with girlfriend Martha Gellhorn. *To Have and Have Not* published.

1938 *The Fifth Column* and *The First Forty-nine Stories* published.

1940 Divorces Pauline, marries Martha. Buys the home Finca Vigia in Cuba. *For Whom the Bell Tolls* published.

1944 Begins affair with Mary Welsh in London. Travels with US troops in France and Germany as World War II correspondent.

1945 Martha Gellhorn divorces him.

1946 Marries Mary Welsh.

1950 *Across the River and into the Trees* published.

1951 Mother (who he refers to as "the bitch") dies.

1952 *The Old Man and the Sea* published.

1953 Injured in two separate plane crashes in Africa.

1954 Receives Nobel Prize for Literature.

1960 Moves to Ketchum, Idaho. Hospitalized for uncontrolled high blood pressure, liver disease, diabetes and depression. The treatment includes shock therapy.

1961 Blows his brains out with a shotgun at home in Idaho.

ERNEST HEMINGWAY, ADMIRING HIS REFLECTED IMAGE, WHILE DRESSED FOR A BOXING MATCH, 1944.

KEY: CHILD ●●●●●➤ ADOPTED CHILD ●●●●●➤ MARRIED ▬▬▬ DIVORCED ▬ ▬ ▬ DE FACTO ▬·▬·▬ SPLIT UP ▬ ▬ ▬ ▬

{ hemingway family tree }

ANSON HEMINGWAY 1844–1926

Anson moved with his parents to Illinois from Connecticut. With two of his brothers he fought for the Union in the Civil War. Of the three brothers, only he survived. After the War he was General Secretary of the local YMCA, before starting a local real estate business which prospered. A Congregationalist, he was an evangelical fire-and-brimstone kind of Christian, and some of his siblings became missionaries.

> *Surely you have other words in your vocabulary besides "damn" and "bitch."*
> GRACE HEMINGWAY
> ON ERNEST'S FIRST NOVEL, **THE SON ALSO RISES**

ADELAIDE EDMONDS 1841–1923

She was something of a Bible basher but, like her husband, she was interested in the sciences, particularly botany and astronomy, which she had studied at college. This enthusiasm for the natural world was conveyed to her descendants.

CLARENCE HEMINGWAY 1871–1928 ☠

The athletic eldest son of Anson and Adelaide, he studied medicine in Chicago and became a general practitioner with a reputation for obstetrics. He was a sharp-tempered, disciplinarian father, whose own depression and harsh, Protestant world view led him to commit suicide with his father's revolver before his 60th birthday. His love of nature and hunting also rubbed off on his son.

ERNEST HALL 1840–1905

After being shot in the thigh during the Civil War, he became well-off through his partnership in a Chicago wholesale cutlery firm. As an Episcopalian, his religion was less constrictive than that of Hemingway's paternal grandparents. While a devout Christian, he nonetheless smoked a pipe. He was also a music lover and a descendant of Edward Miller, a leading 18th-century English musicologist.

GRACE HALL 1872–1951

A singer and music teacher, she once had a promising opera career. While she and Ernest apparently didn't get on, it's from her that Ernest received his rebellious nature. Even though she was married with children, she was something of a proto-feminist, continuing to give musical performances in Chicago and other parts of America, while being known for her disinterest in doing the domestic chores. It has even been rumored she engaged in a lesbian affair.

CAROLINE HANCOCK 1843–95

She consolidated the artistic leanings of her husband. As a singer she had been in demand in Chicago, while her paintings were on the walls of the family home. Ernest Hemingway spent the first 6 years of his life living here and no doubt absorbed his grandparents' love of the arts.

ERNEST AND FIDEL
ERNEST HEMINGWAY CHATS TO CUBAN PREMIER, FIDEL CASTRO, DURING LATE 1959. HOWEVER, IN 1960 HEMINGWAY WAS FORCED OUT OF HIS HOME IN CUBA DUE TO THE ESCALATING TENSIONS SURROUNDING THE CASTRO REGIME, AND HE MOVED TO IDAHO, USA.

ERNEST HEMINGWAY 1899–1961

The undoubted star of the family, this Nobel Prize winner is one of the most celebrated voices in American literature. Ernest's image combined the literary life with that of a man of action. He participated as a journalist and ambulance driver in a number of wars and was a huge fan of fishing and hunting. However, his life was marred by the family tendency toward depression. Self-medication with alcohol proved ultimately counter-productive and, faced with writer's block, he killed himself with a shotgun.

ERNEST'S WIVES & CHILDREN NEXT PAGE

MARCELLINE HEMINGWAY 1898–1963

The eldest of the Hemingway children, Marcelline was quite close to Ernest, even after she married and moved to Grosse Point, Michigan.

MADELAINE HEMINGWAY 1904–95

Nicknamed "Sunny," she seemed to escape the chemical imbalances afflicting many of her family, and lived to the ripe old age of 90. Like many of her relatives she also published a memoir of her life with Ernest who, she claimed was not only her big brother, but also her best friend.

URSULA HEMINGWAY 1902–66

Ernest's favorite sibling, Ursula, married her college contemporary, Jasper Jepson, and spent several years living as an artist in Honolulu, Hawaii. After surviving three cancer operations, and suffering from depression, Ursula committed suicide by drug overdose on October 30, 1966.

CAROL HEMINGWAY 1911–2002

Carol and Ernest had an argument in 1933 over her choice of husband and, after a flurry of nasty letters, they never talked to each other again. She married the man, stayed married to him, had three children, worked as a school teacher and lived to a ripe old age.

'Daddy was so incensed that a son of his would so far forget his Christian training that he could use the subject matter and vulgar expressions this book contained that he wrapped and returned all six copies to the Three Mountains Press in Paris. He wrote to Ernest and told him that no gentleman spoke of venereal disease outside a doctor's office.
MARCELLINE HEMINGWAY
AT THE HEMINGWAYS: A PERSONAL PORTRAIT'

LEICESTER HEMINGWAY 1915–1982

Like Ernest, Leicester was a writer, world traveler, and avid outdoorsman. He worked mainly as a journalist, specializing in articles on fishing and the outdoors for men's magazines, but was also a boat builder. In 1964, he became the founder of New Atlantis, a very small nation off the coast of Jamaica. In 1982, faced with the loss of his legs from diabetes, Leicester shot himself in the head with a revolver.

HILARY HEMINGWAY 1961–

Another relative who has contributed to the enormous Hemingway industry with books such as *Hemingway in Cuba*—although Ernest died just before she was born. She has also published a thriller novel about a UFO cover-up.

ERNEST'S 1ST WIFE

ELIZABETH HADLEY RICHARDSON 1891–1979

When she and Ernest married in 1920, she was 28 years old, 8 years older than him. For the early years of their marriage they were poor, existing on fees from his occasional journalism but primarily on her trust fund. They moved to Paris, where they split up after she discovered his affair with next wife-to-be, Pauline. Feeling guilty, he gifted the royalties for *The Sun Also Rises* to her and their son, Jack, who was 5 years old when they divorced.

ERNEST'S 2ND WIFE

PAULINE PFEIFFER 1895–1951

From a wealthy family, she was a *Vogue* journalist living in Paris when she befriended the Hemingways and began an affair with Ernest. The setting, however, for their own marriage was largely Key West, Florida, where her uncle bought them a home. They had two sons, Patrick and Greg.

ERNEST'S 3RD WIFE

MARTHA GELLHORN 1908–98

Another journalist, she and Ernest began their passionate affair in 1936, before running away to the Spanish Civil War together. The allure of her independent nature wore off for Ernest when he found himself at home in Cuba while she was in England covering World War II. She urged him to come to England, where they fought and he then moved on to his next and final wife, Mary Welsh. Martha was the only wife to leave him, and she went on to become one of the 20th century's greatest war correspondents.

JACK HEMINGWAY 1923–2000

He was born into the bohemian cafes of Paris, where his godparents were Alice B. Toklas and Gertrude Stein, yet he soon acquired his father's love for all things outdoors. In World War II he was parachuted behind German lines and took his fly-fishing kit with him, catching trout before being shot and interned as a POW. After the war, he lived in Idaho, becoming a champion fisherman and hunter who was also heavily involved in environmental issues. He also wrote a memoir of his father, *Misadventures of a Fly Fisherman: My Life with and without Papa*.

BYRA WHITTLESEY 1927–

A good-looking Idaho war widow, known to her friends as "Puck" yet, according to daughter Mariel's memoir *Finding My Balance*, she was a gloomy spirited woman, who didn't get on with her husband—although they stayed married until her death in 1986.

THE HEMINGWAY BOYS
ERNEST HEMINGWAY'S THREE SONS AT THEIR HOME IN IDAHO, USA. FROM LEFT TO RIGHT, JACK "JOHN," PATRICK "MOUSE," AND GREGORY "GIGI."

"By a very conservative count, more than 75 per cent of my family has been alcoholic. This alcoholism, passed along with a passion to write, and the will to survive that passion, is as clearly as much a heritage to me as are my dark eyes. LORIAN HEMINGWAY"

ERNEST'S 4TH WIFE

MARY WELSH 1908–86

She was a journalist whose affair with Ernest began during World War II. They married in Cuba in 1946, her third marriage and his fourth. For most of it, Ernest was afflicted by booze and depression, but were together until his death.

PATRICK HEMINGWAY   1928–

He grew up in Key West, Florida, but caught his father's big game bug. For most of his adult life, he lived in Africa, running a safari company in the savanna. He also accepted politically dangerous positions as honorary game warden for Kenya, Uganda and Tanzania. He retired to Montana where he became the controversial editor of *True at First Light*, his father's fictional memoir of his second African safari, published posthumously in 1999.

JOAN HEMINGWAY   1950–

Nicknamed Muffet, she's lived in the shadows of her younger sisters. She had a bad LSD trip when she was 16 which triggered manic depression, which she has battled throughout her life in conjunction with alcoholism. Her co-authored novel, *Rosebud*, about Palestinian terrorists hijacking a yacht crewed by millionaires' daughters, was made into an Otto Preminger film starring Peter O'Toole and Richard Attenborough. She lives in Idaho near her parents and paints.

GREGORY HEMINGWAY
1931–2001

A champion shooter, doctor and author, he rebelled against his macho dad by flirting with transvestism. Although he married four times and had eight children, he eventually had gender-reassignment surgery and changed his name to Gloria. He also inherited a severe strain of the family's manic depression. He died in a police cell the morning after being arrested drunk and naked on a Florida street with a dress and a pair of high heels in his hand. His 1976 book about his father, *Papa: A Personal Memoir*, is nonetheless considered one of the best portraits of the man.

MARGAUX HEMINGWAY
1955–96

Six feet tall, blonde and gorgeous, Margaux Hemingway burst onto the New York scene aged 19. Her career peaked at age 21 when she got paid $1 million to become Faberge's Fabulous Babe. Her first film, *Lipstick*, was panned—except for her younger sister's role. A year later she was in rehab for alcohol, while her sister Mariel's career began to take off. Margaux struggled with the family double whammy of alcoholism and depression and never really recovered, despite constant attempts to revive her career, such as 1990s *Playboy* centerfold shots. In 1996 she was found dead in her Santa Monica studio apartment. The coroner ruled suicide.

VALERIE DANBY-SMITH   1940–

Sixty-year-old Ernest became infatuated with this young freelance journalist's youth and persuaded her to come to Cuba with him—platonically—as his secretary. Later, he sent her away so he could commit suicide. But she wasn't quite finished with the Hemingway family yet. After Ernest's death, she worked for his wife, Mary Welsh, and the Hemingway literary estate. Then, following an affair with the married Irish playwright and booze artist Brendan Behan, which gifted her a child. She later married Gregory, Papa Hemingway's youngest son. The couple eventually divorced but not before having several children. The memoir of her Hemingway times is called *Running with the Bulls*.

MARIEL HEMINGWAY   1961–

She first came to attention when her sister scored her a role in *Lipstick*. However, she later regretted the move as Margaux's career stagnated while Mariel's took off. She was nominated for an Oscar for her role in Woody Allen's *Manhattan*. But while acting has kept her relatively busy since, she's never quite hit the same peak. For a Hemingway her life seems fairly balanced: she lives in Idaho with her husband and two children and runs a yoga studio.

> THE "HEMINGWAY CURSE" WAS SUCH A HUGE, AWFUL THING FOR ME TO HAVE TO DEAL WITH … THE REALITY IS, BECAUSE THERE ARE GENETIC TENDENCIES TOWARD MENTAL ILLNESS, YOU NEED TO BE AWARE OF THEM.
> MARIEL HEMINGWAY

LORIAN HEMINGWAY   1952–

The daughter of Greg/Gloria Hemingway, she has battled the family demons of alcoholism and depression as well as writing a number of books and finding solace in fly fishing.

CELEBRITY FAMILY TREES 126

FROM INAUSPICIOUS BEGINNINGS IN A NEW MEXICO FRONTIER TOWN, CONRAD HILTON EMERGED TO CREATE THE FIRST INTERNATIONAL HOTEL CHAIN. AS THE NUMBER OF PEOPLE SLEEPING IN HILTON ROOMS GREW, SO DID THE CELEBRITY OF THE OWNERS, AS THEY BECAME ONE OF AMERICA'S RICHEST FAMILIES IN AN INDUSTRY WHICH HAS ALWAYS HAD A DEGREE OF NATURAL GLAMOUR.

THE HILTONS

CONRAD HILTON SENIOR PRACTICING HIS GOLF SWING, 1949.

The Hilton family began to mingle with the rich and famous, while its men developed a taste for Hollywood actresses. Conrad and his wastrel son, Conrad Jr, each married one of the most famous and beautiful women of their day, while third generation Ricky Hilton married a less famous actress. Unlike his relatives, however, Ricky's marriage has been a success. It should also be noted that against the celebrity lifestyle there is a powerful sense of family pervading the Hiltons, best exemplified by the staunchly conservative Barron Hilton, who took over the family business upon the retirement of his dad. While he made Hilton Corporation the biggest gambling company in America, he married a cheerleader and they had eight children together. The marriage lasted until she died. Curiously, the current famous Hilton family—despite the amateur pornographic antics of daughter Paris, and being a two-reality-TV-show family—has maintained some of these values, while simultaneously earning millions from real estate and shameless self-promotion.

HOW THEY RATE

WEALTH ★ ★ ★ ★ ★
For much of the 20th century, the Hiltons were one of the richest families in America. Even today Barron Hilton is a billionaire. However, with eight children and the father's mutterings about leaving all his loot to charity—something over which he fought his own father—the fortune is likely to dissipate; although Ricky Hilton and his daughters, Paris and Nicky, are doing a good job of accumulating fortunes of their own.

HEALTH ★ ★ ★
Slightly better than average and surprisingly few substance abuse problems, with the exception of Conrad Jr.

HAPPINESS ★ ★ ★ ★
Parts of this family seem to have pulled off the difficult trick of being filthy rich and fairly happy at the same time.

FAME ★ ★ ★ ★
Paris, Paris, Paris ... shrewdly milking her 15 minutes for all it's worth. But what's going to happen when the limelight's turned off?

SEXINESS ★ ★ ★ ★
Only if you like them blonde, rich, thin and raunchy—which a lot of people evidently do.

BLACK SHEEP FACTOR ★ ★ ★
Conrad Jr gambled, womanized and drank his way to an early grave. Paris has potential, but her family love her too much.

ECCENTRICITY ★ ★
Not really—a little too all-American, even when they're being bad.

INFLUENCE ★ ★ ★
The Hilton brand is one that came to embody life in the jetsetting age. The influence of Paris Hilton is powerfully apparent in the hairstyle and fashion choices of girls today. Her image is an alluring blend of ditzy femininity and raunch culture, but whether it has staying power is yet to be discovered.

THE HILTON SISTERS

THE ICONIC HILTON SISTERS ARE THE DAUGHTERS OF KATHY AND RICKY HILTON. FOR HER 21ST BIRTHDAY, PARIS (ON THE RIGHT) THREW FIVE BIRTHDAY PARTIES FOR HERSELF: IN NEW YORK, LAS VEGAS, LONDON, HOLLYWOOD AND TOKYO. NICKY (SHORT FOR NICHOLAI), WAS THE FACE OF ANTZ PANTZ UNDERWEAR IN 2005, ALONG WITH ROD STEWART'S DAUGHTER, KIMBERLEY.

LIZ'S HUSBANDS

CONRAD HILTON JR Hotel heir **(1950–51)** (divorced)

MICHAEL WILDING Actor **(1952–57)** (divorced)

MIKE TODD Producer **(1957–58)** (widowed)

EDDIE FISHER Singer **(1959–64)** (divorced)

RICHARD BURTON Actor **(1964–74)** (divorced)

RICHARD BURTON (2nd marriage) **(1975–76)** (divorced)

SENATOR JOHN WARNER **(1976–82)** (divorced)

LARRY FORTENSKY Construction worker **(1991–96)** (divorced)

> 'THE PROBLEM WITH PEOPLE WHO HAVE NO VICES IS THAT GENERALLY YOU CAN BE PRETTY SURE THEY'RE GOING TO HAVE SOME PRETTY ANNOYING VIRTUES.'
> **ELIZABETH TAYLOR**

LIZ TAYLOR FEEDING NICKY HILTON CAKE ON THEIR WEDDING DAY, 1950.

LIZ AND NICKY

If Zsa Zsa was a bona fide celebrity, Liz Taylor was a bona fide star, who melted the heart of many a cinema-going man. However, her list of husbands is almost as daunting as Zsa Zsa's, while her fortune is considerably greater (estimated at over $750 million). Still her marriage to Conrad "Nicky" Hilton was even less successful than Zsa Zsa's marriage to his dad.

When Liz and Nicky met at LA's Mocambo nightclub in October 1949, Nicky was instantly smitten. Liz had already broken off two engagements to army football hero Glenn Davis and millionaire Bill Pawley. Although she still went clubbing with a chaperone, the child star was itching for a taste of adult life. Hilton, a renowned playboy and gambler, had the requisite bad boy charm.

During their courtship, Taylor graduated from high school and made *Father of the Bride*. Three thousand of her fans were outside the Church of the Good Shepherd in Beverly Hills when they married in May 1950, while 600 guests, including columnists, millionaires and stars, had been invited. MGM picked up the wedding tab, including $3500 for a splendidly sexy gown, knowing it was great PR for *Father of the Bride*, which was released at the same time.

Their 3-month European honeymoon was less idyllic. Nicky hated playing second fiddle and being called "Mr Taylor," and indulged in all-night gambling and drinking to assuage the pain, while his 18-year-old wife—considered by some the most beautiful woman in the world—languished and consoled herself with shopping binges. She came home a haggard-looking chain-smoker and that December moved out of their Pacific Palisades house.

A SIMPLE LIFE

In this bizarre reality TV show, which first screened in 2003, Paris Hilton and her friend Nicole Richie—daughter of Lionel—went out into the "real world." Deprived of their credit cards, they traveled round America amusing their audience while they tried to live like normal people. There were three series on Fox. In the first, they worked on a farm, while the second involved a road trip where they ventured across America in a trailer, working odd jobs to support themselves on the way. The third series saw them working as interns in a variety of jobs from funeral parlor to bakery. After this series, Nicole and Paris had a falling out—the likely cause being a private screening Nicole held of her co-star's sex video. Fox dropped the show, but a fourth series—a kind of variation on the theme of *Wife Swap*—has been made by cable channel E! and features the two girls running a variety of households, albeit separately.

PARIS HILTON AND NICOLE RICHIE

'I AM A MARVELOUS HOUSEKEEPER. EVERY TIME I LEAVE A MAN I KEEP HIS HOUSE.'
ZSA ZSA GABOR

ZSA ZSA GABOR

By evolving from a beauty pageant queen and second-rate actress into a pure celebrity in her own right, Zsa Zsa created a realm of possibility her step-granddaughter Paris has seized upon with vigor. While Zsa Zsa's acting career peaked with a supporting role in Orson Welles's *A Touch of Evil*, and an amusing self-parody in 1991's *The Naked Gun 2: The Smell of Fear*—where Zsa Zsa reprised an incident where she was arrested for slapping a policeman—she has been a ground-breaking celebrity, the first in a long line of people who are famous for being famous. To be fair, it should be added that she did this with considerably more verve than most. She has proven herself one of the wittiest Hollywood gold-diggers who ever lived and her second marriage to Conrad Hilton was a masterstroke.

HILTON HOTEL CHRONOLOGY

1907 Conrad Hilton's father, Gus, was a merchant in San Antonio, New Mexico. When his business was hit by the economic downturn of 1907, young Conrad suggested to his parents that they lease out rooms in their large adobe house to travelers. Every night Conrad would go to the train station looking for guests to pay $1 a night for a clean room and home-cooked meals.

1919 With a $5000 inheritance, Conrad Hilton headed to Texas to start a career in banking. When he was in the Mobley Hotel in Cisco he noticed oil workers scrambling for a room. The hotel owner, overwhelmed by the constant demand, sold Conrad the hotel. It was pretty seedy to begin with but Hilton fixed it up to become the first in the Hilton business hotel chain.

1930s By this time Hilton had accumulated eight hotels, but he lost three of them and acquired a debt of $500,000 because of the Great Depression.

1946 Hilton Hotels first listed on the New York Stock Exchange. At the time the company operated fourteen hotels across the United States.

1949 After the downturn of the 1930s, Hilton (right) clawed his way back to prosperity. In 1949, he bought one of the world's great hotels, New York's Waldorf Astoria. That same year, he opened the Caribe Hilton in Puerto Rico, making Hilton Hotels the first international hotel chain.

ZSA ZSA'S HUSBANDS

BURHAN BELGE Press director **(1937–41)**

CONRAD HILTON Hilton Hotel magnate **(1942–46)**

GEORGE SANDERS Actor **(1949–54)**

HERBERT HUTNER Financial consultant **(1964–66)**

JOSHUA S. COSDEN, JR Oil heir and businessman **(1966–67)**

JACK RYAN Inventor associated with Barbie doll **(1975–76)**

MICHAEL O'HARA Lawyer **(1977–82)**

FELIPE DE ALBA The marriage on a ship was bigamous, because she was still married to Michael O'Hara, and it was annulled.

FREDERICK PRINZ VON ANHALT Gold-digger **(1986–)**

"I WANT TO BE A HILTON"

In 2005, Paris's mom, Kathy, starred as the host of *I Want to Be a Hilton*, an *Apprentice*-clone reality television show where the contestants competed for a prize package that included a $200,000 trust fund, a new apartment, a new wardrobe and the opportunity to live the life of high society for a year. The show was originally entitled *The Good Life*, to tie it in to Paris's reality show *The Simple Life*. The contestants resided at a fancy New York hotel and were divided into two teams: "Park" and "Madison." In each episode, the contestants were required to perform certain tasks, ranging from dog grooming, participating in a fashion show and organizing a charity event, while learning etiquette and manners. Kathy Hilton judged the contestants on their success in general etiquette. Losing contestants were despatched at the end of each episode with Hilton telling them: "You're not on the list." The winner of the show ended up with the bizarre prize of living with the Hiltons for a few weeks at their Long Island home.

1954	Hilton bought the entire Statler Hotel chain. At the time, this $111 million deal was the highest real estate transaction in history.
1964	Hilton enjoyed the post-war prosperity and the advent of regular plane travel, expanding the chain to forty American and forty international hotels. However, in 1964, the international hotels were sold to British interests, which became Hilton Group, but it was not run by the Hilton family.
1966	Conrad Hilton retired from running the business and his son Barron took over. Under the stewardship of Barron, the company continued to expand and diversify, most notably into gambling in Las Vegas.
1970	Hilton became the first company listed on the New York Stock Exchange to enter the domestic gaming industry, with the purchase of the Flamingo Hilton–Las Vegas and the Las Vegas Hilton.
1979	Conrad Hilton died. His will left almost all of his fortune to the Catholic Church.
1988	Barron Hilton won a lawsuit against his father's estate on the basis of his role in building the family business.
1996	Stephen F. Bollenbach became President and Chief Executive Officer, marking the end of the Hilton family's running of the company, although Barron remained Chairman. With the acquisition of Bally Entertainment Corporation, Hilton became the world's largest casino gaming company.
2005	The international and American arms of the Hilton chain were reunited when Hilton Hotels Corporation bought back its international assets after 40 years. Today Hilton Hotel Corporation owns, manages and franchises over 500 hotels with 147,667 rooms worldwide.

THE PARIS VIDEO

WHILE SHE HAS APPEARED IN A NUMBER OF MOVIES AND HOSTED HER OWN REALITY TV SHOW, IT WAS THE RELEASE OF PARIS'S AMATEUR PORN VIDEO ON THE INTERNET THAT REALLY PROPELLED HER INTO THE UPPER ECHELONS OF CELEBRITY. HER CO-STAR WAS RICK SALOMON, HOLLYWOOD PLAYBOY, GAMBLER AND ESTRANGED HUSBAND OF ACTRESS SHANNON DOHERTY. WHEN THE FOOTAGE WAS LEAKED, THE HILTON FAMILY PUT OUT A STATEMENT: "THE HILTON FAMILY IS GREATLY SADDENED AT HOW LOW HUMAN BEINGS WILL STOOP TO EXPLOIT THEIR DAUGHTER, PARIS, WHO IS SWEET-NATURED, FOR THEIR OWN SELF-PROMOTION AS WELL AS PROFIT MOTIVES." THEY IMPLIED THAT SALOMON HAD DRUGGED HER, AND THAT HE HAD RELEASED THE MATERIAL TO MAKE MONEY FOR HIMSELF. HE SUED THEM AND WAS AWARDED $10 MILLION. THIS STILL DIDN'T STOP HIM FROM RELEASING SEVERAL VERSIONS FOR SALE ON A PAY-PER-VIEW BASIS OVER THE INTERNET. NOR DID IT STOP PARIS FROM REACHING AN AGREEMENT TO SHARE THE PROFITS. BOTH HAVE MADE HUNDREDS OF THOUSANDS OF DOLLARS FROM THEIR NIGHT OF PASSION.

"The interesting part of Paris is that she's not a celebrity, she's an icon."

DAD RICKY ON PARIS

{ hilton family tree }

AUGUSTUS HALVORSON "GUS" HILTON 1854–1919

A farmer's son from Ullensaker, Norway, he emigrated to the United States in 1870 and settled in San Antonio, New Mexico, where he opened a store and became known as the Merchant King. He also established a stagecoach line which serviced the mining town of White Oaks, 80 miles away.

CONRAD NICHOLSON HILTON 1887–1979

From fairly humble beginnings in a New Mexico frontier town, where his father's fortunes ebbed and flowed dramatically, Conrad Hilton pioneered the concept of the hotel chain. With assets including New York's Waldorf Astoria and Plaza Hotels, the Hilton name became synonymous with executive luxury. The hotels also made him one of America's richest men, while his second marriage to the beautiful Zsa Zsa Gabor undoubtedly added to the glamour of the chain.

CONRAD "NICKY" HILTON JR 1926–69

This first child of the Hilton founder anticipated the party life of great niece Paris. He was an alcoholic and playboy with a taste for actresses. His wives were Elizabeth Taylor and the oil heiress Trish McClintock, but he also had relations with actresses Mamie Van Doren, Clair Kelly, Joan Collins and Natalie Wood. His marriage to Elizabeth Taylor, who he started seeing in her final year of high school, lasted less than a year, while his second was only slightly more successful—the divorce claim citing abuse. Although he was an executive with the family hotel chain, when Conrad senior retired in 1966, it was younger brother Barron who took over the reins. Nicky died 3 years later from a heart attack precipitated by his excessive lifestyle.

MARY GENEVIEVE LAUFERSWEILER 1861–1947

Mary Genevieve was born in Fort Dodge, Iowa, where her father, Conrad, was a German-born cabinetmaker who diversified by opening a Funeral Home in 1856—which is still operated by the Laufersweiler family today.

1ST WIFE

MARY ADELAIDE BARRON 1906–79

She married Conrad in 1925, the same year he started the Dallas Hilton. They had three sons before divorcing in 1934, partly due to the business pressures caused by the Great Depression. She went on to marry Texan, Mack Saxon.

WILLIAM BARRON HILTON 1927–

While his elder brother was putting notches on his bedpost, Barron Hilton was building up the family business's beds, becoming Vice President of Hilton Hotels in 1954. When Conrad retired in 1966, Barron took over running the chain and managed to expand it significantly. His father's gratitude didn't expand to the will, however. When Barron discovered his thrice-married father had left most of his loot to the Catholic Church, he sued and won on the basis that he'd created much of the Hilton wealth. As a Catholic, he was more successful than his father, staying married to one woman until her death in 2004 and fathering eight children. His hobbies include flying planes and gliders, while he also founded the San Diego Chargers football team in 1960.

2ND WIFE

ZSA ZSA GABOR 1917–

The most famous of the three Hungarian Gabor sisters, she was Miss Hungary in 1936. She acted in a number of Hollywood movies but was more famous as a sex symbol, and for successful and shameless gold-digging, than her acting prowess. She married Conrad in 1942 and divorced him in 1946. He was the father of her only daughter and the second of her nine husbands.

> Conrad Hilton was very generous to me in the divorce settlement. He gave me 5,000 Gideon Bibles.
> ZSA ZSA GABOR

CONSTANCE FRANCESCA HILTON 1947–

The only child of any of the three Gabor sisters is the last in the line, as she never had children herself. A dreamed-of acting career failed to eventuate and she has lived her life entirely in the shadow of her famous parents. The only two times she has hit the newspapers are when she's been in court against them. Like Barron, she contested her father's will, but since she hadn't worked for the family company, her claim for a larger share was denied. In 2005 her mother Zsa Zsa filed a suit accusing her of $2 million worth of larceny and fraud.

3RD WIFE

MARY FRANCES KELLY unknown

They remained married until his death.

ELIZABETH TAYLOR 1932–

With almost as many husbands as Zsa Zsa and considerably more acting talent, she married Nicky Hilton in 1950, the year after she graduated from high school. By this time she was already a star from her role in the 1944 film *National Velvet*. After divorcing Nicky in 1951 (unlike Zsa Zsa, she refused alimony), her star continued to rise. The pinnacle of her career came with films such as *Who's Afraid of Virginia Wolf* and *Cleopatra*. However, since the 1970s her career has plummeted into parody, interspersed with weight problems and substance abuse.

PATRICIA "TRISH" McCLINTOCK 1939–

Like Liz Taylor, oil heiress Trish McClintock married Nicky in 1958 when she was still a teenager. Her family had been involved in the oil industry since America's first oilfield in Pennsylvania and the oldest surviving oil well bears the family name. She had two sons with Nicky before divorcing him in 1965 on the grounds that he had caused her extreme mental and physical suffering.

MARILYN HAWLEY 1928–2004

Hilton men have always had a yen for young beauties and Barron was no different. Marilyn was a Santa Monica, California, cheerleader before they married in 1947. It was a marriage that lived up to the promise of "till death do us part." Marilyn died in 2004 after a long battle with multiple sclerosis.

RICHARD "RICKY" HOWARD HILTON 1955–

The sixth of Barron and Marilyn Hilton's eight children, Richard is a successful real estate broker, dealing primarily in high-end residential Californian property. While he's a Hilton heir, he has earned his own millions and shares a $10 million Bel Air mansion and a $6 million Long Island holiday house with his wife, actress and celebrity Kathy Hilton (née Richards). His most famous achievements, however, are undoubtedly his celebrity daughters, Paris and Nicky, and he's certainly a proud father, despite the controversy they've caused.

KATHY RICHARDS 1959–

As an actress in the 1970s she had roles in iconic TV shows, such as *The Rockford Files* and *Happy Days*, but her résumé is somewhat shorter than her younger sisters, Kim and Kyle. Kathy's most recent venture into the limelight was in 2005, when she hosted the reality show, *Who Wants to Be a Hilton*, where contestants fought for the right to live like a Hilton for a year.

 EVERY WOMAN SHOULD HAVE FOUR PETS IN HER LIFE: A MINK IN HER CLOSET; A JAGUAR IN HER GARAGE; A TIGER IN HER BED; AND A JACKASS WHO PAYS FOR EVERYTHING. PARIS HILTON

PARIS HILTON 1981–

Just as the Hilton family looked like it might be sliding into wealthy obscurity, along came Paris. Her capacity to turn herself into an industry is exemplary and, from the looks of things, half the world's young women agree. Paris once described herself as "an actress, a brand, a businesswoman," but is more famous for just being Paris: celebrity slut, amateur pornographer and dog lover. Her show *The Simple Life* with ex-friend Nicole Richie (daughter of Lionel) was a vacuous hit, while her acting credits include horror film *House of Wax*, *Pledge This* and a role as herself in *Zoolander*. She has been linked to a variety of hot young men, including Rick Salomon, former husband of *Beverly Hills 90210* star and bad girl, Shannon Doherty, and co-star of *that* video. A 2005 engagement to shipping heir Paris Latsis didn't last the distance. She replaced him with another Greek heir Stavros Niarchos. In addition to being an heiress, her annual earnings from fragrance and jewellery ranges are in the millions.

> "I don't want to be known as the granddaughter of the Hiltons. I want to be known as Paris."
> PARIS HILTON

NICKY HILTON 1983–

The younger sister of Paris is also a Hollywood party girl, but keeps a lower profile. When offered the chance to join her big sister in *The Simple Life* she refused saying she wasn't interested in the lifestyle. Nicky doesn't seem as interested in celebrity as Paris, perhaps happier to revel in the socialite activities of the heiress class without courting attention. Her hasty 2004 marriage to businessman Todd Meister, which some claimed was a way of distancing herself from her more promiscuous sister, lasted only 5 months before it was annulled. Nonetheless, her fashion labels "Chick by Nicky Hilton" and "Nicky Hilton Beverly Hills" have proven lucrative, even without the notoriety of her sister's self-branding.

★

ONE OF ADOLF HITLER'S DOGS LOOKING AT HIS MASTER'S PORTRAIT.

> I am convinced that nothing will happen to me, for I know the greatness of the task for which Providence has chosen me.
> ADOLF HITLER

THE HITLERS

In many famous political families, even if there is one absolute star, there is usually a plurality of talent—the Churchills, for instance. In others, such as the Bonapartes, the brilliance of one member translates to opportunities for the rest. Rarer is the case where one member emerges from mediocrity to become one of the most powerful people in the world, yet leaves no familial trace of having done so. Adolf Hitler is such a one. The family history is a tale of incest, illegitimacy and petty tyranny and it's a wonder, really, that Adolf ever got the chance to play out his psychopathy on the world stage. Still, once he had climbed to his short-lived pinnacle he showed little interest in bringing his family with him. Perhaps it was because he'd already driven his niece Geli, the one member of his family he genuinely loved—albeit perversely—into an early grave. Or it may well have been that Adolf Hitler viewed his family as something to escape from, rather than to love and celebrate.

HOW THEY RATE

WEALTH ★
Wealth was never a concern. Adolf was only ever really interested in power and the remainder of the family have showed no real facility with money.

HEALTH ★
Reproductive health was especially poor. A lot of infant mortality. There were also three suicides. None of the Hitlers seem to have lived for an amazingly long time.

HAPPINESS ★
Historically not a lot. Most Hitlers have been failures, while the successful ones were filled with rage.

FAME ★ ★ ★ ★
It's a name infamous the world over, yet it has very much been a one-act family with little chance of revitalizing its fortunes.

SEXINESS ★
It's hard to imagine a family with less sex appeal, yet Hitler men managed to get the women when they so desired, and had a penchant for relatives as well as overlapping girlfriends and wives.

BLACK SHEEP FACTOR ★ ★ ★ ★ ★
It doesn't get much blacker than one of the great mass murderers of the 20th century.

ECCENTRICITY ★ ★ ★ ★
In a hatefully neurotic way that led variously to genocide and domestic violence.

INFLUENCE ★ ★ ★ ★ ★
Adolf was behind the deaths of 11 million people. The aftershocks of World War II can still be felt today. Loathsome as he was, he was still one of the 20th century's most influential individuals.

> Make the lie big, make it simple, keep saying it, and eventually they will believe it.
> ADOLF HITLER

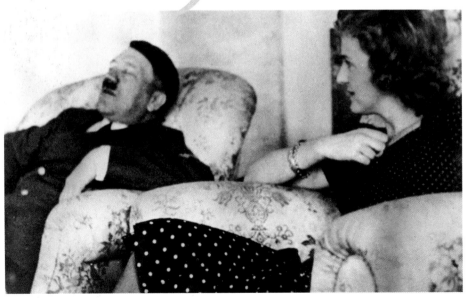

A SLEEPING ADOLF HITLER IS WATCHED BY HIS ADORING MISTRESS, EVA BRAUN, C.1940. DURING THE LAST DAYS OF WORLD WAR II, ON APRIL 29, 1945, THE COUPLE WOULD FINALLY MARRY—THE DAY BEFORE THEY COMMITTED SUICIDE.

A 10-YEAR-OLD ADOF HITLER ARROGANTLY STARES INTO THE CAMERA. THE BOY FEARED HIS FATHER BUT ADORED HIS MOLLYCODDLING MOTHER.

PAULA HITLER INTERVIEWED

The series of interviews Paula Hitler gave to the American Army soon after the war (see the excerpt below), and another she gave to British television in 1960, are the best indicators we have of what the domestic life of young Adolf may have been like.

"The married life of my parents was a very happy one, in spite of their very unlike characters. My father, who was of great harshness in the education of his children and who only spoiled me as the pet of the family, was the absolute type of the old Austrian official, conservative and loyal to his emperor to the skin. My mother, however, was a very soft and tender person, the compensatory element between the almost too harsh father and the very lively children who perhaps were somewhat difficult to train. If there were ever quarrel or difference of opinion between my parents it was always on account of the children. It was especially my brother Adolf who challenged my father to extreme harshness and who got his sound thrashing every day. He was a scrubby little rogue, and all attempts of his father to thrash him for his rudeness and to cause him to love the profession of an official of the estate were in vain. How often on the other hand did my mother caress him and try to obtain with her kindness, where the father could not succeed with harshness!"

ADOLF PRACTICING HIS POSES AS HE LISTENS TO A RECORDING OF HIMSELF SPEAKING, 1925.

THE HITLER MEN

Hitler men were generally unpleasant. When looking at Alois Hitler, who died while drinking his morning beer in the pub, it's easy to imagine that had he lived 100 years later, he would have been a German sex tourist in Southeast Asia. Alois was ambitious and despite a lack of formal education managed to do well in getting into, and climbing the ranks of, the Austro-Hungarian Civil Service. Yet his private life had none of the bureaucratic orderliness, but much of the same egoistic determination.

He married his first wife, Anna, when she was in her fifties, because she had the contacts to help his career. When he married Anna he took his young cousin/niece, Klara Pölzl, with him—and considering what came after, the chances are that, from the outset, she was giving him more than a helping hand. At the same time he fathered a child during an ongoing affair with a barmaid, Fanni Matzelberger. This affair precipitated the breakdown of his marriage to Anna, who obtained a legal separation. When she died, Alois married Fanni, although one of the conditions was that Klara leave the house. He and Fanni had another child, but soon after she contracted tuberculosis. Faced with a bedridden wife and two young children, Alois asked Klara to come back and help him. By the time Fanni died, Klara was already pregnant with their child. The marriage of Alois and Klara maintained a master–servant feel, and the only time Klara battled against him was when she was protecting her children. According to one account she even once lay over the body of her son Adolf and absorbed the blows when Alois was giving him one of his frequent beatings.

THE ENTRY OF THE COLORS, OR SWASTIKAS, AT THE GERMAN NATIONAL SOCIALIST PARTY DAY, NUREMBERG, 1933.

THE TRAGIC TALE OF
GELI RAUBAL

SOME DICTATORS ARE NOTORIOUS FOR THE BENEFITS THEY BESTOW ON THEIR FAMILIES, BUT THE BENEFITS ADOLF HITLER GAVE HIS NIECE, GELI, ENDED UP KILLING HER. GELI CAME WITH HER MOTHER, ANGELA, IN 1928 TO LOOK AFTER HITLER'S HOUSE. BUT THE MASTER OF THE HOUSE SOON BECAME ENAMORED OF GELI AND IT SEEMS LIKELY THEY BECAME AN ITEM. IN A WAY THE SITUATION WAS A MIRROR OF ADOLF'S FATHER AND MOTHER'S RELATIONSHIP—SINCE KLARA WAS ALSO A RELATIVE (POSSIBLY A NIECE) WHO ENTERED THE HOUSEHOLD IN A SERVING POSITION. HITLER TRIED TO KEEP A TIGHT REIN ON GELI, BUT SHE WAS A FREE SPIRIT WHO HAD ALSO HAD AN AFFAIR WITH HITLER'S CHAUFFEUR. HITLER WAS DEEPLY IN LOVE WITH HER AND HE BECAME JEALOUS. FROM HER LETTERS WRITTEN TO THE YOUNG MAN SHE WISHED TO BECOME ENGAGED TO, GELI DID NOT ENTIRELY RECIPROCATE HER UNCLE'S PASSION. BUT WHEN YOU'RE BEING PURSUED BY AN OLDER FAMILY MEMBER WITH THE TACIT CONSENT OF YOUR MOTHER, AND HE ALSO HAPPENS TO BE THE ABSOLUTE DICTATOR OF YOUR COUNTRY, IT'S NOT ALWAYS THAT EASY TO SAY NO. GELI WAS ONE OF THE FEW PEOPLE WITH ENOUGH GUTS TO STAND UP TO ADOLF, WHICH PARADOXICALLY IS WHY HE LOVED HER (IT'S LONELY AT THE TOP WHEN YOU'RE SURROUNDED BY FRIGHTENED YES MEN). IN HER FINAL DAYS, THEY FOUGHT LIKE CAT AND DOG. WHETHER GELI, FEELING TRAPPED BY HIM, DECIDED THE ONLY WAY OUT WAS TO SHOOT HERSELF IN THE HEAD, OR WHETHER ADOLF—WHO BY THE WAY WAS ALREADY SEEING EVA BRAUN—WITHDREW HIS REVOLVER IN A FIT OF PASSIONATE RAGE AND SHOT HER REMAINS UNKNOWN. THE OFFICIAL VERDICT, HOWEVER, WAS SUICIDE. NO SURPRISES THERE.

HITLER CHRONOLOGY

1889 Adolf Hitler born on April 20, in Linz, Austria.

1905 Leaves school without graduating.

1907 Hitler's mother dies, making him an orphan.

1908 Moves to Vienna. Fails to get into art school.

1916 Corporal Adolf Hitler injured in the thigh during the Battle of the Somme. He is sent to Berlin's military hospital.

1918 Hitler, recipient of the Iron Cross (First Class) for his bravery in the Ludendorff Spring Offensive, is blinded by gas and sent to hospital in Munich.

1921 Becomes the leader and 55th member of the German Workers' Party which he renames the National Socialist German Worker's Party (NSDAP).

1923 The National Socialists under Hitler try to overthrow the Stresseman government in the Beer Hall Putsch. More than a dozen Nazis are killed and Hitler is jailed while the Nazi Party is banned.

1924 Finishes his book *Mein Kampf* and is released from prison despite only serving 13 months for treason.

1933 Hitler becomes German Chancellor. The first concentration camp opens in Dachau. Its prisoners are communists and it is run by the SS. Jews are banned from government jobs.

1934 When President Hindenburg dies, Hitler joins the post of President to Chancellor and becomes Führer.

1935 "The Law for the Protection of German Blood and Honour" banned marriages between Aryans and Jews. Jews and non-Jews were also banned from having sexual relations together. The citizenship rights of Jews were removed by the "Reich Citizenship Law." These laws became known as the Nuremburg Laws.

1939 Germany invades Poland, beginning World War II.

1941 Operation Barbarossa—the German invasion of the USSR begins.

1942 After agreement on the "Final Solution" for the Jewish population, the first extermination camp is set up in Poland.

1943 The Germans surrender at Stalingrad in the USSR.

1944 The Allied troops land in Normandy on D-Day.

1945 Hitler marries Eva Braun in his Berlin bunker as the Russians enter the city. The next day she takes poison and he shoots himself in the head. Their bodies are burned. Within a week Germany has surrendered.

HITLER'S HALF-BROTHER, ALOIS JR, LIVED IN HIDING IN HAMBURG AFTER WORLD WAR II, BUT HE RECEIVED MANY THREATENING PHONE CALLS.

> "THE LEADER OF GENIUS MUST HAVE THE ABILITY TO MAKE DIFFERENT OPPONENTS APPEAR AS IF THEY BELONGED TO ONE CATEGORY." ADOLF HITLER

FRATERNAL DELUSIONS

Whether it was a reaction to the petty bourgeois tyranny of their father, both Alois Jr and his younger half-brother had sociopathic personalities with a capacity for fantasy. The same quality that helped one brother become a dictator and genocidal maniac, made the other a petty criminal, bigamist and small-time scammer. Like Adolf, Alois Jr had issues with his dad. Whereas Adolf had the protection of his mother, Klara's preference for her biological son over her step son saw her set Alois senior against Alois Jr. It also meant Alois Jr resented Adolf. Things were so bad that Alois left home at 14 without completing his education. After leaving home he worked as an apprentice waiter until he was arrested for theft and served a 5-month jail sentence in 1900 and another of 8 months in 1902. He then left for Ireland and was working as a waiter when he met 17-year-old Bridget Dowling. Here his penchant for fantasy paid dividends. Having convinced her he was a wealthy hotelier on holiday, they eloped. Her father was furious, however, and threatened to have Alois arrested for kidnapping. Bridget managed to persuade him not to. It wasn't the last time she saved Alois either—though you have to wonder why. He was prone to violent rages and frequently beat her and their infant son. This stopped when he returned to Germany without them to break into the safety razor business and was separated from them by the outbreak of World War I. After the war, he stayed in Germany. His business was doing well, but he didn't send any money back to her. Rather, he got married again without telling Bridget. His new wife was a German, Hedwig Heidemann, and they had a child, Heinz. Somehow the German authorities got wind of the situation and Alois was charged with bigamy. He was only rescued from a third stint in jail because Bridget refused to prosecute. At some point Alois's business became a casualty of German hyperinflation but with his brother Adolf's accession to power, Alois opened a bar in Berlin in 1934 which became a favorite of SS stormtroopers. His son, William Patrick, spent much of the 1930s in Germany and landed a series of unspectacular jobs through his uncle. Alois, however, maintained little contact with his brother, who had the tendency to lord it over him whenever they met. After the war, Alois Jr scrabbled a living based on his proximity to notoriety by signing and selling photos of his brother to tourists.

WILLIAM PATRICK HITLER JOINED THE US NAVY.

hitler family tree

JOHANN GEORG HIEDLER 1792–1857

A journeyman miller, he was the Third Reich's official grandfather of Adolf Hitler, but whether he was his actual biological grandfather remains unknown. In 1842, he married Maria Schicklgruber and became the legal stepfather of her 5-year-old illegitimate son, Alois. It was later asserted that Johann had fathered Alois prior to his marriage to Schicklgruber and in 1876, almost 20 years after his death, Alois was legally declared to have been Johann Georg's son. However some historians believe Johann's brother, Johann Nepomuk Hiedler, was Alois Schicklgruber's biological father.

ALOIS SCHICKLGRUBER HITLER 1837–1903

He spent most of his childhood in his uncle's house. After completing a cobbler's apprenticeship he moved to Vienna to pursue leatherwork. However, he managed to get a job in the Customs Department of the Austrian Civil Service and in a 40-year career climbed the ladder to Higher Collector of Customs, the highest rank open to someone with only an elementary school education. However, while he was respected in his community, at home he was a bad-tempered tyrant who meted out thrashings to his domestic underlings—perhaps as compensation for the crawling to superiors he was forced to perform in his job. He opposed Adolf's desire to be an artist, while his own hobbies were drinking beer with his friends and bee-keeping.

UNCONFIRMED

MARIA ANNA SCHICKLGRUBER 1795–1847

One of eleven children of whom only six made it through infancy, she grew up a Catholic peasant in a poor but pretty area, northeast of Austria. She showed financial shrewdness and probably worked as a servant until she gave birth to her only child, Alois, at the age of 42. She wouldn't tell the priest who had fathered the child, so Alois was recorded as being illegitimate. She moved in with her father and 5 years later married Hiedler. She died 5 years afterward.

2ND WIFE

FRANZISKA "FANNI" MATZELBERGER 1861–84

She was Alois's second wife, after his first marriage to Anna Glassl—an older woman he married for her assets and connections in the civil service. During the marriage, Alois started an affair with "Fanni," a guesthouse maid. Their marriage broke down because of it in 1880. In 1882 Fanni had a child to Alois, named Alois Jr, who they were able to legitimize by getting married as soon as Anna died in 1883. Their daughter, Anna, was born 2 months after the wedding. In 1884, however, Fanni caught tuberculosis and died later that year.

JOHAN NEPOMUK HÜTTLER 1807–88

The possible father of Alois, and definite brother of Johann Georg Hiedler. Even though they chose to spell their surnames differently, they both meant "smallholder," which neither was. While Hiedler was an itinerant journeyman, Hüttler was more prosperous than his older brother and was the owner of a medium-size landholding. Interestingly, Alois went to live with his "uncle," where he received an elementary school education before becoming an apprentice cobbler. This has been used to suggest he was the natural father, not his brother.

UNCONFIRMED

3RD WIFE

KLARA PÖLZL 1860–1907

The third wife of Alois Hitler, she was officially his second cousin, but if Alois's natural father was Hüttler rather than Hiedler, then Klara would have been his niece—an incestuous romance pattern their son would also pursue. When Alois married Anna, Klara joined the household as their maid. When he married Fanni, she made him send Klara back, but when Fanni got sick, Alois brought her back. Only two of their children survived childhood. Klara was a gentle, doting and over-protective mother who adored her son Adolf and tried to compensate for the harshness of her tyrannical husband. She died from breast cancer when she was 47.

EVA MARIA DECKER 1792–1873

The theory that Johan Nepomuk was Alois Hitler's natural father is supported by the fact that he had a taste for older women. His wife Eva was 15 years older than her husband and was 37 when they married in 1829, probably because she was pregnant. They had two children, both daughters.

> 'He had a real dislike of the female sex up to the moment that he was grown up. When mother wanted him to get up in the morning she had only to say to me, "Go and give him a kiss." She said it not very loud, but for him to hear and as soon as he heard the word "kiss" and that he was to get one from me, he was out of bed in a flash because he just could not stand that.' — PAULA HITLER ON BIG BROTHER ADOLF

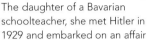

ADOLF HITLER
1889–1945

A poor student and bullied son with an over-protective mother, there was nothing in his early life to suggest the monster he would become. His life changed when he won the Iron Cross in World War I and he went on to become a military genius, whose charismatic philosophical slop was the catalyst for the deaths of over 11 million people. He was the only person in his family to rise above mediocrity. Yet he was still beholden to some familial patterns of his father—female relatives were good for cleaning the house and sleeping with. He brought his half sister in to be his housekeeper, and had a public affair with her daughter, Geli, which ended in her suicide. He never managed children himself and ended his war by committing suicide.

EVA BRAUN   **1912–45**

The daughter of a Bavarian schoolteacher, she met Hitler in 1929 and embarked on an affair with him against her family's wishes. It wasn't easy sailing and she tried to commit suicide in both 1932 and 1935. In 1936 Eva joined Hitler's household on a permanent basis, although the two were never seen together in public since Hitler thought it would jeopardize his popularity with Germany's women. She was fond of photography and nude sunbathing and spent the war in a leisurely fashion, until she joined Hitler in his bunker at the end of the war. She married him on April 29, 1945. They committed suicide the day after the wedding.

> "HE HAS SO OFTEN TOLD ME HE IS MADLY IN LOVE WITH ME, BUT WHAT DOES THAT MEAN WHEN I HAVEN'T HAD A GOOD WORD FROM HIM IN THREE MONTHS?" — EVA BRAUN ON ADOLF HITLER

PAULA HITLER   **1896–1960**

The youngest sibling of Adolf. When their mother died Adolf gave Paula his portion of their orphan's pension. She didn't hear from him for over a decade until he turned up in Vienna in 1921 and took her shopping. She worked for an insurance company in Vienna, but was dismissed in 1930 because of her brother's political activities. When he found out, Hitler started paying her an allowance. In 1936, Adolf asked her to change her name to Paula Wolff, presumably because being his relative put her at risk. Paula never married but, in 2005, historians discovered a memoir supposedly written by Paula, which says she wanted to marry Erwin Jekelius, an Austrian doctor responsible for gassing 4000 disabled people. Apparently, Hitler opposed the match and when Jekelius went to ask him for Paula's hand, he was met by the Gestapo and shipped off to the eastern front from which he never returned.

ADOLF HITLER, C.1889–91

BABY HITLERS

THE INCESTUOUS GENE MIX OF ALOIS HITLER AND HIS SECOND COUSIN KLARA POLZL DID NOT APPEAR TO BE A HEALTHY ONE IN EVOLUTIONARY TERMS. ADOLF WAS THEIR FIRST CHILD TO SURVIVE INFANCY. HIS THREE OLDER SIBLINGS ALL DIED BEFORE HE WAS BORN, TWO OF THEM WITHIN A YEAR AS THE RESULT OF DIPHTHERIA. IN 1894 A BROTHER, EDMUND, WAS BORN, BUT HE DIED FROM MEASLES AT THE AGE OF 6. ONLY HIS SISTER, PAULA, BORN IN 1896, SURVIVED TO ADULTHOOD WITH HIM. NEITHER ADOLF NOR PAULA HAD ANY CHILDREN.

2 CHILDREN: ALOIS & ANGELA NEXT PAGE

{ "THROUGH CLEVER AND CONSTANT APPLICATION OF PROPAGANDA, PEOPLE CAN BE MADE TO SEE PARADISE AS HELL, AND ALSO THE OTHER WAY ROUND, TO CONSIDER THE MOST WRETCHED SORT OF LIFE AS PARADISE."
ADOLF HITLER }

ALOIS HITLER JR 1882–1956

He left home aged 14 and lived an erratic life thereafter. Somewhere between a small-time crook and ne'er-do-well fantasist, he spent time in jail for theft before emigrating to Ireland, marrying and then moving to England. After the failure of a number of business ventures, he left his wife and child to break into the safety razor business in Germany, and became separated from them by World War I. He made a bigamous marriage with a German woman, Hedwig Heidemann, for which he was almost jailed again. They had a son, Heinz. In 1934, he opened a bar in Berlin which he ran until the end of World War II. After the war ended he made money signing photos of his brother, Adolf, and selling them to tourists.

BRIDGET DOWLING 1891–1969

She met Alois Jr at the Dublin Horse Show (where Mia Farrow's mother, Maureen O'Sullivan was discovered) when she was only 17. She swallowed his fib that he was a wealthy hotelier and they eloped. They lived in Liverpool, England, where they had a son. Bridget didn't go to Germany with Alois when she discovered he was violent. Instead, she moved to London and supported herself by taking in lodgers. When Alois was charged with bigamy in 1924, she intervened on his behalf and acceded to a divorce, although her Catholicism was opposed to it. In 1939, she joined her son on a lecture tour of the US where she stayed. She later wrote the factually critized book *My Brother-in-Law Adolf*.

{ "OF MY OTHER BROTHERS AND SISTERS I ESPECIALLY REMEMBER MY STEPSISTER ANGELA AS A BEAUTIFUL GIRL. ALSO SHE WAS WATCHED BY MY FATHER VERY HARSHLY."
PAULA HITLER }

ANGELA HITLER 1883–1949

The only sibling mentioned in Adolf Hitler's *Mein Kampf*, Angela was 6 years older than him but, at various times in their lives, they were close. Although the daughter of Fanni, she was brought up by Klara Pölzl. She married Leo Raubal, a junior tax inspector, and they had three children together: Leo Jr, Geli and Elfriede. When her husband died in 1910, she moved to Vienna. After World War I, she became manager of Mensa Academia Judaica, a residence for Jewish students, where she defended them against anti-Semitic rioters. In 1928, she moved to Obersalzberg and became her brother's housekeeper. At some stage she and brother Adolf fell out. She left him and married a Professor Hamitsch in Dresden. Her brother did not attend the wedding.

HOME SWEET HOME
HITLER'S PARENTS' HOUSE IN LEONDING, AUSTRIA, WHERE THE YOUNG HITLER GREW UP.

WILLIAM PATRICK HITLER
1911–87

Abandoned by his father at the age of 3, he was raised by his mother, but went to Germany to visit Dad in 1929. He returned again in 1933 to try to profit from his uncle's rise to power. His uncle got him a job as a bank clerk. William Patrick then worked for Opel and became a car salesman. None of the jobs matched the grandeur of his anticipated nepotism, though. In 1938, Uncle Adolf promised him a better job if he renounced his British citizenship. Instead William Patrick went back to Britain and wrote an article "Why I hate my Uncle." On the strength of this article he secured a lecture tour in America. When war broke out in Europe, William Patrick, joined by his mother Bridget, stayed. In 1942, he joined the American navy and fought against his uncle. After the war he married a German emigrant, changed his surname to Stewart Chamberlain, lived in Long Island, and started a successful blood pathology laboratory.

HEINZ HITLER c.1920–45

Adolf called this son of Alois Jr, and his bigamous marriage to Hedwig Heidemann, his favorite nephew. It did Heinz no good though. Although he received an education at one of the National Socialist's elite schools, it filled him with such patriotic fervor that he volunteered as an Officer for the Russian Front and never returned—the speculation being that he died while a POW of the Russians.

LEO RUDOLF RAUBAL   1906–79

Leo Rudolf had a job in Salzburg, Austria, and frequently came to Hitler's estate, Berchtesgaden, to visit his mother when Hitler was in Berlin, but would leave when it became known that Hitler was on his way. He accused Hitler of causing his sister, Geli's, death and refused to speak to him again as long as he lived.

ANGELA "GELI" RAUBAL ☠
1908–31

She joined her mother, Angela, in 1928 when she became Adolf's housekeeper. However Adolf took a shine to Geli, and it is likely she was his lover. But Geli had another love interest she wanted to marry. Whether out of jealousy or over-bearing patriarchy, Hitler refused to let her. She was one of the few people who stood up to him, but it caused her downfall. After a fiery argument between them, she ended up with a bullet in her head.

STEWART CHAMBERLAIN

WILLIAM PATRICK HITLER'S CHOICE OF POST-WAR SURNAME WAS INTERESTING, IT'S HARD TO IMAGINE IT WAS A COINCIDENCE THAT THE NAME HE CHOSE—THE DOUBLE-BARRELED STEWART CHAMBERLAIN—WAS ALSO THE NAME OF THE ARYAN RACIAL THEORIST, HOUSTON STEWART CHAMBERLAIN, WHO HITLER ONCE DESCRIBED AS "THE PROPHET OF THE THIRD REICH" AND WHO, ALTHOUGH ORIGINALLY AN ENGLISHMAN, BECAME A GERMAN CITIZEN WHO ARGUED THE CAUSE OF RACIAL PURITY AND THE GERMAN VOLK, AND MARRIED WAGNER'S DAUGHTER. ONE WONDERS THEN WHETHER WILLIAM PATRICK'S CHOICE OF POST-WAR PROFESSION OF BLOOD PATHOLOGY MIGHT HAVE ALSO BEEN INSPIRED—DESPITE HIS MESSY FAMILY HISTORY—BY NOTIONS OF RACE AND BLOOD. WHAT'S ALSO INTERESTING IS THAT, EVEN THOUGH HE FOUGHT AGAINST HIS UNCLE, AND FOR A WHILE EARNED AN INCOME BAD-MOUTHING HIM, HE GAVE HIS OLDEST SON THE SECOND NAME OF "ADOLF." BUT THEN THE REST OF THE FAMILY HAD BEEN STRIKINGLY MEDIOCRE, AND SCARCELY WORTH REMEMBERING.

ALEX STEWART CHAMBERLAIN   1949–

The oldest of the surviving Long Island Hitler clan, he has worked as a social worker. Although his father was publicly opposed to Hitler, Alex was given the second name of Adolf.

LOUIS STEWART CHAMBERLAIN   1951–

He has a gardening business. According to some reports, all three living brothers have decided not to have children in order that the male Hitler line dies out with them.

HOWARD STEWART CHAMBERLAIN   1957–89

Howard was an Internal Revenue Service officer who was killed in car crash while on duty.

BRIAN STEWART CHAMBERLAIN   1965–

He works in the same gardening business as his brother Louis. He has claimed that, while his brothers might have conspired to end the family line, they didn't tell him. Nonetheless, he remains childless.

★

THE KENNEDYS

JOHN F. AND BOBBY AT A SENATE HEARING ON LABOR RACKETEERING, 1957.

WITHIN THE SPACE OF A CENTURY THE KENNEDY FAMILY GREW FROM POOR, BOG-IRISH IMMIGRANTS INTO AMERICA'S PRE-EMINENT POLITICAL FAMILY. ALTHOUGH THEY MAY HAVE BEEN OUTSTRIPPED BY THE BUSH DYNASTY IN TERMS OF HOLDING OFFICE, NO OTHER FAMILY HAS ENTERED THE POPULAR IMAGINATION TO THE EXTENT OF THE KENNEDYS WITH THEIR CHARM, AMBITION, TRAGEDY, IDEALISM, RUTHLESSNESS, SCANDAL AND GOOD WORKS.

I n true Irish fashion, the family made its initial money selling booze, then made even more bootlegging it during Prohibition. In true American fashion, their wealth grew exponentially as a result of savvy speculation on the stock market. Yet, balancing this worldly performance was a powerful sense of spiritual purpose and the obligation to do good works. Few families have done as much for charity as the Kennedys. At a political level this created a Kennedy aura which combined ruthless pragmatism, a Macchiavellian sense of destiny with genuine idealism—a quality that has largely been lost in the 30-second-grab, spin-doctored politics of today. Of course this idealism lost its chance to be made a reality with the assassinations of JFK and Bobby, and the allure of the Kennedys is partly beause they represent unfulfilled political potential. Yet, there is also a seamier, self-interested side to the Kennedys, prepared to sacrifice others (even their own) in the pursuit of the family's interest. The sad fate of Rosemary Kennedy is an example. Then again, few families have been as unlucky as the Kennedys, and the superstitious might think the Kennedy Curse is a consequence of hubris, of being stubborn enough to hold onto a dream.

HOW THEY RATE

WEALTH: ★ ★ ★ ★
Not short of a dollar but more interested in power, fame and public works than money.

HEALTH: ★ ★ ★
Their longevity is generally good, but they are extremely accident prone, while there is evidence of an addictive streak running through the family.

HAPPINESS: ★
Considering what has happened to them, it's hard to imagine them getting too much of a chance to be happy.

FAME: ★ ★ ★ ★
Huge at the time, though the pinnacle of Kennedy fame has probably passed.

SEXINESS: ★ ★ ★ ★ ★
Yes. JFK was a Presidential sex symbol and he cashed in on it, too. Male Kennedys are known for their womanizing. The good Catholics among them, both male and female, have shown their sexiness by the large size of their families.

BLACK SHEEP FACTOR: ★ ★ ★ ★
Heroin addiction, murder, serial adultery, election fraud. This is a family with a lot of Black Sheep moments.

ECCENTRICITY: ★
More of the all-American style charm.

INFLUENCE: ★ ★ ★ ★
On the surface their influence has been profound, though an argument might be made that the Kennedy myth exceeds the reality of their achievement. Still they are hardly lightweights on the world scene.

MONROE SINGS *HAPPY BIRTHDAY*, 1962.

JFK CHRONOLOGY

1917 Born May 29.

1940 Harvard honors thesis on UK's Hitler Appeasement published as a book, *Why England Slept*.

1941 Joins US navy.

1943 Earns medal for rescuing his crew when their boat is sunk by the Japanese during World War II.

1946 Elected to the US House of Representatives.

1952 Elected to US Senate as senator from Massachusetts.

1953 Marries Jacqueline Bouvier.

1955 Almost dies during a back operation.

1956 Loses his bid for the Democratic nomination for Vice President.

1957 Daughter Caroline born. Wins Pulitzer Prize for Biography with *Profiles in Courage*, which chronicles politicians who risked their careers for the sake of their convictions

1960 Defeats Richard Nixon by a very slim margin to become the 35th President of the United States. (Kennedy won by a margin of 0.2 percent with 49.75 percent of the votes against Nixon's 49.55 percent.)
Son John born.

1961 Becomes the second-youngest American president ever. Bay of Pigs crisis after botched CIA-instigated invasion.

1962 Cuban Missile Crisis.

1963 Sends the Alabama National Guard to the University of Alabama to protect two African–American students who won a court order against segregation to study there.
Son Patrick is born but dies after 2 days.
Signs the Nuclear Test Ban Treaty.
Assassinated by Lee Harvey Oswald.

COLLATERAL DAMAGE

AS THE THIRD SON OF ELEVEN CHILDREN, DAVID KENNEDY MIGHT HAVE FELT AGGRIEVED AT BEING LOST IN THE MIDDLE, BUT HIS FATHER, BOBBY, ALSO A THIRD SON, KNEW THIS AND PAID HIS DREAMY, INTROVERTED SON A BIT OF SPECIAL ATTENTION. WHEN HE BEGAN CAMPAIGNING FOR THE 1968 PRESIDENTIAL PRIMARIES, HE TOOK 13-YEAR-OLD DAVID WITH HIM. WHILE CALIFORNIANS WERE CASTING THEIR VOTES, DAVID AND BOBBY WENT FOR A SWIM AT MALIBU. DAVID GOT CAUGHT IN AN UNDERTOW AND BOBBY SWAM OUT AND RESCUED HIM. AS BOBBY KENNEDY WAS ANNOUNCING HIS VICTORY IN THE PRIMARY, DAVID WAS BACK AT THE HOTEL ROOM, ALONE, PROUDLY WATCHING HIS DAD ON TV. THEN HIS DAD WAS SHOT IN FRONT OF HIS EYES. IN THE CONFUSION THAT FOLLOWED, DAVID WAS FORGOTTEN, AND IT WASN'T UNTIL SEVERAL HOURS LATER THAT HE WAS FOUND IN A STATE OF SHOCK, STILL STARING AT THE TV, BY THE ASTRONAUT JOHN GLENN AND AUTHOR THEODORE WHITE. DAVID WAS UNABLE TO SPEAK FOR DAYS AND THE EVENTUAL DECLINE OF THIS SENSITIVE BOY INTO A DRUG HAZE, WHICH ENDED WITH HIS OVERDOSE DEATH, HAD ITS ORIGINS IN THIS ONE APPALLING MOMENT.

> And so, my fellow Americans ... ask not what your country can do for you ... ask what you can do for your country. My fellow citizens of the world ... ask not what America will do for you, but what together we can do for the freedom of man.
> JOHN F. KENNEDY, INAUGURATION SPEECH

PATRICIA KENNEDY AND HER MOVIE-STAR HUSBAND, PETER LAWFORD, 1965.

THE SKAKEL CURSE

PEOPLE TALK ABOUT THE KENNEDY CURSE BUT THE FAMILY OF BOBBY'S WIFE, ETHEL, HAS A SOLID CLAIM ON A CURSE OF THEIR OWN. THE SKAKELS FIRST CAME INTO CONTACT WITH THE KENNEDYS WHEN ETHEL AND JEAN KENNEDY WERE COLLEGE ROOMMATES IN MANHATTAN. HOWEVER, IT WAS ETHEL'S OLDER SISTER, PATRICIA, WHO FIRST DATED BOBBY KENNEDY. WHEN THEY BROKE UP, ETHEL AND BOBBY STARTED TO GET IT ON AND THE TWO WERE MARRIED IN 1950. WHEN BOBBY WAS ASSASSINATED, ETHEL WAS PREGNANT WITH HER ELEVENTH CHILD. BY THEN TRAGEDY HAD STRUCK THE SKAKELS AS WELL AS THE KENNEDYS. IN 1955 ETHEL'S PARENTS WERE KILLED IN A PLANE CRASH. HER BROTHER GEORGE, WHO HAD TAKEN OVER HIS FATHER'S LUCRATIVE COAL COMPANY—THE GREAT LAKES CARBON CORPORATION—DIED IN 1966, ALSO IN A PLANE CRASH, WHILE SISTER PATRICIA DIED SOON AFTER FROM CANCER AGED ONLY 39. YET THE STRANGEST TWIST IN THE SKAKEL FORTUNES CAME IN 1975 WHEN TEENAGER MARTHA MOXLEY WAS FOUND CLUBBED AND STABBED TO DEATH WITH A GOLF IRON SOON AFTER SHE'D BEEN MUCKING AROUND WITH THOMAS SKAKEL, ONE OF ETHEL'S GREENWICH CONNECTICUT NEPHEWS. AFTER WHAT MANY BELIEVE WAS A POLICE COVER-UP, BECAUSE OF THE FAMILY'S POLITICAL INFLUENCE, IN 2002, MICHAEL SKAKEL, WHO AS A TEENAGER HAD COMPETED WITH BROTHER THOMAS FOR MARTHA'S AFFECTION, WAS FOUND GUILTY OF THE MURDER HE COMMITTED WHEN HE WAS 15 AND WAS SENTENCED TO 20-TO-LIFE IN JAIL MORE THAN 25 YEARS AFTER THE CRIME.

CATHOLICISM AND THE KENNEDYS

In this day and age it's easy to forget the degree of sectarian enmity that has existed between Catholics and Protestants for much of the past 400 years. But in the mid-20th century it still had a powerful effect on the way American society worked. The Kennedys were Boston Irish. For much of their time in America the Irish had been looked down on in America, yet they fought back through the Democrat party and its affiliations with institutions such as New York's Tammany Hall. Rose Kennedy's father, "Honey Fitz," was the first Irish-born Mayor of Boston, which had historically been ruled over by established families, often descended from the original Puritan pilgrims. When JFK was elected President, he was the first (and only) President of the USA to be a Catholic. As part of his campaigning, he had to assure Protestant voters that he believed in the absolute separation of church and state and wouldn't be taking orders from the Pope.

In the Kennedy family, however, things weren't always so tolerant. Rose Kennedy disapproved of Kick's marriage on the grounds that she was marrying a Protestant. She was so incensed when Kick openly started seeing a married man that she told her daughter she would be going straight to hell, and effectively disowned her. She didn't even go to Kick's funeral. The Catholicism of the Kennedys can also be noticed in the number of children there tend to be in most branches of the Kennedy family—Bobby and Ethel topped the charts there with eleven. The Irish also have a reputation for clannishness and the Kennedys are a classic example. While competitive, they are also often found to be helping each other out.

It should also be noted that their Catholicism is partly responsible for the idealism that pervades the Kennedys. In terms of charitable works, they are one of the most active dynasties America has ever had. Their causes include the disabled, children, providing heating for the poor and protecting the environment. However, considering the fate that's been dealt to so many Kennedys, you sometimes wonder how they could believe in God at all.

ROBERT F. KENNEDY WITH WIFE ETHEL AND CHILDREN, 1957.

THE KENNEDY CURSE

There are few families who have been hit with as much tragedy as the Kennedys. As they became one of America's most famous families, they simultaneously seemed to become a kind of disaster magnet—one that would have destroyed the bonds between many other family units.

JFK AND JACKIE WITH BABY CAROLINE, 1958.

PLANE CRASH DEATHS

The chances of dying in a plane crash are very small. You are more likely to be run over while crossing the road. Unless you happen to be flying with a Kennedy ...

1944 Joseph Kennedy Jr—the World War II bomber he is flying explodes.
1948 Kick Kennedy and Earl Fitzwilliam—their plane flies into French mountain.
1955 Ethel Skakel's parents killed in plane crash.
1964 Teddy Kennedy survives a plane crash that kills his aide, Edward Moss
1966 Ethel Skakel's brother George killed in a plane crash.
1999 John Kennedy Jr, his wife and her sister die when the plane he is flying crashes on the way to Rory Kennedy's wedding in Martha's Vineyard.

CAR ACCIDENTS

1969 Edward Kennedy drives off a bridge at Chappaquiddick, killing a Kennedy aide, Mary Jo Kopechne.
1973 Joseph P. Kennedy II, son of Bobby and Ethel, is the driver of a car in an accident which leaves one of its occupants permanently paralyzed.

ASSASSINATIONS

1963 JFK is shot by Lee Harvey Oswald.
1968 Bobby Kennedy is shot by Sirhan Sirhan.

TRIALS

1969 Paul Michael Hill is wrongly convicted as an IRA terrorist. He later marries Courtney Kennedy following the quashing of his conviction in 1990.
1991 William Kennedy Smith is charged with but acquitted of rape.
2002 Kennedy cousin Michael Skakel is charged and convicted of the 1975 murder of Martha Moxley.

DRUGS

1984 Bobby's son David dies from an overdose in Miami. The following fourth-generation members of the Kennedy family have also had drug problems: Chris Lawford, Patrick Kennedy and Robert F. Kennedy Jr.

MEDICAL AND MISCELLANEOUS

1941 A failed lobotomy further damages Rosemary Kennedy, who's confined to a nursing home.
1963 Patrick Bouvier Kennedy, son of JFK and Jackie, dies 2 days after his premature birth.
1973 Edward M. Kennedy Jr, Ted Kennedy's son, loses a leg to cancer.
1997 Michael Kennedy, son of Bobby Kennedy, dies in a Colorado skiing accident.

BOBBY WITH HIS CHILDREN, 1964.

'He didn't even have the satisfaction of being killed for civil rights. It had to be some silly little Communist.' JACKIE KENNEDY ON JFK'S DEATH

ROSE AT CAPOTE'S MASKED BALL, 1966.

THE GLASS IS HALF FULL

One of the reasons why the Kennedys have endured so well is their streak of idealism and the powerful language they often use to express it. This excerpt from a speech Bobby Kennedy gave to students at the University of Cape Town in South Africa is a wonderful example.

"This world demands the qualities of youth, not a time of life but a state of mind, a temper of the will, a quality of the imagination, a predominance of courage over timidity, of the appetite for adventure over the love of ease. It is from numberless diverse acts of courage and belief that human history is shaped. Each time a man stands up for an ideal, or acts to improve the lot of others, or strikes out against injustice, he sends forth a tiny ripple of hope, and crossing each other from a million different centers of energy and daring, those ripples build a current which can sweep down the mightiest walls of oppression and resistance ... Idealism, high aspirations and deep convictions are not incompatible with the most practical and efficient of programs. It is not realistic or hardheaded to solve problems and take action unguided by ultimate moral aims and values, although we all know some who claim that it is so. In my judgment, it is thoughtless folly. For it ignores the realities of human faith and of passion and belief—forces ultimately more powerful than all of the calculations of our economists or our generals. While efficiency can lead to the camps at Auschwitz, or the streets of Budapest, only the ideals of humanity and love can climb the hills of the Acropolis."

"MY BROTHER [BOBBY] NEED NOT BE IDEALIZED, OR ENLARGED IN DEATH BEYOND WHAT HE WAS IN LIFE, TO BE REMEMBERED SIMPLY AS A GOOD AND DECENT MAN, WHO SAW WRONG AND TRIED TO RIGHT IT, SAW SUFFERING AND TRIED TO HEAL IT, SAW WAR AND TRIED TO STOP IT. THOSE OF US WHO LOVED HIM AND WHO TAKE HIM TO REST TODAY, PRAY THAT WHAT HE WAS TO US AND WHAT HE WISHED FOR OTHERS WILL SOME DAY COME TO PASS FOR ALL THE WORLD. AS HE SAID MANY TIMES, IN MANY PARTS OF THIS NATION, TO THOSE HE TOUCHED AND WHO SOUGHT TO TOUCH HIM: 'SOME MEN SEE THINGS AS THEY ARE AND SAY WHY. I DREAM THINGS THAT NEVER WERE AND SAY WHY NOT.'" QUOTE FROM TED KENNEDY'S EULOGY OF BROTHER BOBBY

"The courage of life is often a less dramatic spectacle than the courage of a final moment; but it is no less a magnificent mixture of triumph and tragedy." JFK

JOHN F. KENNEDY IN HIS CAR, MOMENTS BEFORE THE ASSASSINATION BY LEE HARVEY OSWALD IN 1963

{ kennedy family tree }

PATRICK JOSEPH KENNEDY   1858–1929

The son of poor Irish Catholics who emigrated in a "coffin ship" to Boston, his father died in a cholera epidemic soon after his birth. He was the first Kennedy to get a formal education and won a scholarship to Boston College. He was a successful saloon owner who became a bootlegger during Prohibition. The first in a long line of Kennedy politicians, he was elected to both the Massachusetts House of Representatives and Senate.

JOSEPH PATRICK KENNEDY
1888–1969

Joseph Patrick made his money during the stock market boom of the 1920s and pulled it out before the 1929 crash. He simultaneously operated as a Hollywood financier and had a stormy affair with the actress Gloria Swanson. As the son of a spirits importer, he made an illicit fortune supplying bootleg booze during the Prohibition era (1920–33). When Prohibition was repealed, he turned to politics. He was a backer of Franklin D. Roosevelt, who appointed him Ambassador to Great Britain from 1938 until 1940, but he lost favor for not supporting America entering the war.

JOHN FRANCIS "HONEY FITZ" FITZGERALD
1863–1950

He dropped out of Harvard Medical School to support his family after his father's death and entered the insurance business before finding his way into politics. He won a seat in the Massachusetts Senate in 1892 and upgraded to the US House of Representatives 3 years later. He became Boston's first "Irish" Mayor in 1906. His administration was noted for its cronyism and graft, while Fitzgerald became infamous for his affair with the cigarette girl Toodles Ryan. The combination of these things cost him the election of 1914. He won a seat in the US House of Representatives in 1918 but lost it because of systematic election fraud which included hiring thugs to threaten voters.

ROSE ELIZABETH FITZGERALD
1890–1995

She married Joseph Kennedy in 1914 after a 7-year courtship. They had nine children of whom four would pre-decease her. Deeply religious, she shepherded her family through their many triumphs and tragedies until she died aged 104.

> ❝ NOW, I THINK THAT I SHOULD HAVE KNOWN THAT HE WAS MAGIC ALL ALONG. I DID KNOW IT—BUT I SHOULD HAVE GUESSED THAT IT WOULD BE TOO MUCH TO ASK TO GROW OLD WITH AND SEE OUR CHILDREN GROW UP TOGETHER. SO NOW, HE IS A LEGEND WHEN HE WOULD HAVE PREFERRED TO BE A MAN.
> JACKIE KENNEDY
> ON HUSBAND JFK ❞

JOSEPH PATRICK KENNEDY JR
1915–44

His father had high hopes of a political career for his eldest son. He left Harvard Law School before his final year to become a US navy pilot. He earned his wings in 1942 and was sent to England where he flew missions as a bomber pilot. In July 1944, he heroically volunteered for a dangerous special mission designed to test a possible counter to Germany's V2 rockets. However, the plane he was flying laden with explosives blew up. Kennedy's body was never recovered.

JOHN FITZGERALD KENNEDY 1917–63

His early life showed both prodigious talent and tremendous resolve. Despite poor health from Addison's disease (a hormonal disorder) and osteoporosis, he joined the navy and became a hero when he rescued his men when their boat was rammed by a Japanese destroyer. He entered the House of Representatives in 1946, moved to the Senate in 1952 and married Jackie in 1953. His 1956 nomination for the vice presidency failed, but he succeeded in becoming President against Richard Nixon in 1960. His presidency was dominated by international incidents such as the Bay of Pigs fiasco and the subsequent Cuban Missile Crisis. He was also instrumental in starting the Space Race, and sending the National Guard into the South to enforce Civil Rights. As a funky young couple, the Kennedys bridged politics and celebrity—something also noticeable in JFK's serial womanizing. However, the most resonant moment of his presidency was his assassination while being driven through Dallas in a convertible, on November 22, 1963.

2 CHILDREN NEXT PAGE

ROSE MARIE "ROSEMARY" KENNEDY 1918–2005

Whether she was mentally handicapped or merely stigmatized as such for being slow in a family of powerful intellects, remains a moot point. However, she was competent enough to perform math and keep a diary. Yet adolescent mood swings and wild behavior made her a potential embarrassment to this image-conscious and ambitious family and her parents put her in for a lobotomy, which they had been told would cure her problems. Instead it reduced her to an incontinent, infantile state and she was packed off to a residential care unit in Wisconsin where she lived until her death 55 years later.

JACQUELINE LEE BOUVIER 1929–94

Her high school yearbook quoted her ambition as "not to be a housewife." She became the White House wife instead. The daughter of a wealthy family, in 1947–48 she was named Debutante of the Year. After graduating from college, she worked as a photographer for the *Washington Times-Herald*, which was when she met her husband-to-be at a dinner party. As First Lady she modernized both the role and the White House. She displayed immense dignity when JFK was assassinated. In 1968, she married shipping magnate Aristotle Onassis. They remained married until his death in 1975, though the marriage had unofficially ended.

KATHLEEN AGNES "KICK" KENNEDY 1920–48

Known to her family as Kick, apparently because she was fun to be around, she worked for the British Red Cross during the war and married William Cavendish, heir to the Duke of Devonshire. Her mother, a staunch Catholic, was against the match on the grounds he was a Protestant. Four months after their marriage, he was killed by a German sniper (his brother Andrew, who was married to Deborah Mitford, inherited the title). Kick then became the mistress of another English aristocrat, the married 8th Earl Fitzwilliam. Mrs Kennedy was even more appalled. As Kick and Fitzwilliam were flying to France to seek her father's blessing, their plane crashed into a mountain. Kick's mother and siblings did not attend her funeral.

ROBERT SARGENT SHRIVER 1915–

After fighting in the US navy during World War II, he married Eunice Kennedy in 1953 and entered political life through working on his brother-in-law Jack's political campaigns. Like his wife, he was interested in philanthropic activity and was appointed the first director of the Peace Corps in 1961. He was selected by the Johnson administration to be the US Ambassador to France, a position which he held 1968–70. He also made unsuccessful runs for Vice President in 1972 and later President in 1976.

EUNICE MARY KENNEDY 1921–

Perhaps out of sympathy or even guilt for the fate of Rosemary, Eunice Kennedy has spent most of her professional life helping the disabled, and especially the mentally retarded. In 1968, along with Anne McGlone Burke, she was one of the founders of the Special Olympics. She married Robert Sargent Shriver in 1953 and they had five kids.

3 CHILDREN: MARIA, MARK & ANTHONY PAGE 149

4 MORE CHILDREN: ROBERT, PATRICIA, JEAN & EDWARD NEXT PAGE

4 MORE CHILDREN OF ROSE & JOSEPH PATRICK

PATRICIA KENNEDY 1924–

She shared her father's interest in Hollywood and moved there with the intention of becoming a movie producer, only to find herself producing religious programs. She met the actor Peter Lawford through her brother Jack and the two married in 1954, becoming a Hollywood glamour item. It was a turbulent marriage, however, where her religion came up against his boozing ways. They eventually split, by which time Patricia had her own alcohol problems.

PETER LAWFORD 1923–84

The son of actors, he was a contract player for MGM studios, but came to notoriety as a member of Frank Sinatra's "Rat Pack," whose suave yet wild behavior became legendary. After he and Patricia Kennedy divorced in 1966, he married a further three times. Lawford continued working in Hollywood and was a frequent guest on television game shows until life in the fast lane caught up with his liver and kidneys.

> "I thought they'd get one of us, but Jack, after all he's been through, never worried about it. I thought it would be me."
> BOBBY KENNEDY

ROBERT FRANCIS KENNEDY 1925–68

Bobby followed in his brother's footsteps, serving in the navy during World War II. After finishing law school he was campaign manager for his brother's Senate and presidential campaigns. Between campaigns he worked for Senator Joe McCarthy and earned a reputation for toughness when he stood up to mobster Jimmy Hoffa in his subsequent job as chief counsel to the Senate Labor Rackets Commission. When Jack won office, he appointed Bobby Attorney General. After JFK's assassination, Bobby was elected to the Senate in 1964 where he became known for advocating the civil rights cause. He was assassinated by Sirhan Sirhan in 1968 after winning the Californian primary to become the Democrat presidential candidate in that year's election.

ETHEL SKAKEL 1928–

Ethel was college roommates with Jean Kennedy but it was her sister Patricia who first dated Bobby. When they broke up, however, she and Bobby started hanging out and they were married in 1950. At the time of Bobby's assassination she was pregnant with her eleventh child. After her husband's death, Ethel founded the RFK Memorial Organization, a nonprofit charitable organization which is devoted to human rights and activism. She is a deeply religious Catholic who is also active in grassroots welfare, particularly for disadvantaged children.

JEAN ANN KENNEDY 1928–

Like her sister, Eunice, she has been active in promoting the disabled. Whereas her sister helped disabled sports, Jean founded Very Special Arts, an organization devoted to providing artistic programs to disabled people. She has also dabbled in politics and was Ambassador to Ireland during the Clinton administration, from 1993 until 1998.

EDWARD MOORE KENNEDY 1932–

The only surviving Kennedy son, Teddy was elected to the US Senate in 1962, representing Massachusetts, and has been there ever since. His hopes for higher honors vanished in 1969 when he drove off a bridge, then abandoned the scene of the accident leaving a dead girl in the passenger seat. He was defeated in his one attempt to nominate for the Democratic presidential candidacy by Jimmy Carter in 1980.

3 CHILDREN OF EUNICE & ROBERT SHRIVER

SAYING GOODBYE
IN ONE OF THE MOST FAMOUS PHOTOGRAPHS OF THE 1960S, ON HIS THIRD BIRTHDAY, JFK JR SALUTES AS THE CASKET OF HIS FATHER, THE LATE PRESIDENT JOHN F. KENNEDY, IS CARRIED FROM ST. MATTHEW'S CATHEDRAL IN WASHINGTON, DC.

JOHN FITZGERALD KENNEDY JR 1960–99
JFK Jr, or John-John, worked in the Manhattan district attorney's office and for many Kennedy causes, but left this behind in 1995 to launch the political magazine *George*. He died on July 16, 1999 in a crash with his wife, Carolyn Bessette Kennedy, and her sister Lauren, while piloting his own plane to a family wedding in Martha's Vineyard.

CAROLINE BOUVIER KENNEDY 1957–
While working at the Metropolitan Museum of Art, she met her husband, Edwin Schlossberg, a cultural historian and designer. She is currently president of the Kennedy Library Foundation and chairperson of the American Ballet Theater.

MARIA OWINGS SHRIVER 1955–
This television journalist is married to Californian Republican Governor, movie star and former Mr Universe Arnold Schwarzenegger. They have four kids.

ARNOLD SCHWARZENEGGER 1947–
His father and older brother used to call him Cinderella. He went on to become Mr Universe, while his father and brother were both killed in alcohol-related car accidents. He branched out of body-building into Hollywood action films with roles such as *Conan the Barbarian* and *The Terminator* before diversifying into comic roles in films such as *Kindergarten Cop*. Then he decided to join his family-in-law's business: politics and, as Governor of California, is the only Kennedy relation to hold office as a Republican.

MARK KENNEDY SHRIVER 1964–
He served as a Democratic member of the Maryland House of Delegates for two terms. After an unsuccessful campaign to nominate for the US House of Representatives in 2002, he is currently an executive for the Save the Children charity.

ANTHONY PAUL KENNEDY SHRIVER 1965–
After studying theology at University, he has followed his mother into becoming an activist for the mentally handicapped. In 1989, he founded Best Buddies, an international organization that helps the handicapped to find work and overcome social difficulties. He is married to a Cuban-born former ballerina, Alina Mojica, and is tipped to hold political office in Florida.

CHRISTOPHER KENNEDY LAWFORD 1955–
After overcoming problems with substance abuse, he became a lawyer before changing direction at the age of 30 to follow his father into acting. He was a mainstay on the soap opera *All My Children* in the 1990s and has played minor parts in a number of major movies since.

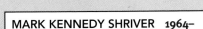

9 CHILDREN: KATHLEEN, ROBERT JR, MARY, JOSEPH, DAVID, MICHAEL, MARY, DOUGLAS & RORY NEXT PAGE

SON: PATRICK JOSEPH PAGE 151

SON: WILLIAM PAGE 151

KATHLEEN HARTINGTON KENNEDY

1951–

The eldest daughter of Bobby and Ethel Kennedy's eleven children, she was also the first Kennedy woman to hold political office in her own right. She was Deputy Assistant Attorney during the Clinton administration before serving two terms as Maryland's Lieutenant Governor under Parris Glendening from 1995 to 2003. She ran for Governor in the 2002 elections but lost to the Republican Bob Ehrlich after a campaign which was criticized by her party for being weak.

KERRY KENNEDY MARRIES ANDREW CUOMO, 1990.

ROBERT FRANCIS KENNEDY JR   **1954–**

He graduated from Harvard with a major in political science before following his father's footsteps and studying law at the University of Virginia. In 1983 he was arrested for heroin possession. After getting clean and performing 800 hours of community service, he has become a prominent environmental lawyer and academic.

MARY COURTNEY KENNEDY   **1956–**

Her second husband is Paul Michael Hill, an Irishman who, as one of the Guildford Four, spent 15 years in prison after being wrongly convicted of the IRA's 1974 bombing which killed five people. The conviction was secured on the basis of confessions extracted after the British police had tortured them.

JOSEPH PATRICK KENNEDY II   **1952–**

He founded the Citizens Energy Corporation, a non-profit organization that helps supply inexpensive heating to the poor. In 1987, he was elected to the US House of Representatives from Massachusetts where he served until stepping down in 1999 to return to nonprofit work. He became the subject of controversy in 1993, when he tried to annul his 12-year, two-child marriage to town planner Sheila Rauch Kennedy so he could marry again in the church. Unimpressed, Sheila wrote a book, *Shattered Faith*, about the hypocrisy of this action. He has since remarried.

DAVID ANTHONY KENNEDY   **1955–84**

This sensitive third son was thrown off balance by his father's assassination and never really recovered, with serious drug problems accompanying him from early adolescence to his death in Miami's Brazilian Court Hotel, from a cocaine and Demerol overdose.

MICHAEL LEMOYNE KENNEDY   **1958–97**

He helped manage his uncle Ted Kennedy's Senate campaign in 1994. In 1997 he was investigated for statutory rape after an alleged affair with the family's babysitter. He split up with his wife and died later the same year in a skiing accident in Colorado.

BOBBY WITH SON ROBERT JR, AT HICKORY HILL, 1957.

MARY KERRY KENNEDY 1959–

She established the Robert F. Kennedy Center for Human Rights in 1987 and is the Chairman of the Board for Speak Truth to Power, a human rights advocacy group, named after her book of the same name. She is married to Andrew Cuomo.

ANDREW MARK CUOMO 1967–

He was the US Secretary of Housing and Urban Development (HUD) from 1997 until 2001 and has campaigned unsuccessfully for the Democratic nomination for Governor of New York, a position held by his father, Mario Cuomo, from 1983 to 1995.

DOUGLAS HARRIMAN KENNEDY 1967–

He is a FOX TV journalist who has a bi-monthly TV show called *Douglas Kennedy's American Stories.*

TOGETHER WITH HER MOTHER, ETHEL, AND BROTHERS DOUGLAS AND ROBERT JR, RORY KENNEDY PLACES SOME YELLOW ROSES ON HER FATHER, BOBBY'S, GRAVE.

RORY ELIZABETH KATHERINE KENNEDY 1968–

Born 6 months after her father's assassination, she is a documentary filmmaker. She once was a partner in a production company with Vanessa Vadim (Jane Fonda's daughter). It was en route to her wedding with Mark Bailey that John F. Kennedy Jr and his wife died when their plane crashed.

> 'DADDY WAS VERY FUNNY IN CHURCH BECAUSE HE WOULD EMBARRASS ALL OF US BY SINGING VERY LOUD. DADDY DID NOT HAVE A VERY GOOD VOICE. THERE WILL BE NO MORE FOOTBALL WITH DADDY, NO MORE SAILING WITH HIM, NO MORE RIDING AND NO MORE CAMPING WITH HIM. BUT HE WAS THE BEST FATHER THEIR [SIC] EVER WAS AND I WOULD RATHER HAVE HAD HIM FOR A FATHER FOR THE LENGTH OF TIME I DID THAN ANY OTHER FATHER FOR A MILLION YEARS.'
>
> DAVID KENNEDY
> AFTER HIS FATHER'S DEATH

WILLIAM KENNEDY SMITH 1960–

This second son of Jean Kennedy Smith made headlines when he was accused of committing rape in Palm Beach in 1991 after a night on the town with Uncle Ted and cousin Patrick. He was acquitted after a nationally televised trial and is currently a doctor.

PATRICK JOSEPH KENNEDY 1967–

He recovered from a teenage cocaine addiction to become the youngest Kennedy family member to win office when he won a seat in the Rhode Island House of Representatives in 1988, at age 21. In 1994, he was elected as a Democrat to the US House of Representatives where he remains.

SON OF JEAN

SON OF EDWARD

THE KRUPPS

BERTHA KRUPP, WIFE OF GUSTAV, WITH HER CHILDREN, C.1912.

HOW THEY RATE

WEALTH ★ ★ ★ ★ ★
Immensely wealthy over a long period of time, especially given the family's strict adherence to primogeniture (where the oldest son gets the lot).

HEALTH ★ ★
Too much time spent in foundries, and there was a unhealthy tinge to the obsessiveness which drove their success.

HAPPINESS ★
Too Protestant, too repressed, too obsessed with work and familial duty.

FAME ★ ★ ★
Yes, but the Krupps are not as conspicuous on the world stage as some of the US industrial dynasties.

SEXINESS ★
Quite difficult to imagine. There is, however, a decadent homosexual strain running through the family.

BLACK SHEEP FACTOR ★ ★ ★ ★
The winner is Arndt von Bohlen und Halbach, who told his father he wasn't interested in the family business and would rather be a playboy—thus ending the Krupp dynasty.

ECCENTRICITY ★ ★ ★ ★ ★
Friedrich, with his self-destructive obsession, Alfred and his inspiring manure, Fritz and his impersonation of Tiberius's little fishes (young boys) on Capri. The repressions of the job and their dour religion made the Krupp personalities flower in strange, not always wonderful, ways.

INFLUENCE ★ ★ ★ ★
Yes, but not particularly good. Alfred Krupp is considered the father of modern warfare. Without Krupp, Germany mightn't have had the military wherewithal to take on the world twice in 30 years. Even America realized they needed Krupp to rebuild West Germany as a bulwark against communism. But since then, Krupp has become just another multinational.

For more than 400 years the Krupp family did business in Essen, Germany. Their fortune grew from a combination of mercenary speculation, idealistic industrialism and sinister political affiliations. It started with the Black Plague property buy-up of Arndt Krupp in 1599. From there the Krupp family built their riches on trading goods and expanding their landholdings. They emerged relatively unscathed from the chaos of the Thirty Years War and by the 1950s were known as the "uncrowned kings of Essen."

Yet making their way into the ranks of the great industrial steel barons almost cost Friedrich Krupp everything the family had. However, his son Alfred had the technical genius to make cast steel work and the lucky timing of the rail era's demand for steel. His son, Fritz, despite a fondness for young boys, compounded the fortune with his financial genius, until scandal caught up with him. The family then became intricately linked in the martial plans of the German state, not least because of the Kaiser-arranged marriage between Fritz's daughter Bertha, and Gustav, a German diplomat. Krupp grew close to Hitler and would forever be tainted with their abuse of slave labor. Nonetheless, Gustav's son Alfried managed to revive the family fortunes, despite being jailed as a war criminal. The glory was short lived. Hit by a double whammy of financial problems and a decadent son, in 1968 Krupp lapsed into public ownership and Alfried, last of the Krupp steel barons, died soon after.

KRUPP CHRONOLOGY

1587	Arndt Krupp arrives in Essen.
1599	Arndt makes a fortune buying property during the Black Death.
1618-1648	Anton Krupp produces 1000 gun barrels a year during the Thirty Years War.
1650	The Krupps survived the many upheavals of the period largely unscathed, and by 1650 were sufficiently wealthy to be known as the "uncrowned kings of Essen."
1811	Friedrich Krupp founds the family's cast steel factory and, in the intervening years, almost goes broke because of it.
1847	Prussia receives Alfred Krupp's first steel cannon.
1870	Krupp guns defeat Napoleon III.
1900	Fritz Krupp builds a navy for Kaiser Wilhelm.
1902	Fritz Krupp commits suicide.
1914	Big Bertha cannons, named after Bertha Krupp, crush Belgium in World War I.
1919	Bertha's husband, Gustav, named a war criminal by the Allies.
1920	Gustav Krupp begins secret German rearmanent.
1931	Alfried Krupp joins Hitler's SS.
1933	Krupp finances Hitler.
1943	RAF raids on Essen.
1944	Alfried rules over 100,000 slave laborers.
1945	Americans capture Krupp factory at Essen—Alfried, Gustav and Bertha Krupp are interned.
1948	Nuremberg War Crimes Tribunal sentences Alfried Krupp to 12 years' jail.
1951	Americans release Alfried and return his assets.
1963	Alfried becomes the most powerful industrialist in the Common Market.
1967	Krupp completes Germany's first nuclear power plant, but the company finances collapse and Alfried Krupp dies.
1968	The company is dissolved into public ownership.
1999	Krupp and Thyssen merge to form a giant German steel conglomerate.

IN 1999 THE KRUPPS MERGED WITH THE VON THYSSENS TO CREATE THYSSEN KRUPP. TODAY THE COMPANY MAKES SOME OF THE MOST SOUGHT-AFTER KITCHEN APPLIANCES IN THE WORLD.

> THE PURPOSE OF WORK SHOULD BE THE COMMON GOOD. THEN WORK BECOMES A BLESSING, WORK IS THEN PRAYER.
> ALFRED KRUPP

CASHING IN ON THE BLACK DEATH

When Arndt Krupp first came to Essen in 1587, it was a small, densely packed medieval town, presided over by the Abbess of a nearby monastery. Sanitary conditions were appalling, with people just throwing the slops from their chamber pots into the street. The tightly packed houses caused a lack of sunlight (nature's disinfectant) to filter into homes, and provided ideal conditions for the spread of disease. When the Black Death arrived in 1599, those houses with infected members were sealed off with the sick inside. Many people fled and, in order to finance their flight, disposed of their assets at bargain prices. Others, in true apocalyptic spirit, decided to liquidate their assets in order to enjoy a final binge before eternity. Arndt Krupp bought from both and amassed enough property to enable his family to gain political control over the town. Despite a few slippages, this control would persist for almost 400 years. There are more than 100 streets in Essen today that are named after Arndt and his descendants.

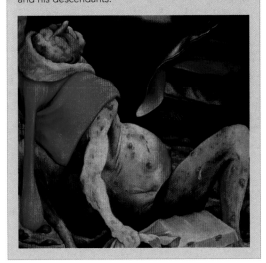

{ GUSTAV KRUPP WAS ORIGINALLY NAMED GUSTAV VON BOHLEN UND HALBACH. HOWEVER, FOLLOWING HIS MARRIAGE TO BERTHA KRUPP, KAISER WILHELM II GAVE HIM PERMISSION TO ADD KRUPP TO HIS NAME. }

FROM CAST STEEL ALCHEMY TO THE CANNON KING

At the turn of the 19th century, only England had the secret for the manufacture of cast steel. As such, they had a monopoly over a large range of products and were famous for their Sheffield steel. The challenge of making cast steel started to obsess Friedrich Krupp and, to the alarm of his relatives, he sacrificed much of the family's profitable business and holdings to pursue this Holy Grail. In 1811 he opened his foundry and, while he had managed to make cast steel by the time he died in 1826, it was in uncommercial quantities and the foundry had a total of seven, largely idle, staff. Alfred Krupp took over the family business when he was just 14, but he was even more obsessive than his father had been. Alfred pioneered the manufacture of hot rolled steel and put grooves in the rolls to make forks and spoons—the sale of which enabled him to improve his technology and expand the business. At the Great Exhibition in London in 1851, he caused a stir by exhibiting the largest cast steel ingot ever cast up to that time (4300 pounds). More importantly for business, he also exhibited a three-pounder, cast-steel, muzzle-loaded gun. Any trouble he had selling his new-fangled steel cannons ceased when their superiority over Louis Napoleon's bronze armory was proved during the Franco-Prussian War. It was with these guns, and the railroads with their demands for steel, that the company really took off. Having started with seven workers, when Alfred Krupp died, he had more than 21,000 men working under him.

"BIG BERTHA," THE KRUPP-DESIGNED CANNON WITH A RANGE OF 75 MILES.

ALFRED AND HIS FETISHES

THE CANNON KING WASN'T JUST A BRILLIANT AND DRIVEN INDUSTRIAL INNOVATOR, HE WAS A FORMIDABLY ECCENTRIC CHARACTER. FOR SOMEONE WHO MADE HIS FORTUNE OUT OF FOUNDRIES, HE WAS MORBIDLY AFRAID OF FIRE. WHEN HE BUILT HIS MASSIVE AND REMARKABLE HILLSIDE VILLA, WHICH WAS TO BECOME THE FAMILY SEAT, HE CONSTRUCTED IT ENTIRELY FROM STEEL AND STONE SINCE WOODEN BEAMS COULD BURN. BECAUSE HE WAS ALSO AFRAID OF CATCHING PNEUMONIA, HE HAD ALL THE WINDOWS PERMANENTLY SEALED TO PREVENT ANY DRAFTS. THE ONLY DRAFTS HE PLANNED REVEAL HIS TRUE PERVERSITY. DEEPLY INTERESTED IN ODORS, HE THOUGHT THE SMELL OF HORSE MANURE WAS INSPIRING. SO WHEN HE DESIGNED HIS CASTLE, HE PLANNED FOR HIS STUDY TO BE ABOVE THE STABLES SO THE WAFT OF DUNG COULD REACH HIM. WHILE HE LIKED MANURE, HE BELIEVED HIS OWN BREATH TO BE TOXIC, AND TRIED TO ALWAYS STAY ON THE MOVE SO HE WOULDN'T BE OVER-EXPOSED TO IT. WHILE THE ODDITY OF SUCH A BELIEF IN A MAN WHO SPENT MOST OF HIS LIFE IN A FOUNDRY IS REMARKABLE, THE MOST SALIENT CONSEQUENCE WAS A PROFOUND MISTRUST OF SLEEPING. ALFRED ALSO HAD A MANIA FOR EFFICIENCY, AND HERE HIS INSOMNIA HELPED. HE WAS A COMPULSIVE WRITER AND, AFTER A HARD DAY IN THE FOUNDRY, HE WOULD GO HOME AND SPEND THE NIGHT IN BED WRITING LETTERS AND BUSINESS MEMORANDA.

THE KRUPPS AND NAZI GERMANY

While many Germans remember the Krupps as the inventors of a uniquely German industrialism, for most of the world they are stained with the ignominy of their Nazi collaboration. In some ways the conditions for this were set by the harsh terms of the Treaty of Versailles, which prevented the re-armament of Germany, thus denying Krupp the right to make weapons. Krupp officially began manufacturing agricultural instead of military equipment but, as any economist will tell you, the profit margins aren't quite the same. As a result, Krupp were secretly engaged in re-armament projects from 1919 onward, mainly through partnerships and subsidiaries in other countries. Krupp evaded Allied arms inspectors by making U-boats in Spain and Japan, machine guns in Sweden and tanks in Russia. The ascendancy of Hitler, with his expansive industrial and military dreams, was something of a godsend. Although Gustav Krupp, a former diplomat and a snob, initially resisted, Hitler made the synergy of their ambitions clear. For Gustav, supporting Hitler made good business sense. However, it was his son, Alfried, who became the most dedicated Nazi. While Gustav waited until Hitler became Chancellor before throwing his lot in with the Nazis, Alfried had joined the SS, Hitler's bodyguard, in 1931. When war broke out, Alfried was considered too important to fight, and while two of his four brothers were killed, he remained in Essen, working the business with his father, who was no longer in good health. The really nasty Krupp activities were largely down to Alfried. As the war progressed, Krupp became an exploiter of slave labor from the concentration camps and even set up a fuse factory in Auschwitz. Of the estimated 100,000 slave laborers Krupp employed, only about 30,000 survived. Furthermore, they weren't shy of using Nazi tactics to achieve their business aims. When Robert Rothschild persisted in refusing to sign his French tractor factory over to Krupp, he was apprehended, sent to Auschwitz and gassed. After the war, Alfried Krupp was sentenced to 12 years' jail for war crimes and had his assets were confiscated. Perhaps it should have been for longer. However, he only served 3 years—saved by the American priority of building up the West German economy as a bulwark against the threat emerging from behind the Iron Curtain. A few years after his release, Alfried Krupp was once again Germany's richest man.

ALFRIED KRUPP BEING HELD BY US SOLDIERS FOR QUESTIONING, JANUARY 1945.

THE PERFECT DIAMOND
THE 33.19-CARAT "KRUPP DIAMOND" WAS ONCE OWNED BY VERA KRUPP. CONSIDERED THE MOST PERFECT DIAMOND IN THE WORLD, IT NOW BELONGS TO LIZ TAYLOR.

> ‘JUBILEERS AND CO-WORKERS! WE SHALL BE THANKFUL TO FATE THAT WE WERE AND ARE PERMITTED TO BE EYE AND ACTION WITNESSES OF THE GREAT TURNING POINT IN OUR GERMAN HISTORY, AND WE SHALL THANK ESPECIALLY THE DIVINE DESTINY THAT IT HAS PRESENTED US WITH A MAN LIKE ADOLF HITLER.’
> GUSTAV KRUPP

KEY: CHILD ••••••▶ ADOPTED CHILD ••••••▶ MARRIED ▬▬▬ DIVORCED ▬ ▬ ▬ DE FACTO ▬•▬•▬ SPLIT UP ▬ ▬ ▬

krupp family tree

ARNDT KRUPP 💰
unknown–1624

The first Essen Krupp arrived in 1587 and joined the Smiths' Guild. He became one of the city's wealthiest men when he backed himself to survive the Black Death and bought up the assets of families who fled.

ANTON KRUPP 1588–1661

His father-in-law was a gunsmith and Anton followed him into the trade. He was manufacturing 1000 gun barrels a year during the Thirty Years War (1618–48).

GEORG KRUPP 1590–1623

He and his young wife both died during an epidemic leaving their young son, Matthias, an orphan.

MATTHIAS KRUPP 1621–73 💰

He consolidated the Krupp family holdings in Essen by buying the fields east of the city walls, which would later become the site for the Krupp gun factory. In Matthias's time, the Krupp family became patrician and were influential in Essen's municipal government, where Matthias was the long-running Town Clerk.

ARNOLD KRUPP 1662–1734

His brother Georg inherited his father's position of town clerk and held it for 63 years. But Arnold went one step further by becoming Mayor. Another brother looked after the family business. The Krupps were never a fantastically fertile family and only Arnold managed to have children—two fairly unremarkable sons.

FRIEDRICH JODOCUS KRUPP 1706–57

His brother Heinrich Wilhelm inherited the position of Town Clerk and lost all his money in ill-advised mining speculation. At 45, Friedrich was not much better. His wife had died and he had run the family business down to the extent where it had effectively become a grocery store. However, he managed to hang on to the family landholdings and, most importantly, produce an heir, when he married Helene Amalie, 26 years his junior, who almost immediately became pregnant. This mission successful, he died soon after.

HELENE AMALIE ASCHERFELD 1732–1810

Her husband, Friedrich, had run down the family business drastically yet, once he died, Helene Amalie, with her son as her accountant, showed remarkable energy and aptitude in rebuilding the family fortune, which her grandson was unfortunately soon to squander.

PETER FRIEDRICH WILHELM KRUPP 1753–95

More than anything else he was his mother's little helper. She ran the show while he occupied the family's traditional seat in the municipal government. Before he died at the age of 42, he managed to marry and produce a son, Friedrich, who he would leave for Helen Amalie to teach the ropes of the business.

FRIEDRICH KRUPP 1787–1826

His grandmother rescued the Krupp wealth from the incompetence of her husband but this didn't prevent her from leaving it to her incompetent grandson. He approached the problem of making cast steel as if it were a Holy Grail but, by the end of his life, had made little progress except in the depletion of the family's bank balance.

> Let us all follow him now also, our Leader, our Reich—and People's Chancellor.
> GUSTAV KRUPP ON ADOLF HITLER

KRUPP AT NUREMBERG
AT THE TRIALS AT THE COURT IN NUREMBERG, GERMANY, JULY 13, 1948, ALFRIED KRUPP VON BOHLEN UND HALBACH LISTENS TO THE PROCLAMATION OF HIS SENTENCE. ACCUSED OF LOOTING, ROBBERY AND SLAVE LABOR. ALFRIED WAS SENTENCED TO 12 YEARS IN JAIL AND ALL HIS PROPERTY WAS CONFISCATED. HOWEVER, AFTER THE REVISION OF HIS SENTENCE IN 1953, ALL HIS NUMEROUS COMPANIES, WEALTH AND PROPERTY WERE RESTORED TO HIM AND WITHIN A FEW YEARS OF HIS RELEASE, THE KRUPP COMPANY WAS THE TWELFTH-LARGEST CORPORATION IN THE WORLD.

GUSTAV KRUPP VON BOHLEN UND HALBACH 1870–1950

Despite being a former diplomat, Gustav, who was renowned for his obsession with efficiency, was at least nominally in charge of Krupp between 1902 and 1943. He was close to the Kaiser and was the major German arms manufacturer during World War I. After the Treaty of Versailles, he made tanks, while pretending they were a kind of agricultural tractor. Krupp also subverted the treaty by making submarines in Spain and developing weapons in Sweden. He was initially against Hitler, but was lured on the promise that the Nazis were good for weapons production and would act against the trade-unionist left. As Chairman of the Association of German Industrialists, Gustav was instrumental in bringing other big business over to the Nazis. By that time Krupp were using slave labor from the concentration camps during the war, however, Gustav was already senile.

ALFRED KRUPP 1812–87

An eccentric, obsessive workaholic, Alfred Krupp became known as the "Cannon King" and in many ways was the founder of modern warfare. Inheriting his father's failing foundry at age 14, he benefited from the onset of the rail era, then began designing cannons to improve the quality of his steel. In the Franco–Prussian War, Krupp's steel guns proved vastly superior to Louis Napoleon's bronze armory and, by his death, he had supplied arms to forty-six nations. While the Krupps profited from the misery they brought to millions, Alfred was also an enlightened employer who introduced sick pay, free medical benefits and retirement schemes for workers and their families.

FRIEDRICH "FRITZ" ALFRED KRUPP 1854–1902

Where Alfred's genius lay in technique, Fritz's genius lay more in the financial management of a large conglomerate. In this he was extremely successful. Aided by a bellicose world, in his 15-year reign Krupp expanded from 21,000 workers to 43,000 and diversified into new businesses, such as making warships and armor-plating. Although married with children, Fritz was homosexual—a crime in Germany at the time—and he committed suicide after his romps with the painter Christian Wilhelm Allers, which took place on the Italian island of Capri, were leaked to the press.

ALFRIED KRUPP VON BOHLEN UND HALBACH 1907–67

The last of the Krupps to run the company, he was also the most reprehensible. A paid-up Nazi from the early days, he was instrumental in setting up Krupp factories using slave labor in places such as Auschwitz. Of the estimated 100,000 laborers who worked for Krupp, around 70,000 died as a consequence of the appalling conditions they worked under. At the end of World War II, Krupp was jailed for 12 years for war crimes; a light sentence in itself. Yet he was released after only 3 years, because the Americans sought to use the Krupp industrial powerhouse against the communist threat. Alfried quickly became Germany's most powerful industrialist, yet he lost control of the company in a financial crisis and died soon after.

BERTHA KRUPP 1886–1957

When her father died she became the wealthiest woman in Europe, but it wasn't possible to leave Germany's largest weapons manufacturer in the hands of a 16-year-old girl. It was Kaiser Wilhelm who found her a husband, the German diplomat Gustav von Bohlen und Halbach. It was for Bertha that the "Big Bertha" gun that pounded the Allies in World War I was named. Although her husband was head of Krupp, some have argued that he was something of a figurehead and that Bertha, along with her son, Alfried, were the true forces in the business.

ARNDT VON BOHLEN UND HALBACH 1938–86

He abandoned his position as heir to Krupps for a life among the jetset and oscillated between homes in Florida, Germany and Morrocco's bohemian Marrakech. As such he wasn't permitted to adopt the name Krupp, and it died out with him. Although he married an Austrian princess, it was primarily for form's sake and he was known as a gay playboy until he died from jaw cancer in his forties.

THE MITFORDS

*V*ogue magazine once said, "The Mitford girls were probably the most spectacular sister act of the twentieth century." It's hard not to agree. From the tranquility of the English Cotswolds, the six Mitford sisters (who also had one brother) burst into society, leaving a trail of controversy wherever they went. Their parents were the eccentric product of eccentric Victorian politician parents, one of who was stigmatized by divorce, the other by illegitimacy. If this produced the urge for rural obscurity, their beautiful, clever and willful daughters would sorely disappoint them. Nancy would immortalize the family in her fiction, Unity would develop a fatal crush on Hitler, while Diana—after a divorce from a literary-minded beer heir—would find her soulmate in British Facist leader, Oswald Mosley. The only son, Tom, was killed in World War II, while Pam was a quiet kind of Fascist who retreated back to a rural life. Jessica counterpointed her Fascist sisters by eloping with the communist nephew of Winston Churchill before becoming known as America's Queen of the Muckrakers for her pioneering exposé journalism. The only sane one, perhaps, was Deborah, who married the heir to the Duke of Devonshire and has sagely helped manage their immense Chatsworth estate. Subsequent generations have lived in the shadows of their spectacular parents to some extent. But then again, how could you avoid it?

FROM LEFT TO RIGHT, SISTERS UNITY, DIANA AND NANCY MITFORD, 1932.

HOW THEY RATE

WEALTH ★ ★ ★
Enough well-aged money not to care too much about it.

HEALTH ★ ★ ★
Fairly hardy aristocratic stock, if they aren't killed early. They're usually good for at least 80 years

HAPPINESS ★ ★ ★
Too extreme in their passions to be overly concerned with happiness, although they were definitely capable of enjoying a good time.

FAME ★ ★ ★
Very famous in their time, but now they are more historical cult figures with a fan-club appeal.

SEXINESS ★ ★ ★ ★ ★
Diana was rated the most beautiful woman in Britain, while most of the sisters shared her penetrating blue eyes. They broke most of the social taboos of their day as well, and it's hard not to want to sleep with a beautiful rebel. It's almost as if they were the rock stars of their era.

BLACK SHEEP FACTOR ★ ★ ★ ★
The family black sheep seems to be socialist sister, Jessica. However, Diana with her unrepentant Fascism and love for Oswald Mosley probably takes the cake.

ECCENTRICITY ★ ★ ★ ★ ★
Oh Yes! They were known in their day as "the mad mad Mitford sisters." They are probably the most eccentric family, certainly the most eccentric generation of a family, in this book.

INFLUENCE ★ ★
More connected than influential. Diana and Unity were two of the only people to be close to both Hitler and Churchill, but achieved little from it. Jessica did somewhat better as a social activist in the Civil Rights Movement in America, while Deborah runs the most visited stately manor in Britain.

UNITY (AGED 9) AND JESSICA (AGED 6), 1923. THE TWO SISTERS WERE VERY CLOSE, DESPITE A SITUATION WHICH SAW THEM TIT-FOR-TAT ETCHING SWASTIKAS AND HAMMERS AND SICKLES RESPECTIVELY INTO THE WINDOW PANES OF THE SITTING ROOM THEY SHARED.

ITFORDS TO THE LEFT, MITFORDS TO THE RIGHT

JESSICA MITFORD IN BERMEO, SPAIN, 1937.

Despite growing up in the isolated, if somewhat idyllic, rusticity of England's Cotswolds with its rolling green hills and picturesque villages, the Mitfords were prone to extremism from the beginning. Both Nancy and Jessica were socialists, while Diana, Tom, Unity and Pamela were all to the right. The Mitford parents, who met Hitler on a trip to Germany, were initially ardent supporters, but later split—with their mother Sydney remaining a fan, while father David reinistated Germans at the top of his list of most hated foreigners. The Mitford sisters often still managed to be friends with each other, even if their political oppositions were played out with considerable enmity.

"ALWAYS BE CIVIL TO THE GIRLS, YOU NEVER KNOW WHO THEY MAY MARRY" IS AN APHORISM WHICH HAS SAVED MANY AN ENGLISH SPINSTER FROM BEING TREATED LIKE AN INDIAN WIDOW.
NANCY MITFORD

MITFORD AND SWINBURNE

While the Mitford girls' paternal grandfather was called Algernon, Britain's most famous 19th-century Algernon was the poet Algernon Charles Swinburne. He was actually a cousin of Algernon "Bertie" Mitford. When Swinburne was sent to Eton, Mitford, who was already there, was given the task of looking after the new boy, and the two became good friends.

> *I am not, and never have been, a man of the right. My position was on the left and is now in the centre of politics.*
> OSWALD MOSLEY

MOSLEY THE FICKLE FASCIST

OSWALD MOSLEY MIGHT HAVE BEEN A FASCIST, BUT HE CERTAINLY WASN'T A FAITHFUL ONE. A MAN OF RESTLESS ENERGY, HE WAS A HARLOT WITH POLITICS AND WOMEN. DURING HIS YOUNGER DAYS, HIS PERSONAL CREED WAS "VOTE LABOUR, SLEEP TORY." WHILE MARRIED TO HIS FIRST WIFE, CIMMIE, HE CONDUCTED AN AFFAIR WITH HER YOUNGER SISTER, BABA METCALFE, AT THE SAME TIME AS HE AND DIANA MITFORD WERE SEEING EACH OTHER. WHEN CIMMIE DIED, IT WAS BABA, NOT DIANA, WHO GOT TO "COMFORT" HIM. DESPITE THE RESERVATIONS OF HER HUSBAND, GEORGE. DIANA HAD TO WAIT IN THE WINGS BEFORE SHE MADE HER MOVE. THEIR MARRIAGE DID NOT BRING AN END TO OSWALD'S AFFAIRS. AT ONE POINT, TO HOUSE HIS EXTRA-CURRICULAR ACTIVITIES, HE RENTED A BACHELOR PAD 5 MINUTES' WALK FROM HIS HOUSE, COMPLETE WITH A MASSIVE BED ON A RAISED DAIS THAT WAS SET INTO A CURTAINED ALCOVE. WHILE MOSLEY MIGHT HAVE BEEN IN DEMAND BY THE BORED WIVES OF THE ENGLISH ARISTOCRACY, MANY OTHER PEOPLE THOUGHT HE WAS ABSURD. INDEED AFTER THE WAR HE BECAME MORE OF A FIGURE OF FUN THAN A THREAT TO THE NATIONAL INTEREST.

THE PURSUIT OF LOVE and LOVE IN A COLD CLIMATE

The Mitford sisters were undeniably remarkable, but their cult is largely to do with the novels of the eldest sister, Nancy. Her most famous novels are *The Pursuit of Love* and *Love in a Cold Climate*, which are thinly veiled depictions of her own family. Written from the outside perspective of a cousin, the Mitfords become the Radletts whose vague mother mirrors her mother Sydney Bowles, while Uncle Matthew, inclined to erratic rages and hunting his children with bloodhounds when he can't find a fox, is a caricature of her father, David. The novel deals with growing up in such a household, while the second, unsurprisingly, deals with the eldest daughter's entry into adult society and her initiation and experience of romantic love. Brilliantly written and very witty, the books offer a sharp portrait of a mode of life whose vector of possibility was drawing to a close in the build-up to World War II.

NANCY MITFORD IN HER PARIS APARTMENT, 1956.

CLOSE ENCOUNTERS OF THE MITFORD KIND

THE DUCHESS OF DEVONSHIRE (DEBO), 1980.

1. MITFORD AND KENNEDY

The Mitfords were at the epicenter of mid-20th-century English society. They were relatives of Churchill, friends of Hitler, and also came into contact with the Kennedys. In the build-up to World War II, Joseph Kennedy Sr was the US ambassador to Great Britain. His son Joseph Kennedy Jr was acquainted with at least one of the Mitfords. While Deborah Mitford became the Duchess of Devonshire, it was very nearly Joseph Jr's sister, Kick Kennedy who did so. Kick was married to William Cavendish, the heir, and the older brother of Andrew (who was married to Debo). William, however, was killed by a sniper in Belgium during World War II before he had the chance to inherit the title.

2. MITFORD AND CHURCHILL

David Mitford's cousin was Clementine Ogilvy Hozier, who happened to become Winston Churchill's wife. The Mitford children would often go to stay at the Churchills' house, which is where Jessica first encountered Esmond Romilly, who she would later elope with.

3. MITFORD, MOSLEY AND MI5

It was partly the testimony of the eldest sister, Nancy, that had Fascist-lover and husband of Oswald Mosley, Diana Mitford, interned for most of World War II. Nancy told MI5 that Diana was: "far cleverer and more dangerous than her husband ... sincerely desires the downfall of England and democracy generally and should not be released."

She went on to say that Diana "will stick at nothing to achieve her ambitions, is wildly ambitious, a ruthless and shrewd egotist, a devoted Fascist and admirer of Hitler." Combined with the opinion of Diana's former father-in-law, Lord Moyne (father of Bryan Guinness), this was enough to get Diana locked up with Mosley. They were both eventually released into house arrest because of Mosley's health.

Apparently, after the war Diana, who knew what her sister had done, had forgiven her herself, but still had to keep it a secret from her husband, Mosley because, if he had known, he would never have allowed Nancy into their house ever again.

ESMOND ROMILLY WITH HIS WIFE, JESSICA, AT THEIR HOME, 1939.

"THE GREAT ADVANTAGE OF LIVING IN A LARGE FAMILY IS THAT EARLY LESSON OF LIFE'S ESSENTIAL UNFAIRNESS." NANCY MITFORD

{ mitford family tree }

ALGERNON BERTRAM FREEMAN-MITFORD, 1ST BARON REDESDALE   1837–1916

His childhood was ruptured by his mother abandoning the family, and he was at Eton by the age of 9. A brilliant linguist, he entered the Foreign Office in 1858, and had postings to Russia, China and Japan. While in Japan, he was among the first Westerners to witness a *hara kiri*, the ritualistic suicide by disembowelment. Between 1874 and 1886 he was Secretary for the Office of Works. He was also a Conservative Member of Parliament between 1892 and 1895, and in 1902, he was elevated to the peerage and made Baron Redesdale.

CLEMENTINE OGILVY   1854–1932

Bertie first proposed to her in America and, when she refused, he went buffalo hunting instead. However, she accepted the second time round and they had nine children. Her niece, also Clementine Ogilvy, would become Winston Churchill's wife. Something of a stuffy snob, she disapproved of her husband's eccentric friend Thomas Bowles, but didn't put up too much resistance to her son marrying his daughter.

DAVID MITFORD, 2ND BARON REDESDALE 1878–1958

His daughters competed for the attention and affection of this somewhat daffy, outdoorsy hounds-and-foxes member of the English landed gentry. Deeply eccentric and unpredictable, he was prone to illogical fits of rage. He was also renowned for his strong opinions and irrational prejudices against foreigners (especially Germans), Jews, Roman Catholics and boys who tried to woo his daughters. He lost a lung fighting in the Boer War but still fought in World War I, where his older brother's death made him heir to the baronetcy and family estates.

THOMAS BOWLES   1841–1921

Although an illegitimate child, Bowles was adopted into his father's official family by his stepmother when his birth mother died. Unable to go to a public school like his half brothers, he was educated in France. He and Bertie Mitford met and became friends, which is how their children David and Sydney met and ultimately married. Bowles was the founder of two magazines, *Vanity Fair* (not the US title) and *The Lady*. He was also a Conservative Member of Parliament, a passionate sailor, and an advocate of British naval supremacy.

JESSICA EVANS-GORDON   1852–87

Her father, Major-General Evans-Gordon, didn't take a shine to his prospective son-in-law, at one stage banning him from the house. Yet Thomas and Jessica were deeply in love and determined to be married. Jessica was intellectually engaged with her husband's political and publishing careers. She was less engaged with being a mother, preferring to leave the child-rearing to nannies and governesses. Child-bearing was constitutionally difficult for her and she died as a consequence of a surgeon's abortion of her fifth pregnancy, something she had undertaken without seeking Thomas's consent.

SYDNEY BOWLES   1880–1963

Her father was eccentric and her mother died when she was young. Although she had a reputation for being a stuffy snob—generational compensation perhaps for her dad's illegitimacy—she was also acquainted with the unconventional from an early age, such as living for long periods of time with her widowed father, brothers and sisters on the family yacht. In her marriage, however, she was the practical one. She met David when she was 14 and he 17, but their romance didn't begin in earnest until he returned injured from the Boer War, during which Sydney's boyfriend of the time had been killed.

> "AN ARISTOCRACY IN A REPUBLIC IS LIKE A CHICKEN WHOSE HEAD HAS BEEN CUT OFF; IT MAY RUN ABOUT IN A LIVELY WAY, BUT IN FACT IT IS DEAD."
>
> NANCY MITFORD

NANCY MITFORD 1904–73

The eldest of the Mitford sisters she was an author most famous for her rendition of her family and her often flippant approach to romantic subjects. Her semi-autobiographical novels of her upbringing, *The Pursuit of Love* (1945) and *Love in a Cold Climate* (1949), were enormous successes and contributed much to the Mitford mystique. The former sold over 200,000 copies and has never been out of print since. Her love life was not so fortunate. A first marriage ended in divorce while, the love of her life, French statesman Gaston Paweski, decided to marry someone else. In politics, she was to the left, and her novel *Wigs on the Green* (1934) was a thinly veiled critique on her Fascist-loving sister Unity.

> To fall in love you have to be in the state of mind for it to take, like a disease.
> NANCY MITFORD

PAMELA MITFORD 1907–1994

Perhaps the least-renowned of the Mitford sisters, as a child Pamela's ambition was to be a horse, so it was perhaps no surprise that she ended up marrying Derek Jackson, a physicist who was also an amateur jockey. They divorced after 14 years, had no children and, in later life, Pam became a noted chicken breeder who also looked after her sisters when they were ailing.

DEREK JACKSON 1906–82

Independently rich through his inheritance of shares in the British newspaper *News of the World*, he was a brilliant physicist who made important advances in the field of spectroscopy. In his spare time he was a talented amateur jockey who sometimes rode in the famous Grand National horse race, and had a keen eye for horseflesh. Despite having open sympathy for Fascism and the Nazis, he joined the British Air Force and was decorated for bravery by the American, French and British governments. Pamela Mitford was his second wife, his first being Poppet, daughter of painter Augustus John and stepmother of Talitha Pol. The day after Pam and Derek married, his twin, Vivian, an astrophysicist, died in a sledging accident. After he divorced Pam he married a further three times and had one child.

THOMAS MITFORD 1909–45

The only son surrounded by a sea of sparkling sisters, his career in the law was interrupted by World War II. Sharing to some extent Unity, Pam and Diana's affinity for the Nazis, when it became clear England was winning the war, he requested a posting to Burma rather than have to invade Germany and preside over their civilians. He was later killed in action in Burma.

DIANA MITFORD 1910–2003

She was married with two children to Bryan Guinness, writer, Irish aristocrat and beer heir, when she started an affair with Britain's leading Fascist, Oswald Mosley. When she divorced Guinness her parents thought it shameful, but her sisters thought it was exotic. Diana and Oswald married in Germany with Hitler and Goebbels as the only guests. During World War II they were interned by the British and, after the war, they mainly lived in Paris where they were neighbors and friends of the Duke and Duchess of Windsor. Unlike many, Diana never renounced her Fascist beliefs and remained a supporter of British right-wing movements until her death.

SON JONATHON GUINNESS NEXT PAGE

BRYAN GUINNESS, 2ND BARON MOYNE 1905–92

When he and Diana were first married, they were prominent in London's arts scene. Evelyn Waugh dedicated *Vile Bodies* to them. Bryan was something of a renaissance man, combining acclaimed literary production with a seat on the board of the family brewing company. After divorcing Diana, he married Elisabeth Nelson with whom he had a further nine children.

SON MAX MOSLEY NEXT PAGE

OSWALD MOSLEY 1896–1980

Mosley was elected a Conservative Member of Parliament in 1918 at the age of 21, an independent MP in 1922, and lost as a Labour candidate to appeaser Neville Chamberlain in 1924 by 77 votes, before becoming a Labour MP in 1926— only to resign in 1930 when they refused to adopt his economic solutions. Following a study trip to Italy and Germany in 1931, he returned to Britain to create the British Union of Fascists. After the war he persisted in politics, but his activities were largely impotent, although he was selected the Twentieth Century's Worst Briton in *BBC History* magazine.

3 MORE CHILDREN: UNITY, JESSICA & DEBORAH NEXT PAGE

3 OTHER CHILDREN OF DAVID & SYDNEY

UNITY VALKYRIE MITFORD 1914–48

She fell under the influence of her older sister Diana and also became an ethusiastic Fascist. She met Adolf Hitler when the two sisters went to the 1933 Nuremberg Rally and quickly became part of his inner circle. But when war between Britain and Germany broke out, she was so distraught she wrote a farewell letter to Hitler and shot herself in the head. The bullet failed to kill her but left her brain-damaged and she was smuggled back to England. She lived on an English island until she died from complications arising from the bullet still lodged in her head.

1ST HUSBAND

ESMOND ROMILLY 1918–1943

He and his brother Giles, nephews of Winston Churchill, caused a stir at the elite Wellington College when they declared themselves pacifists and refused to join the Officer Training Corps. Esmond became known as the "Red Menace" for distributing communist propaganda to the adolescent upper classes. He ran away from school to work in a London communist bookshop, but was arrested. When his mother told the judge he was uncontrollable, he was placed in a remand home. On the outbreak of the Spanish Civil War, Esmond joined the International Brigades. He fought in Madrid then went back to England. He returned as a journalist with his girlfriend, Jessica Mitford. They later married in Spain in 1937. When World War II broke out, he and Jessica moved to the United States. Esmond joined the Canadian Air Force and was killed when his plane was shot down over the North Sea.

> *UNITY MITFORD IS ONE OF THE MOST UNUSUAL WOMEN I HAVE EVER MET. SHE IS NOT AT ALL PRETTY, WITH VERY BAD TEETH AND TERRIBLY FAT, HOWEVER WITH A CERTAIN FINE ARYAN LOOK. SHE DOESN'T IMPRESS YOU WITH PERSONALITY BUT RATHER SEEMS TO BE IN A STATE OF HIGH NERVOUS TENSION IN WHICH SHE HAS NOT GREAT INTEREST IN OTHER THINGS BUT THINKS ONLY OF THE FÜHRER AND HIS WORK. SHE NEVER REFERS TO HIM AS HITLER BUT ALWAYS AS THE FÜHRER AND LOOKED AT ME RATHER FUNNILY WHEN I CALLED HIS NAME IN VAIN.* JOSEPH KENNEDY JR

2ND HUSBAND

ROBERT TREUHAFT 1912–2001

The son of Hungarian immigrants, he found his way to Harvard where he studied law. Unable to fight in World War II for medical reasons, he was working for the Office of Price Administration when he met Jessica Mitford. They joined the American Communist Party, moved to California and married in 1943. Treuhaft was a powerful legal advocate for civil rights and labor causes. Senator Joe McCarthy described him as one of the most subversive lawyers in the country. Both he and Jessica refused to testify to McCarthy's un-American activities committee. Treuhaft lost his faith in Soviet-style communism and left the party in 1958. Yet he maintained his commitment to social justice in his work as a lawyer for the American underdog.

JESSICA "DECCA" MITFORD 1917–96

She was the most conspicuously left-wing of her family. She usurped her sisters Diana and Unity in the black sheep stakes when she eloped to Spain with Esmond Romilly, Winston Churchill's nephew. They moved to America and when Esmond was killed fighting in World War II in the Canadian Air Force, Jessica stayed. She was a member of the American Communist Party and later married the lawyer and labor activist Robert Treuhaft. She became famous for works of exposé journalism, such as her 1963 classic on the funeral industry, *The American Way of Death*.

> "You may not be able to change the world, but at least you can embarrass the guilty." JESSICA MITFORD

CONSTANCIA ROMILLY 1941–

She followed the politics of her mother and became a veteran of the American civil rights movement. Her first husband was the black rights activist James Forman.

BENJAMIN TREUHAFT 1947–

He became a piano tuner in New York City and has tuned pianos for Elton John and Vladimir Horowitz. He also started the left-wing philanthropic project "Send a Piana to Havana."

DEBORAH "DEBO" MITFORD 1920–

The only surviving Mitford sister, in 1941 she married Andrew Cavendish, the man who became the 11th Duke of Devonshire. More in the aristocratic mold of her father than the rest of the family, she has presided over Chatsworth, the Duke's Devonshire seat, which is open to the public and receives more than 500,000 visitors a year. She runs a produce business and has also published a number of books about Chatsworth.

ANDREW CAVENDISH, 11TH DUKE OF DEVONSHIRE 1920–2004

The second son of the 10th Duke of Devonshire, he married Deborah Mitford in 1941. During the war he was a Major in the Coldstream Guards and earned the Military Cross for action in Italy. He became heir to the title when his older brother William (husband of Kathleen "Kick" Kennedy) was killed by a sniper. After the war, he stood unsuccessfully for Parliament and, through his seat in the House of Lords, was appointed to a number of ministerial positions by his uncle, Harold Macmillan. He was also known as something of a playboy who kept a number of young mistresses. At his death, he was the 73rd-richest person in Britain. The Duke had a significant collection of contemporary art, and was particularly known for his patronage of Lucian Freud.

JONATHAN GUINNESS 1930–

He acquired his mother's political tastes and has been a stalwart of the Conservative Monday Club, which is a right-wing grouping in the party. In his working life, he was a merchant banker, yet he has also written a number of books including *The House of Mitford*, which he penned together with his daughter, Catherine. A colorful old-style Tory, he had an official family in London and an unofficial one with his mistress in Penzance, Cornwall, England.

MAX MOSLEY 1940–

The second son of Diana and Oswald, he qualified as a barrister, but his true passion was racing cars. After retiring as a reasonably successful Formula One driver, he entered the business side of things and is currently the President of the Federation Internationale de Automobile (FIA), the regulatory body for the Formula One World Championship among other things.

PEREGRINE ANDREW MORNAY CAVENDISH 1944–

He succeeded to the dukedom on his father's death in 2004. He was appointed a CBE for his services to horse racing in 1997.

> "When jobs come up I'm still... Wow! Weird! Sometimes I see myself and I have no idea why they booked me."
> STELLA TENNANT

MODEL MITFORDS

DIANA MITFORD (RIGHT) WENT FROM BEING CONSIDERED THE MOST BEAUTIFUL WOMAN IN ENGLAND TO BEING THE MOST HATED. NONETHELESS, SOME OF HER BEAUTY HAS BEEN HANDED DOWN THROUGH GENERATIONS. HER GREAT GRANDDAUGHTER, VIA HER SECOND SON, DESMOND GUINNESS, IS THE MODEL JASMINE GUINNESS. ANOTHER MITFORD MODEL IS THE GRAND-DAUGHTER OF DUCHESS DEBO, STELLA TENNANT (FAR RIGHT), WHO DISPLACED CLAUDIA SCHIFFER IN 1996 AS THE FACE OF CHANEL.

THE NEHRU-GANDHIS

It all begins with Motilal Nehru, a prosperous barrister who is instrumental in the Independence movement led by Mahatma Gandhi. His son, Jawaharlal ("Pandit") is also a central player in Indian Independence and, as the leader of the Congress Party, becomes the country's first prime minister. Also no slouch, Pandit's sister becomes the ambassador to the USSR, then goes on to be the first female female President of the United Nations General Assembly. Two years after Pandit's death his daughter, Indira, becomes Prime Minister, while her son Sanjay is her closest adviser. She will be the second-longest serving Indian prime minister after her father. Following her assassination, her son Rajiv becomes PM. Then following his assassination, his Italian-born widow, Sonia, rises to rescue the Congress Party, is offered the Prime Minister's job but demurs. With two of the next generation primed for Congress Party political honors, and a renegade branch of the family prominent in the opposition party, the Nehru-Gandhi dynasty show signs of continuing major influence over the world's largest democracy and second-most populous nation for many years to come.

> FORGET THE KENNEDYS AND THE BUSHES, THIS IS THE PREMIER POLITICAL DYNASTY OF THE 20TH CENTURY.

HOW THEY RATE

WEALTH ★★★
They've had it but have never seemed to be obsessed by it.

HEALTH ★★★
Fairly reasonable given the stress of their jobs, the jailings in the early generations and the assassinations in the later.

HAPPINESS ★★★
It's difficult to imagine there being great happiness in a family where political duty so often overrides individual desire and destiny. However, an admirable strain of happiness and forbearance can be found in the generosity of Motilal, the marriage and writings of Pandit, and the marriage of Rajiv and Sonia before politics staked its claims.

FAME ★★★★★
The most famous name in India, idolized by hundreds of millions, hated by almost as many, and renowned on the world political stage over four generations.

SEXINESS ★★
With someone like Pandit, the paternal and spiritual charisma perhaps overrides the sex appeal. Some of the women have been rather good looking, but they are hardly Bollywood lust objects.

BLACK SHEEP FACTOR ★★★
Sanjay and his brood are the Black Sheep of the Nehru-Gandhi dynasty. Not only was he an unelected thug who behaved both stupidly and appallingly during the Emergency Years, but his widow and son defected from the Congress Party to the BJP.

ECCENTRICITY ★
Charming and idiosyncratic, or haughty and withdrawn, but there are no serious manifestations of eccentricity, except perhaps for Sanjay's fatal hobby of flying stunt airplanes, which might even have been an attempt to outdo his commercial pilot older brother.

INFLUENCE ★★★★★
They have presided over the world's second-most populous nation for most of its independent history, something they were instrumental in bringing about.

JAWAHARLAL, BETTER KNOWN AS "PANDIT" (MEANING "TEACHER") NEHRU, ADDRESSES A CROWD OF SUPPORTERS FROM THE BALCONY OF HIS HOUSE IN SIMLA, INDIA, 1945.

LIVING THE HIGH LIFE IN ALLAHABAD

When Motilal Nehru decided to abandon his elitist English ways and live like an Indian, he was faced with the task of reforming an extremely lavish lifestyle. He was very successful as an Allahabad barrister, had become the town's wealthiest citizen and bought a huge forty-two-room house on the outskirts of town, which he called Anand Bhavan (Abode of Happiness). He was the first in the area to install electricity and running water, and he also added an indoor swimming pool. His house had three kitchens and there were often big dinner parties where Christian, Muslim and Hindu guests were all served according to their religious customs. It took scores of servants, including a bona fide English governess, Miss Hoover, to run the household. Anand Bhavan had beautiful gardens, a tennis court, an orchard and a riding ring. Behind it were woodlands where family members would often go hunting on horseback with rifles. Motilal had a keen eye for horses, particularly Arabians, but this didn't prevent him from becoming the first person in the district to own a car when he imported one from England in 1904.

PANDIT NEHRU WITH HIS PARENTS, 1899.

Friends and comrades, the light has gone out of our lives, and there is darkness everywhere, and I do not quite know what to tell you or how to say it. Our beloved leader, Bapu [father] as we called him, the father of the nation, is no more. Perhaps I am wrong to say that; nevertheless, we will not see him again, as we have seen him for these many years, we will not run to him for advice or seek solace from him, and that is a terrible blow, not for me only, but for millions and millions in this country.
PANDIT NEHRU ON THE DEATH OF MAHATMA GANDHI

HOW THE NEHRUS BECAME GANDHIS

While Mahatma Gandhi in many ways was Pandit Nehru's political father, the family's inheritance of the Gandhi name has no direct relation to the father of Indian Independence. The Nehrus first became Gandhis with the marriage of Indira Nehru to Feroze Khan. While the Nehrus were high-caste Brahmins from Kashmir, the Khans were Muslim. For Pandit Nehru the marriage was politically disadvantageous, yet he opposed it because he thought they were incompatible. In this he proved correct, and the couple were to spend most of their married life living apart. By all rights Indira should have become a Khan. Yet Feroze's mother was a Parsi (Persian), whose maiden name had been Ghandi—a name not uncommon among Parsis. While Nehru was ideologically in favor of inter-caste marriage, in order to mitigate political damage, he suggested the couple take the name Ghandi instead. They agreed and the spelling changed to the Hindu-friendly "Gandhi." In a sense, the name change was a positive political symbol in itself. The couple, both of whom became politicians, represented the cultural hopes of a newly independent India, and what better way to mark this than by acquiring the name of its spiritual father.

FUTURE PRIME MINISTER, INDIRA, 1956.

THE OTHER GREAT GANDHI

ALTHOUGH SHE WAS NOT A BLOOD RELATIVE OF THE NEHRUS, THE ADOPTION OF MAHATMA'S NAME BY INDIRA AND HER HUSBAND FEROZE WAS AT LEAST PARTLY A GESTURE OF RESPECT TO A MAN CONSIDERED THE SPIRITUAL FATHER OF THE INDIAN NATION, AND WHO WAS ALSO A CLOSE COLLEAGUE OF BOTH HER FATHER AND GRANDFATHER. MAHATMA GANDHI (1869–1948) WAS ONE OF THE MOST REVERED PEOPLE OF THE 20TH CENTURY. HE PIONEERED THE TACTICS OF NON-VIOLENT RESISTANCE AND CIVIL DISOBEDIENCE, WHICH WERE NOT ONLY THE MEANS BY WHICH INDIA ACHIEVED INDEPENDENCE, BUT BECAME THE TEMPLATE FOR ALL MANNER OF POLITICAL CAMPAIGNS—MOST NOTABLY PERHAPS, THE CIVIL RIGHTS MOVEMENT IN THE US, CHAMPIONED BY MARTIN LUTHER KING. IN DOING SO, GANDHI POLITICALLY OUTWITTED THE LIKES OF WINSTON CHURCHILL—A NOT INCONSIDERABLE ACHIEVEMENT. PANDIT NEHRU IN PARTICULAR WAS VERY CLOSE TO GANDHI, WHO VIEWED HIM AS A POLITICAL SON. HE RARELY WENT AGAINST GANDHI'S OPINIONS IN THE CONGRESS PARTY. A NOTABLE OCCASION, HOWEVER, OCCURRED DURING THE EARLY DAYS OF INDEPENDENCE, WHEN NEHRU PRAGMATICALLY ACCEDED TO THE PARTITION OF INDIA AND PAKISTAN IN ORDER TO PREVENT WHAT HE THOUGHT WOULD END UP IN A HINDU–MUSLIM CIVIL WAR. GANDHI, WHOSE HOPES FOR A UNITED NATION WERE EMBODIED IN HIS NEW NAMESAKES, WAS DEVASTATED. GANDHI EVENTUALLY PAID FOR HIS CONCILIATORY ATTTUDE WITH HIS LIFE WHEN A HINDU EXTREMIST ASSASSINATED HIM BECAUSE OF HIS OVERTURES TO PAKISTAN.

> ' I THINK THE YEARS I HAVE SPENT IN PRISON HAVE BEEN THE MOST FORMATIVE AND IMPORTANT IN MY LIFE BECAUSE OF THE DISCIPLINE, THE SENSATIONS, BUT CHIEFLY THE OPPORTUNITY TO THINK CLEARLY, TO TRY TO UNDERSTAND THINGS.
> PANDIT NEHRU '

HANDCUFFED TO HISTORY

For the Nehru-Gandhi dynasty, politics has often proved a poisoned chalice. Pandit Nehru once described his destiny as being "handcuffed to history." His daughter, Indira, moved in to fill the breach left by his sudden death, and found respite in politics from an otherwise lonely existence. For a long time Indira's son, Rajiv, looked like he'd escaped the burden of the family inheritance. But then his brother, Sanjay, wiped himself out in a stunt plane crash, and soon after his mother was in his ear about the importance of continuing the family business. His Italian wife, Sonia, was not impressed. She said, "For the first time, there was tension between Rajiv and me. I fought like a tigress—for him, for us and our children, above all, for our freedom."

But to no avail. Rajiv became Prime Minister of India when his mother was assassinated by her own bodyguards. After a corruption-tainted government, Congress lost the 1989 election. Rajiv was campaigning for the Congress Party when he was assassinated by a bomb hidden in a basket of flowers. It might have meant the end of the Nehru political dynasty, yet, after resisting the idea for a number of years, Sonia Gandhi entered the political fray, followed by her son, Rahul. Behind them was her daughter, Priyanka. Is it a case of politics in the blood—a cross-generational addiction? Or do the Nehru-Gandhis remain handcuffed to history? Or perhaps it's an ongoing case of the sacrifices of one generation being expiated by the next? Whichever way you see it, there's a good chance of the Ghandis playing a crucial role in Indian politics for many years to come.

THE FAMILY OF ASSASSINATED INDIAN PRIME MINISTER, INDIRA GANDHI, AT HER FUNERAL, 1984.

JAWAHARLAL "PANDIT" NEHRU AND HIS WIFE, KAMALA, ON THEIR WEDDING DAY, 1920.

NEHRU'S ROSE

WHEN JAWAHARLAL'S FATHER WROTE TO HIM IN ENGLAND, TELLING HIM HIS BRIDE, KAMALA, A 12-YEAR-OLD GIRL FROM A CONSERVATIVE KASHMIRI FAMILY, HAD BEEN CHOSEN, NEHRU WASN'T IMPRESSED. WHILE HE DIDN'T OPENLY REBEL, HE WAS OPENLY APPREHENSIVE ABOUT MARRYING SOMEONE HE HAD NEVER MET. THE MARRIAGE WAS SET FOR FEBRUARY 8, 1916—A DATE CHOSEN BY THE FAMILY ASTROLOGERS. THE COUPLE SPENT THEIR HONEYMOON IN KASHMIR, BUT FOR MOST OF IT NEHRU WAS CLIMBING MOUNTAINS WITH A COUSIN. HOWEVER, FROM SUCH INAUSPICIOUS BEGINNINGS, THE MARRIAGE EVOLVED INTO A VERY HAPPY ONE, EMANATING DEEP LOVE AND MUTUAL RESPECT. WHEN KAMALA WAS ON HER DEATH BED WITH TUBERCULOSIS, SHE GAVE HER HUSBAND A ROSE. FOLLOWING HER DEATH, NEHRU PICKED A FRESH ROSE EVERY MORNING IN HER MEMORY, AND WORE IT IN HIS BREAST POCKET.

NEHRU-GANDHI CHRONOLOGY

1947–64 Motilal Nehru's son, Jawaharlal Nehru, serves as first Prime Minister of an independent India, until his death in 1964.

1965–77 Indira Gandhi, daughter of Pandit Nehru, serves as India's third Prime Minister.

1980–84 Indira Gandhi serves another term as Prime Minister.

1980 Sanjay Gandhi, Indira Gandhi's second son, is elected to Parliament. He later dies in plane crash.

1984 Indira Gandhi is assassinated by her Sikh bodyguards. Her son Rajiv Gandhi becomes Prime Minister.

1984–89 Rajiv Gandhi serves as Prime Minister.

1988 Maneka Gandhi, widow of Sanjay, becomes General Secretary of the socialist Janata Dal party.

1989 Maneka Gandhi elected to Parliament.

1991 Rajiv Gandhi, now leader of opposition Congress, is assassinated by Tamil Tigers from Sri Lanka while campaigning to return Congress to power.

1998 Rajiv Gandhi's Italian-born widow, Sonia, becomes president of Congress.

1999 Sonia Gandhi is elected to India's Parliament.

2004 Rahul Gandhi, son of Rajiv and Sonia Gandhi, is elected to Parliament. Sonia Gandhi retains her seat and is poised to become India's first foreign-born Prime Minister, but decides to cede the job to Manmohan Singh, a Sikh economist.

> "My grandfather once told me that there are two kinds of people: those who work and those who take the credit. He told me to try to be in the first group; there was less competition there."
> Indira Gandhi

INDIAN STATESMAN JAWAHARLAL "PANDIT" NEHRU MOVES THE RESOLUTION FOR AN INDEPENDENT REPUBLIC IN A HISTORIC MOMENT AT THE CONSTITUENT ASSEMBLY IN NEW DELHI, INDIA, FEBRUARY 8, 1947. JUST 6 MONTHS LATER HE WOULD DELIVER HIS FAMOUS "A TRYST WITH DESTINY" SPEECH IN THE VERY SAME ROOM.

NEHRU'S DESTINY SPEECH

August 14, 1947, on the eve of India's Independence: "Long years ago we made a tryst with destiny, and now the time comes when we shall redeem our pledge, not wholly or in full measure, but very substantially. At the stroke of the midnight hour, when the world sleeps, India will awake to life and freedom. A moment comes, which comes but rarely in history, when we step out from the old to the new, when an age ends, and when the soul of a nation, long suppressed, finds utterance. It is fitting that at this solemn moment, we take the pledge of dedication to the service of India and her people and to the still larger cause of humanity.

At the dawn of history, India started on her unending quest, and trackless centuries are filled with her striving and grandeur of her success and failures. Through good and ill fortune alike, she has never lost sight of that quest, forgotten the ideals which gave her strength. We end today a period of misfortunes and India discovers herself again. The achievement we celebrate today is but a step, an opening of opportunity to the greater triumphs and achievements that await us. Are we brave enough and wise enough to grasp this opportunity and accept the challenge of the future?

That future is not one of ease or resting but of incessant striving so that we may fulfill the pledges we have so often taken and the one we shall take today. The service of India means the service of the millions who suffer. It means the ending of poverty and ignorance and poverty and disease and inequality of opportunity. The ambition of the greatest men of our generation has been to wipe every tear from every eye. That may be beyond us, but as long as there are tears and suffering, so long our work will not be over."

INDIRA'S TOP FIVE POLITICAL IMPACTS

★ IMPORTED THE IDEAS OF NORMAN BORLAUG'S GREEN REVOLUTION WHICH ORIGINATED IN MEXICO. THE RESULTANT IMPROVEMENT IN CROP EFFICIENCY TURNED INDIA FROM A NET FOOD IMPORTER TO AN EXPORTER AND SAVED AN ESTIMATED 1 BILLION LIVES.

★ IN 1974, INDIA ANNOUNCED TO THE WORLD ITS FIRST SUCCESSFUL TEST OF A NUCLEAR BOMB, WITH THE BIZARRE NICKNAME OF "SMILING BUDDHA."

★ INDIRA'S POPULARITY WAS TREMENDOUSLY ENHANCED IN 1971 WHEN, UNDER HER LEADERSHIP, INDIA TRIUMPHED IN THE WAR AGAINST PAKISTAN.

★ WHEN THE HIGH COURT OF ALLAHABAD (WHERE HER GRANDFATHER MOTILAL HAD PRACTICED LAW) ORDERED INDIRA TO VACATE HER SEAT BECAUSE OF ILLEGAL ELECTIONEERING, SHE DECLARED A STATE OF EMERGENCY (1975–77) WHICH LED TO VIOLENCE AND THE AUTOCRATIC WHIMS OF HER THUGGISH SON, SANJAY, BEING IMPLEMENTED.

★ HER SECOND STINT AS PRIME MINISTER WAS DOMINATED BY ATTEMPTS TO SOLVE THE PROBLEMS OF SIKH SEPARATISTS IN THE PUNJAB. HER HEAVY-HANDEDNESS POLARIZED THE SITUATION, CAUSING MANY DEATHS, INCLUDING HER OWN.

PRIME MINISTER INDIRA GANDHI WITH HER SON, SANJAY, 1980.

{ nehru-gandhi family tree }

MOTILAL NEHRU
1863–1948

This first member of the Nehru political dynasty was a lawyer from a Kashmiri Brahmin family. His father died a couple of months before he was born and he was raised by his older brother, Nand Lal, a lawyer whose career Motilal successfully followed to become wealthy. However, he abandoned many of his elitist anglicized habits to become one of Mahatma Gandhi's most prominent supporters. He was twice President of the Indian National Congress, which later became the Nehru-Gandhi-dominated Congress Party. However, being a generation older than Gandhi and his son, Jawaharlal, he was more moderate in his political positions and clashed with both of them on occasion. Still, he was arrested by the British with his son in 1930, only to be released because of his frail health. He died the following year.

JAWAHARLAL "PANDIT" NEHRU
1889–1964

He was the first Prime Minister of India when it gained independence in 1947, and he held the position until his death in 1964. His education, however, was very English, including boarding at the elite Harrow School (where Winston Churchill, the great enemy of Indian independence, had also boarded), and studying law in London, before entering politics. He had a close relationship with Gandhi and was imprisoned several times in the struggle for independence. Once he became Prime Minister he led India through the difficult days of partition with Pakistan, and grew the economy via a middle ground philosophy of planned capitalism, as well as founding the Non-Aligned Nations Movement.

INDIRA GANDHI
1917–84

As a child Indira was socially isolated by her father's position. She attended elite schools and colleges, including Oxford. Her marriage to Feroze Khan was tempestuous and after a few years she moved back in with her father, only to reunite with her husband after he had a heart attack in 1958, taking him to recuperate in Kashmir with their sons. While she had been her father's chief support during his career, her husband's death enabled her to enter politics herself. Following her father's death, she became Indian Prime Minister 1966–77 and for a second time between 1980 and 1984. Her stewardship was highly controversial and was marked by her isolated personality and emotional dependence on her son Sanjay. She frequently resorted to authoritarian and undemocratic measures, such as the declaration of a State of Emergency and Martial Law in 1974 that would have had her father turning in his grave. She was eventually assassinated by two of her Sikh bodyguards.

VIJAYA LAKSHMI NEHRU PANDIT
1900–90

Following independence, this sister of Jawaharlal had a number of major diplomatic and domestic postings. In 1947 she became India's envoy to the Soviet Union before becoming India's Ambassador to the United Nations. She was the first woman to be President of the United Nations General Assembly in 1953 and was Governor of the Indian state of Maharashtra from 1962–64. However, her political career foundered after her brother's death.

FEROZE KHAN GANDHI   1912–60

His marriage in 1942 to Indira Nehru wasn't welcomed by her parents for personal and political reasons, including the fact that his family was Muslim. After abandoning his studies at the London School of Economics in 1930, he became involved in the independence movement and was jailed. He later became editor of *The National Herald*, a Congress Party-friendly newspaper founded by Nehru. When the 1947 elections were held, Feroze stood for Parliament and, with Indira as his campaign organizer, succeeded in winning a seat. He became known as an anti-corruption campaigner and, on occasion, caused his father-in-law's government serious embarrassment, such as when his exposure of an insurance scandal caused the Finance Minister to resign.

KRISHNA HUTHEESING
1907–67

Pandit Nehru's youngest sister was also heavily involved in the struggle for independence. She and her husband were both jailed in the cause, but after independence went on to be authors rather than politicians. Krishna's books include the family memoir, *We Nehrus*, and a biography of her niece, Indira.

NAYANTARA SAHGAL   1927–

The middle of three daughters born to Vijaya Lakshmi Pandit, she received an elite American college education and has published a number of non-fiction works on Indian politics. As an author, however, she is most famous for her English language novels, which advocate the emancipation of women in Indian society.

> Without peace, all other dreams vanish and are reduced to ashes.
> PANDIT NEHRU

RAJIV GANDHI   1944–91

While his younger brother was playing Svengali to mother, Indira, Rajiv was leading a blissfully unpolitical life as a commercial airline pilot with a beautiful Italian wife. However, because of Sanjay's death due to poor piloting, his mother's determination to perpetuate the political dynasty saw him stand for election and enter Parliament in 1981. When Indira was assassinated in 1984, he took over the leadership of the Congress Party and became Prime Minister. Rajiv pioneered India's burgeoning high-technology sector but was otherwise an unspectacular Prime Minister and lost office largely due to corruption problems in 1989. In 1991 he was campaigning to win back office when he was blown to smithereens by a Tamil Tiger separatist, angry at Rajiv's interventions in Sri Lanka.

SONIA GANDHI   1946–

Born in Italy, she has been a reluctant participant in India's political life. She tried to stop her husband entering politics and, when he was assassinated, she resisted attempts to get involved in the Congress Party until 1997 when it appeared that, without a Gandhi at its helm, oblivion was around the corner. In 1998, she became Congress Party President, the fifth member of the family to do so. She was elected to Parliament in 1999, but Congress suffered an embarrassing defeat to the Hindu Nationalist Bharatiya Janata Party (BJP), who were fond of stigmatizing her foreign origins. In 2004 she led the Congress Party to an election victory but, instead of becoming Prime Minister, she (quite wisely) appointed Manmohan Singh, a Sikh economist to the job.

SANJAY GANDHI   1946–80

Although his mother's clear favorite, Sanjay Gandhi is the villain of the Gandhi-Nehru political dynasty. During his mother's premiership, he was her closest adviser and managed to use his political connections for fraudulent money-making schemes. He has also been accused of engaging in prostitution and the assassination of political opponents. He earned the loathing of many Indians for his thuggish behavior during the authoritarian years of "The Emergency" (1975–77). Several ministers resigned rather than receive orders from this unelected beneficiary of his mother's nepotism. Still, his influence was felt in acts such as the clearing of a mainly Muslim Delhi slum at the cost of thousands of lives, and his family planning program, which involved the forced castration of men. When Indira lost the election at the end of the Emergency era, Sanjay advocated re-imposing martial law, but the army and possibly his mother were against it. He was finally elected to Parliament in 1980, but died not long after when he crashed a stunt plane he was flying against meteorological advice.

> *She was mother not only to me but to the whole nation. She served the Indian people to the last drop of her blood.*   RAJIV GANDHI ON HIS MOTHER, INDIRA

RAHUL GANDHI   1970–

After studying development economics at Harvard and Oxford, Rahul became a Congress Party member of the Indian Parliament in the 2004 election, but has since resisted encouragement to take a more prominent role in the party—though it has been argued that this is a way of keeping his image clean in order to lead the party in the future.

PRIYANKA VADA   1972–

She was instrumental behind the scenes in her mother's 2004 campaign, and her beauty made her a Congress Party poster girl, but thus far she has resisted standing for election—though there are rumors the resistance might be waning.

MANEKA GANDHI   1956–

The widow of Sanjay Gandhi was a model and editor of *Surya India* magazine, before entering politics in 1982 after her husband's death. When Indira Gandhi chose her son Rajiv rather than Maneka to inherit Sanjay's political mantle, Maneka went and joined Janata Dal, the opposition to Congress, and and rose to the status of Minister for the Environment in the cabinet of V. P. Singh (1989–91). With a memory apparently as long as an elephant for a grievance, she traded in her political independent status and won a seat as part of the Bharatiya Janata Party in the 2004 election. Together with her son, Varun, they are a stubborn embarrassment to the rest of the family. She is also India's leading animal rights activist.

VARUN GANDHI   1980–

The only son of Maneka Gandhi, Varun joined his mother in 2004 by campaigning for the BJP. While too young to stand for elected office in the election, he is currently a member of the BJP National Executive and one of the main political campaigners of the party. In 2000, he also published *The Otherness of Self*, a co-written book of poetry and criticism.

THE TOLSTOYS

> *IF IT IS TRUE THAT THERE ARE AS MANY MINDS AS THERE ARE HEADS, THEN THERE ARE AS MANY KINDS OF LOVE AS THERE ARE HEARTS.*
> LEO TOLSTOY

HOW THEY RATE

WEALTH ★ ★ ★
Frequently a kind of asset-rich, cash-poor aristocratic family. The penchant of the men for losing large sums on the gambling table didn't much help either, but still they always seemed to have enough to get by without having to sell too many serfs.

HEALTH ★ ★ ★
For a family whose acquired name means "fat," and who seemed rather fond of the bottle, they show solid longevity and the capacity to breed large numbers of children.

HAPPINESS ★ ★
It's difficult to know. As a general rule, Russians are quite fond of feeling sad.

FAME ★ ★ ★
Only one world-beater, but in Russia a different story altogether. Nikolai Tolstoy has also managed to inveigle his way to becoming a British intellectual celebrity, while Tatyana Tolstaya is extremely popular in Russia.

SEXINESS ★ ★
Perhaps not the best feature of this family, although they were rather adept at having illegitimate children, and enjoyed a romp with the occasional peasant.

BLACK SHEEP FACTOR ★ ★ ★ ★
Without doubt Feodor, "The American" who was an astonishingly badly behaved character. In political terms, however, the Soviet era writer Aleksey—who was a lackey of Stalin and was complicit in the disappearance of some of his colleagues.

ECCENTRICITY ★ ★ ★ ★ ★
Top-class, and most of the time they seemed to enjoy themselves in being it.

INFLUENCE ★ ★ ★
Leo Tolstoy wrote two of the world's greatest novels and his non-violence was a big influence on Gandhi. Otherwise, the influence of the Tolstoys has primarily been restricted to Russia, where they have been influential in political, cultural and military matters over a long period of time.

PYOTR ANDREYEVICH TOLSTOY 1645–1729.

The Tolstoys have been present in Russian culture for almost 700 years, although the family only achived prominence during the 17th century, which is also when they acquired their current surname, which means "fat."

The family became Counts under the reign of Peter the Great of Russia, due to the loyal services offered by Pyotr Tolstoy, but lost favor on the death of Tsarina Catherine, only to have their land and titles restored some 30 years later. In imperial Russia the Tolstoys were renowned for their unruly behavior and they were not shy of a good fight, on the battlefield or off. However, by the 19th century it became clear that their talents lay in artistic pursuits, even if art and wildness were shown not to be mutually exclusive. The Tolstoys have rated highly in the literary pantheon, and Leo's great grandniece, Tatyana Tolstaya, continues to do so today. However, it is Leo Tolstoy who is undoubtedly the star of this family. British poet and critic Matthew Arnold remarked that a work of Tolstoy is not a work of art, but rather a piece of life. And Russian writer Isaak Babel said that if the world could write by itself, it would write like Tolstoy.

WHILE THE GREAT RUSSIAN WRITERS TOLSTOY AND DOSTOEVSKY ADMIRED, AND WERE EQUALLY INFLUENCED BY, EACH OTHER'S WORK, THEY NEVER ACTUALLY MET IN PERSON. TOLSTOY ALLEGEDLY BURST INTO TEARS WHEN HE LEARNED OF DOSTOEVSKY'S DEATH.

ORIGINS OF THE TOLSTOYS

LEO TOLSTOY'S MOSCOW HOUSE.

According to family legend, the Tolstoys first arrived in Russia in 1353 when a nobleman named Indris arrived from the Holy Roman Empire with his two sons and 3000 men. He settled in Chernigov (today in the Ukraine) which had been incorporated that year into the powerful Grand Duchy of Lithuania—although his origins were from further west, most likely from Germany. After Indris's arrival, the family remained relatively obscure. They came to attention, however, when the great grandson of Indris, Andrei Kharitonovich, migrated to Moscow in 1686. He earned the favor of the Great Prince Vasily who gave him the affectionate nickname "Tolstoy," meaning fat—no doubt due to the capacity for eating and drinking that can be found in many of his descendants.

> **EVERYONE THINKS OF CHANGING THE WORLD, BUT NO ONE THINKS OF CHANGING HIMSELF.**
> LEO TOLSTOY

LEO IN PEASANT GARB, 1909.

CURSE OF THE TOLSTOYS

The Tolstoys came to social eminence when Andrei Kharitonovich married into the Miloslavsky family, who had married into the Romanov royal line. Yet it was his second son, Pyotr, who would become the family's first Count, through his service to both Peter the Great and the Tsarina Catherine I (Catherine the Great). Family allegiances were often a dangerous thing in the convoluted world of Russian politics and, when Peter the Great was battling to become Tsar, Pyotr only just saved his neck by switching allegiances at the last moment. Indeed, while Peter valued the abilities of this Tolstoy, he never completely trusted him and, on one occasion, was heard to remark to Pyotr, "Ah head, head, were you not so clever I should had cut it off long ago."

Conflict over succession was frequent. Peter the Great was a difficult father and his son and heir, the Tsarevich Alexei, had rebelled, taking up openly with his Finnish peasant girl mistress, Afrosinya, running away and dodging his father's demands to prove himself on the battlefield. Peter threatened to deprive Alexei of the succession and, when Alexei agreed, Peter changed the terms, ordering him either to become a decent soldier or abandon his mistress and enter a monastery. He gave his son 6 months to think about it, then was overjoyed when he received news the son would be coming to join his father in the fight against Sweden. But Alexei never arrived.

In 1716, a vexed Peter sent Pyotr Tolstoy to track Alexei down. Pyotr found him in Naples, Italy, under the protection of the Holy Roman Emperor Charles V. In a series of delicate negotiations, which included the Tsar's written guarantee of his son's safety, Pyotr managed to persuade the Tsarevich to return to his father on the proviso he was allowed to marry Afrosinya—who was pregnant—before he got back to St Petersburg. When they returned, Alexei was presented to his father as a prisoner and pleaded for his pardon and the chance to live a quiet life in the countryside with Afrosinya. No such luck. Alexei was gently interrogated by Tolstoy to find out who had helped him defy the will of the Tsar. Thinking he was safe, the Tsarevich spilled the beans. When Peter saw the list of who was involved he lost his temper. High-ranking members of society were exiled, tortured, whipped, had body parts amputated and stakes driven up their backsides. Concerned that the Tsarevich had revealed so much openly, the Tsar asked Tolstoy to torture him to find out what else he knew. After a couple of days Alexei confessed to the desire to kill his father, and was sentenced to death. He died, probably smothered with a pillow by Tolstoy and his torture gang. According to legend, when Alexei was being tortured, he cursed the two-faced Pyotr Tolstoy through to his twenty-fifth generation. Public opinion blamed Tolstoy, too, and it was commonly thought that the family's subsequent problems were a consequence of this curse.

ALEKSEY II

A WRITER WHO WON THE RUSSIAN STALIN PRIZE FOR LITERATURE THREE TIMES, ALEKSEY II WAS A STAUNCH COMMUNIST. DURING WORLD WAR II HE WAS A PROLIFIC AUTHOR OF PATRIOTIC ARTICLES FOR THE SOVIET REGIME. HOWEVER, SOME OF HIS LITERATURE HAS BEEN PANNED FOR BEING TOO OVERTLY EROTIC.

> WAR IS SO UNJUST AND UGLY THAT ALL WHO WAG IT MUST TRY TO STIFLE TH VOICE OF CONSCIENCE WITHIN THEMSELVES.
>
> LEO TOLSTOY

KNOWING THAT HER NEPHEW LEO WAS A VEGETARIAN, HIS AUNT WROTE TO ASK THAT MEAT BE SERVED DURING HER STAY WITH HIM. WHEN SHE CAME DOWN TO HER FIRST DINNER, SHE WAS HORRIFIED TO FIND A MEAT CLEAVER ON THE TABLE AND A LIVE CHICKEN TIED TO HER CHAIR.

FEODOR
"THE AMERICAN" TOLSTOY

THE UNDOUBTED BLACK SHEEP OF A FAMILY FAMOUS FOR WILDNESS, THE STORY OF HOW FEODOR EARNED HIS NICKNAME IS GREAT. IN 1803, FACED WITH SIGNIFICANT TRADING SETBACKS THE RUSSIAN–AMERICAN COMPANY DECIDED TO SEND TWO SHIPS TO ASSERT AUTHORITY ON RUSSIA'S FAR-EASTERN COAST. AT THE LAST MOMENT, TSAR ALEXANDER DECIDED TO INCLUDE A DIPLOMATIC MISSION TO JAPAN ON THE BOATS. HIS INITIAL CHOICE OF PARTY INCLUDED FEODOR PETROVICH TOLSTOY, WHO WAS LATER TO BECOME A FAMOUS ARTIST. WHEN HE DECLINED, ALEXANDER ARBITRARILY SUBSTITUTED FEODOR IVANOVICH TOLSTOY, WHO WAS KNOWN AS A DUELIST, WOMANIZER AND MILITARY MISCREANT. THE SHIPS SAILED TO THE ATLANTIC VIA ENGLAND, AND WERE THE FIRST OFFICIAL RUSSIAN SHIPS TO SAIL IN THE SOUTHERN HEMISPHERE. HAVING ROUNDED CAPE HORN, THE SHIP MOVED NORTH. IT STOPPED AT THE MARQUESAS WHERE FEODOR BECAME THE FIRST RUSSIAN ARISTOCRAT TO BE TATTOOED. ON BOARD SHIP, HE ALLEVIATED THE BOREDOM BY PLAYING PRANKS SUCH AS STICKING A DRUNKEN PRIEST'S BEARD TO THE DECK WITH THE CAPTAIN'S SEAL. IN SOME OF THESE CAPERS HE WAS HELPED BY HIS PET ORANGUTAN, WHO HE WAS SO FOND OF THAT IT WAS OFTEN SAID THAT THE APE MUST BE ONE OF HIS MANY MISTRESSES. THE CAPTAIN TURNED A BLIND EYE UNTIL FEODOR STARTED INCITING MUTINY AMONG THE MEN. HE WAS WARNED TO DESIST, THEN THREATENED WITH BEING DUMPED ON AN ISLAND WHEN HE DIDN'T. WHEN HE STILL REFUSED TO COMPLY, HE WAS UNLOADED ON AN ISOLATED ISLAND OFF ALASKA. HE WAS RESCUED FROM THERE BY TLINGIT NATIVES AND LIVED WITH THEM FOR SOME MONTHS UNTIL HE GOT BORED AND ATTRACTED A PASSING SHIP BY LIGHTING A BONFIRE. THE SHIP DROPPED HIM BACK TO THE KAMCHATKA PENINSULA, FROM WHERE HE MADE HIS WAY ACROSS SIBERIA TO RUSSIA BY BOAT, HORSE AND ON FOOT. THE RUSSIANS WERE AMAZED AT HIS RETURN AND HE WAS LIONIZED IN VERSE BY HIS FRIENDS—MOST NOTABLY THE POET PUSHKIN.

BADIM MAKAROFF AND BORIS SERGIEVSKY, HANDING OVER A LETTER TO THE TOLSTOY FOUNDATION, VIA A VAULT, 1956. THE LETTER PROVED THAT STALIN WAS AT ONE TIME AN AGENT OF CZARIST SECRET POLICE.

LITERARY TOLSTOYS

STILL FROM THE 1956 MOVIE *WAR AND PEACE*.

1. LEO

The Tolstoys have long enjoyed an affinity with the written word and even today Tolstoys can be found scribbling out a living. By far the most famous, however, is Leo Tolstoy who wrote two of the world's greatest novels, before becoming a spiritual philosopher whose ideas had a direct impact on the thinking of Mahatma Gandhi.

WAR AND PEACE One of the great historical epics in 19th century literature, this immense novel deals with the interwoven lives of six families set against the tableau of Napoleon's Russian campaign. With its vivid characters and magnificent detail, it has often been considered the greatest novel ever written.

ANNA KARENINA A Russian companion to Flaubert's *Madame Bovary*, Tolstoy's most popular novel chronicles the tragic story of a woman who leaves her husband for her lover.

2. ALEKSEY

Leo Tolstoy was not the first writer in the family to become famous. Diplomat and poet Aleksey Tolstoy became famous during the mid-19th century for his verse, plays and historical fiction. While he is little remembered outside of Russia, his trilogy of plays based on the lives of the Tsars was famous in his day, and the composers Rachmaninov and Mussorgsky based works on his poems. His novel *Prince Silver* remains a work with which Russians introduce their children to serious literature.

3. ALEKSEY II

Another Tolstoy black sheep, he became a lackey of Stalin. Born with not just Tolstoy, but also Turgenev, blood in his veins, he started out writing symbolist poetry He was exiled for some years following the Bolshevik Revolution, but he later returned to Russia. During the 1930s and 1940s he was one of the two most popular Soviet authors. His masterpiece is his novel trilogy *Ordeal*, which chronicles a group of Russian intellectuals first resisting, then coming to understand and support, the people's revolution. He also wrote two plays about Ivan the Terrible which were allegories of Stalin, an unfinished prose epic *Peter the Great*, and he was a pioneer in the field of science fiction with his novels *Aelita* and *Engineer Garin's Death Ray*.

4. NIKOLAI TOLSTOY

Part of the Tolstoy diaspora who settled in England he has become a famous Conservative historian. He has written books on Arthurian England, 20th-century England, and Russia, including *The Tolstoys: Twenty Four Generations of Russian History*.

4. TATYANA TOLSTAYA

The latest in the long line of literary Tolstoys, this granddaughter of Aleksey II achieved fame with her short story collections *On the Golden Porch* (1990) and *Sleepwalker in a Fog* (1992) and has received acclaim for her dystopian novel *Slynx* (2000), a post-apocalyptic allegory. She is one of Russia's most popular contemporary authors and a popular television host as well.

LEO TOLSTOY AT WORK IN THE STUDY AT HIS HOME IN YASNAYA POLYANA, RUSSIA, 1905.

KEY: CHILD ┄┄┄▶ ADOPTED CHILD ┄┄┄▷ MARRIED ━━━━ DIVORCED ━ ━ ━ DE FACTO ━·━·━ SPLIT UP ━ ━ ━

{ tolstoy family tree }

ANDREI TOLSTOY
unknown–1698

He left the provincial home of Chernigov to try his luck in Moscow, became a Royal favorite and earned the nickname Andrei "the fat" which in Russian is "Tolstoy." He also managed to marry into a powerful family with royal connections.

COUNT PYOTR ANDREYEVICH TOLSTOY
1645–1729

This statesman brought his family to prominence by backing Peter the Great and became his ambassador to Turkey. After helping capture and execute Alexei, the Tsar's errant son, who had fled to Naples, Pyotr was made a Count and became Peter's Minister for Commerce, a Privy Councilor and chief of his Chancellery of Secret Investigations. A clever politician and skilled intriguer, when Peter died Pyotr became the right-hand man of the Empress Catherine (Catherine the Great). When she died, however, he picked the wrong horse as successor; his titles were stripped and he was exiled to a remote and dingy monastery in the White Sea, and died 2 years later.

ILYA TOLSTOY 1725–1820

IVAN TOLSTOY 1747–unknown

PETER TOLSTOY 1746–1822
He rose through the military ranks to become head of the War Commissariat under Catherine the Great.

IVAN TOLSTOY
1644–1713

He was a Governor of Azov, a Black Sea garrison town, from where he fought with the Russian forces and defeated the Turks and Cossacks. The branch of the Tolstoys that descended from Ivan eventually settled in England, where their most famous member is the controversial, Conservative historian Count Nicholas Tolstoy.

IVAN TOLSTOY 1685–1728
He was the favorite son of his father. When Pyotr heard from his monastery of exile that Ivan had died, it broke his will to live and he died not long after.

> What a strange illusion it is to suppose that beauty is goodness! A beautiful woman utters absurdities: we listen, and we hear not the absurdities but wise thoughts.
> LEO TOLSTOY

ANDREI TOLSTOY 1721–1803

FEODOR TOLSTOY 1726–60

STEPAN TOLSTOY 1756–1809

PETER TOLSTOY 1798–1872

ALEXANDER TOLSTOY 1821–1906

NIKOLAI TOLSTOY 1849–1900

{ LEO TOLSTOY'S WIFE, SOFIA, PAINSTAKINGLY WROTE OUT REVISIONS OF THE MANUSCRIPT OF **WAR AND PEACE** EIGHT TIMES BY HAND. SHE SAID OF HER HUSBAND, "I AM A SOURCE OF SATISFACTION TO HIM, A NURSE, A PIECE OF FURNITURE, A WOMAN—NOTHING MORE." }

NIKOLAI TOLSTOY 1794–1837

FEODOR TOLSTOY 1782–1846

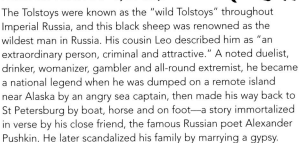

The Tolstoys were known as the "wild Tolstoys" throughout Imperial Russia, and this black sheep was renowned as the wildest man in Russia. His cousin Leo described him as "an extraordinary person, criminal and attractive." A noted duelist, drinker, womanizer, gambler and all-round extremist, he became a national legend when he was dumped on a remote island near Alaska by an angry sea captain, then made his way back to St Petersburg by boat, horse and on foot—a story immortalized in verse by his close friend, the famous Russian poet Alexander Pushkin. He later scandalized his family by marrying a gypsy.

ALEXANDER TOLSTOY 1777–1819

Another of the wild Tolstoys, he was famous for his pranks but died an invalid as a results of wounds received fighting against the French in 1812.

CONSTANTIN TOLSTOY 1780–1870

FEODOR PETROVICH 1783–1873

Although the Tolstoys were more famous for literature, this one shocked his family by abandoning a promising naval career to became an artist, but then attracted the favorable attention of the Tsar and went on to earn acclaim for his series of medals commemorating historical events.

LEO TOLSTOY
1828–1910

His parents died when he was 9 and he was raised by relatives. His youth was spent drinking, whoring and gambling. His gambling debts got so bad that in 1850 he joined an artillery regiment and began to write. In 1857, he traveled abroad and developed an interest in education. When he returned to Yasnya Polyana, the family seat, he started a school for peasants. He married Sofia (Sonya) in 1862, who bore him thirteen children. He also started work on his two classic novels: *War and Peace* (1869) and *Anna Karenina* (1877). In the later stages of his life, Tolstoy went through a powerful spiritual conversion, turning his feudal estate into a kind of Christian commune. He espoused ideas of passive engagement, which were influential on Mahatma Gandhi, and was excommunicated from the Russian Orthodox Church. After leaving his estate to one of his disciples, he became an ascetic wanderer until he caught a chill and died at the remote railroad crossing of Astapovo.

PRASKOVIA TOLSTOY 1831–87

Feodor's only child of twelve to survive until adulthood, she was murdered by her cook.

ALEKSEY TOLSTOY 1817–75

He spent most of his life at the Tsar's court, serving first as the Master of Ceremonies, then as Grand Master of Royal Hunting. He retired from service in 1861 to dedicate more time to writing poetry. While he wrote across a number of genres he was most acclaimed for a trilogy of historical dramas, modeled after Pushkin's *Boris Godunov*.

ALEKSEY TOLSTOY 1883–1945

Not long after he was born his mother, a children's writer who was also a relative of novelist Ivan Turgenev, ran away with her lover and it wasn't until he was 13 years old that Aleksey would discover he was a Tolstoy. He escaped to Paris when the Bolshevik Revolution broke out, but became a communist in Berlin and returned to Russia where, after a period of suspicion, he established himself as a leading Soviet writer. He became chairman of the Soviet Writer's Union in 1936 and won the Stalin Prize for literature three times. Aleksey concentrated mainly on historical fiction, which he sometimes adapted for Stalinist purposes, but he also published memoirs and science fiction.

TATYANA TOLSTAYA 1951–

The granddaughter of Aleksey, her mother was the influential poet, Natalia Tolstaya, and Tatyana took her name perhaps to avoid the artistic and aristocratic stigma of her grandfather's pedigree. She has become one of Russia's most popular contemporary writers and has also been host of a TV show, *The School for Scandal*, which interviews prominent Russians.

INDEX

Page numbers in italics refer to photographs

ACKNOWLEDGMENTS

This book would not have happened without the help of a number of people. Most particularly I would like to thank my publisher Will Kiester for his enthusiasm for the project and encouragement during the writing process. My editor, Ariana Klepac, was invaluable: without her acumen, goodwill and stamina this book wouldn't have happened. Lauren Camilleri has also done a wonderful job giving the book its visual character. Otherwise, I would like to thank my trivia-loving friends either for suggesting or being sounding boards for many of the weird and wonderful tales contained within.

Publisher: William Kiester
Editor: Ariana Klepac
Concept and design: Lauren Camilleri
Photo researchers: Ariana Klepac, Amanda McKittrick
Production: Megan Alsop

Cover photographs: All images copyright © Getty Images
Internal photographs: All images copyright © Getty Images; except pages 12, 13 (t), 14 (t), 16 (b), 19 (l & r), 21 (tl), 26, 32, 34, 35 (b), 36 (b), 37 (c), 38 (l), 40 (t & b), 53 (b), 56 (b), 59 (b), 62 (b), 64 (b), 69 (l), 70 (t), 72 (c & b), 73 (t & b), 74 (t), 75 (t & b), 76, 78 (t), 79 (b), 81 (l), 82 (t, c & b), 83 (t), 85 (b), 91 (tr & br), 99 (t), 101 (t), 102 (t), 104 (cr & br), 105, 107 (t, c & b), 110 (r), 112 (t & c), 113, 115 (t & b), 116 (t), 125 (cr & br), 129, 130 (tl & bl), 131 (tl), 135 (t & b), 136 (t & b), 137 (t, c & b), 138 (l), 139 (t & b), 146 (t), 149 (tl), 150 (tr), 151 (t), 154 (b), 156, 162 (tl & br), 164 (t), 165 (br), 173 (l & r), 177 (t), 179 (cr) © APL/Corbis; 174 © The State Hermitage Museum, Russia. (NB: t=top, c=center, b=bottom, l=left, r=right)

2006 Barnes & Noble Publishing

ISBN-13: 978-0-7607-8312-2
ISBN-10: 0-7607-8312-8

Printed and bound in China by Toppan Printing Co. Ltd.

1 3 5 7 9 10 8 6 4 2